The Freudian Subject

Mikkel Borch-Jacobsen

The Freudian Subject

TRANSLATED BY CATHERINE PORTER

Foreword by François Roustang

Stanford University Press   Stanford, California

The Press is grateful to the French Ministry
of Culture for a grant assisting the preparation
of this translation.

The Freudian Subject was originally published in
French in 1982 under the title *Le Sujet freudien,*
© 1982 by Flammarion. The Foreword has
been prepared specially for this edition by
François Roustang.

Stanford University Press   Stanford, California
© 1988 by the Board of Trustees of the Leland
Stanford Junior University
Printed in the United States of America
Original printing 1988

Last figure below indicates year of this printing:
00   99   98   97   96   95   94   93   92   91

CIP data appear at the end of the book

Contents

Foreword

This book is clear. It states its thesis at the outset. It attempts to demonstrate that thesis on the basis of texts which it follows step by step; it does not take the easy way out and select passages that would serve its own interest. After spelling out at length its point of departure and the path it has chosen to follow, it does not hesitate to draw conclusions. Because the book presents itself so well, because it holds the reader's attention without proceeding too slowly or too quickly, I am not convinced that it needs to be presented by me.

Still, the fact must be faced: this is a difficult book. Not difficult to read—I have just noted its clarity—but difficult to understand and even, I think, difficult to "take." Difficult for psychoanalysts and others who have long since adopted the vocabulary and habits of thought bequeathed by Freud. These readers—of whom I am one—have recognized Freud's genius and have not stopped to criticize it. They have had trouble enough understanding the subtleties, the twists and turns, the changes of heart in that massive work which is still in the process of impregnating our culture. With a thinker of Freud's stature, one does not quibble over details: it is better to watch what he does and use the power of his thought in the continuing effort to understand the many obscure phenomena that he has helped us confront and that he has ultimately restored to the realm of rationality.

Now here is Mikkel Borch-Jacobsen, boldly jarring the Freudian edifice and proposing to reread it from beginning to end so as to show how it coheres in its very inconsistencies. Borch-Jacobsen presents Freud as the victim of a concept of the human subject, inherited from previous generations, that led him toward a series of brilliant solutions to false problems. According to this book, Freud failed to notice that the human subject is radically "altered," that it is never what it is except because it is other, because it is other to itself, because it is its own other, although it is never able to represent that other to itself.

It is as though Freud had always been on the right track. It was he, after all, who did all he could to dislodge the ego from its position of self-sufficiency, trying to be a new Copernicus who would stop the Sun of otherness from revolving around the egoistic Earth. But the premises available to him led him to attribute to the unconscious all that he took away from consciousness; in the process, he failed to see that the new center he was proposing suffered from the same centripetal defect he had attributed to the conscious ego. This leads to a claim of self-sufficiency, not for consciousness but for the unconscious. And this self-sufficiency brings us back to the illusion of completeness and mastery, with the unconscious as new master.

Out of this reasoning a whole series of insoluble problems arises, as Borch-Jacobsen makes clear: the problem of desire going astray in the search for its object; the problem of the social bond that is magnified in paranoia; the problem of the formation of groups, which brings us around to hypnosis. I shall not pursue these points, which are abundantly and forcefully developed in Borch-Jacobsen's book.

Are my own preexisting prejudices returning to make me ask, or reiterate, certain questions? The pleasure of seeing the Freudian machinery dismantled leaves some room for reservations. I wonder, for example, whether Borch-Jacobsen's model is not too large a garment in which to cloak Freudian psychoanalysis. To put it another way, does not the philosophical method proceed too quickly to the ultimate solution, so that questions arising in a clinical context are submerged by the exemplary truth? The response will be, rightly, that false problematics can only lead to therapeutic disasters. Hence I shall formulate my objection differently. Is the philosophical that operates within the transcendental capable of making room, really, for the empirical? Let me take just one example.

According to the logic of Borch-Jacobsen's argument, one must declare not only that transference is finally identical with hypnosis, but also that the hypnotic state is constitutive of the human subject, and that it is therefore useless to hope that transference can be dissolved. We might just as well say that the ego can finally constitute itself independently of the other that defines it without being able to master that other, much less to put itself in the other's place.

That is uncontestable. Uncontestable, yes, but precisely at the level of philosophical principles and their transcendent generality. At the empirical level, the uncontestable is divided into several statements. There is no doubt that, at the end of treatment, the alteration of the subject turns out to be intact if the human subject is defined as altered. There is no way around that, so in this sense the transference remains. But this by no means implies that the transference to a particular analyst—the state of hypnosis, of suggestion, of dependency with respect to that analyst—remains unchanged, that is, retains the form with which it began. The altering other that the psychoanalyst was charged with representing (and it had to be represented, for a time, to emerge from the neurosis) can be dismissed to the benefit of that other who now permits the subject to function without needing to be represented. In this second sense the transference comes to an end, which in no way contradicts Borch-Jacobsen's thesis, but situates it in its proper place.

Let me go even further. It is because Borch-Jacobsen has formulated his thesis that we shall be led, if we listen to him, to spell out just what belongs in our domain, and to understand more precisely the difficulties and, eventually, the solutions we encounter in our practice. There is no better way to mark the interest of a book than to observe that it forces us to rethink what we have been taking for granted and to find more adequate formulations for what we do.

François Roustang

Note on Abbreviations

Unless otherwise noted, all excerpts from Freud's works are quoted from James Strachey, ed., *The Standard Edition of the Complete Psychological Works of Sigmund Freud*, 24 vols. (London, 1953–74). *The Standard Edition* is subsequently referred to as *SE*.

Only works that constitute an entire volume of *SE* appear in italics; all others, regardless of the form in which they were originally published, appear in quotation marks throughout.

The following frequently cited works in *SE* are abbreviated, in both in-text citations and the Notes, and the *SE* volume number omitted, since it is given here:

"Beyond Pleasure"	"Beyond the Pleasure Principle," *SE* 18
"Child"	"A Child Is Being Beaten," *SE* 17
"Creative Writers"	"Creative Writers and Day-Dreaming," *SE* 9
Dreams	*The Interpretation of Dreams*, *SE* 4 and 5
"Ego and Id"	"The Ego and the Id," *SE* 19
"Group Psychology"	"Group Psychology and the Analysis of the Ego," *SE* 14
"On Narcissism"	"On Narcissism: An Introduction," *SE* 14
"Psycho-Analytic Notes"	"Psycho-Analytic Notes on an Autobiographical Account of a Case of Paranoia (Dementia Paranoides)," *SE* 12
"Three Essays"	"Three Essays on the Theory of Sexuality," *SE* 7

Also abbreviated are the following two works:

Origins   *The Origins of Psycho-Analysis, Letters to Wil-
                     helm Fliess, Drafts and Notes: 1887–1902,* ed.
                     Marie Bonaparte, Anna Freud, and Ernst Kris
                     (New York, 1954)

Letters   *The Freud-Jung Letters: Correspondence Be-
                     tween Sigmund Freud and C. G. Jung,* ed. Wil-
                     liam McGuire, trans. Ralph Manheim and
                     R. F. C. Hull (Princeton, N.J., 1974)

The Freudian Subject

Dramatis Personae

At the end of the fourth chapter of *The Interpretation of Dreams*, which deals with distortion in dreams, Freud returns to the formula that concluded the analysis of the dream of "Irma's injection": *After a complete interpretation, every dream turns out to be the fulfillment of a wish*. The formula is justly famous, for it sums up Freud's entire thesis on dreams and fantasies: here, in these bizarre scenes wrested from sleep, in the fantasies of daydreaming, is where desire is fulfilled and "realized," properly speaking. And so this is where the investigator must turn, plunging into the intermediary world between night and day in order to bring what is nocturnal, unconscious, out into the open. We shall follow that path here: according to another celebrated formula, dreams are the *via regia*, the royal road to the unconscious.

But we know, too, that this road is not a direct one. Dreams are obscure; in them, desire does not speak clearly. Thus Freud adds two parentheses to his initial formula, correcting his statement as follows: *"A dream is a (disguised) fulfillment of a (suppressed or repressed) wish"* (*Dreams*, p. 160). The earlier formula dealt directly with the dream's latent thought, the unconscious dream-thought in which a wish is fulfilled (for example: "I am not responsible for Irma's illness"). The second comes at the conclusion of a chapter that attempts to explain why so many dreams, in their manifest content, appear to invalidate the thesis of the wish-dream (because no wish seems to be fulfilled in the dream, or even because the dream runs counter to a wish, as in the case of counter-wish-dreams). This clarifies the point of view from which Freud is looking at distortion in Chapter 4. He is not yet concerned with describing the modalities of distortion in dreams, or the disturbances introduced into dream-thoughts by a dream-work that, for its part, "does not think" (he deals with these in Chap. 6); he is concerned, rather, with a preliminary question: Why is there distortion, and who benefits from it?

The answer, in its essence, is well known. It is the ABC of psychoanalysis: "Everyone has wishes that he would prefer not to disclose to other people, and wishes that he will not admit even to himself" (p. 160). On this point, the psychology of dreams converges with the psychology of neurosis, which Freud had been exploring since his *Studies on Hysteria*. For if the dream-wish has to be distorted, if its discourse has to be purified, it is for the same reason that it is "converted" in hysterical symptoms, "transposed" in obsessive ideas, "rejected" in psychotic hallucinations: because it is inadmissible, irreconcilable, with the conscious, social, orderly ego.[1]

And what is supremely irreconcilable, of course, is sexuality. The dream analyses in *The Interpretation of Dreams* do not all lead to a specifically sexual desire—far from it, and we shall return to this point. Still, the connections Freud repeatedly establishes between dream processes and neurotic processes provide clear evidence that in his mind the "etiology" of dreams is ultimately sexual, just as the etiology of neuroses is sexual. Thus a (pre)conscious wish from the previous evening may well trigger a dream and even occupy center stage in it, but such a wish, according to Freud, could never have formed the dream on its own, without the contribution of a clandestine investment or cathexis. This dream "capitalist," to use the celebrated comparison, always turns out to be an infantile wish, which is unconscious because it is repressed, and repressed because it is sexual (pp. 552–53, 560–61, 605–7, and so on).

Wishes are rooted in the forbidden, by way of sexuality: this is supposed to account for distortion. If the wish is never clearly represented to consciousness, no inherent opacity on the part of the wish is to blame. The wish is not clearly represented because access to consciousness is *denied* it by an "agency" assigned the task of sorting out representations at the entrance to the preconscious-conscious system; significantly, Freud compares the work of this agency to political censorship. The dream's indecipherability thus stems first of all from an elision, a subtraction of the dream-thoughts from consciousness: according to Freud, foreign newspapers with passages blacked out at the Russian border are unreadable in the same way (pp. 142–43, n. 3).[2] Next we have to add the efforts the wish makes to conceal its thoughts and bypass censorship:

A similar difficulty confronts the political writer who has disagreeable truths to tell to those in authority. If he presents them undisguised, the authorities will suppress his words—after they have been spoken, if his pronouncement was an oral one, but beforehand, if he had intended to make it in print. A writer must beware of the censorship, and on its account he must soften and distort the expression of his opinion. [p. 142]

What these "analogies" presuppose is obvious: the newspaper is legible before the censor's scissors make holes in it; the writer knows what he wants to say before he starts to play the game of concealment. In other words, dream-thoughts are indeed thoughts, *cogitationes*, and they are perfectly intelligible ones (Freud insists on this repeatedly). Nothing sets them apart from conscious representations except the simple fact that repression keeps them inaccessible to consciousness:

When we bear in mind that the latent dream-thoughts are not conscious before an analysis has been carried out, whereas the manifest content of the dream is consciously remembered, it seems plausible to suppose that the privilege enjoyed by the second [censoring] agency is that of permitting thoughts to enter consciousness. . . . This enables us to form a quite definite view of the "essential nature" of consciousness: we see the process of a thing becoming conscious as a specific psychical act, distinct from and independent of the process of the formation of a presentation or idea; and we regard consciousness as a sense organ which perceives data that arise elsewhere. [p. 144]

Thus we have come right back to the fundamental hypothesis of psychoanalysis, whose scandalous and enigmatic aspects are revived by the merest reminder: the subject is not conscious of all "its" thoughts, is not present in all "its" representations, not even virtually or potentially. In the move from *cogito* to *me cogitare*, the logic is faulty, for "I" have thoughts (*Gedanken*), "I" make representations (*Vorstellungen*) that do not appear to *me*, are never given to *me* in any experience or perception whatsoever. The *cogitatio*—Freud's term for it is the "psychical"[3]—exceeds and overflows consciousness at every turn, where consciousness is understood as certainty and presence of self in representation. This thinking thinks *without me*, without ceasing to think, moreover (as we see, for example, when it calculates, or makes a joke). *It* thinks, then—and it *thinks*. The Freudian unconscious, Lacan asserts,

> has nothing to do with the so-called forms of the unconscious that preceded it, not to say accompanied it. . . . To all these forms of unconscious, ever more or less linked to some obscure will regarded as primordial, to something preconscious, what Freud opposes is the revelation that at the level of the unconscious there is something at all points homologous with what occurs at the level of the subject—this thing speaks and functions in a way quite as elaborate as at the level of the conscious, which thus loses what seemed to be its privilege.[4]

The debate over the Cartesian *Cogito* and its subsequent history begins, of course, right here. ("It is here," Lacan continues a little further on, "that the dissymmetry between Freud and Descartes is revealed. It is not in the initial method of certainty grounded on the subject. It stems from the fact that the subject is 'at home' in the field of the unconscious.")[5] But the difficulties begin here as well. For once it has been established that "it"—or the *id*—thinks without my knowing, without the ego's knowing, anything about it, then we have to ask: Who is It? *Who* is thinking, in this instance (who, then, is thinking me)? Is this unconscious thinking therefore a thinking attributable to no subject?

Let us not pursue the argument as to whether this *cogitatio* without ego is Structure, Signifier, or Language, as it is frequently claimed to be today: it could be shown that this Structure (a signifying combinatorial, mathematical or mathetic), though it excludes all "subjectivism" and all "egoism," is precisely *the* Subject in the modern, Cartesian sense—as Lacan himself knows perfectly well, and even argues.[6] Let us remain instead on the properly Freudian level of the question. We want to know, then, *who* represents unconscious thoughts to him/her/itself. Indeed, if the "content" of the unconscious is defined essentially as representation, as *Vorstellung* (and in fact, according to Freud, repression involves the ideational representative of an instinct), can we avoid asking *in front of* what, in front of what "agency," this *Vor-stellung* is posited or presented?

What is this psyche, the "psychical" in which an instinct comes to represent itself as representation (*Vorstellung*) and affect (*Affekt*), unless it is, still and always, a subject? Unless it is, more precisely, the subject of representation apart from which the wish or instinct *is* nothing, simply does not appear.[7] And then, if it is true, as Heidegger has conclusively shown,[8] that the subject, for the Moderns, is the subject *of representation*, do we not have to begin to wonder about the radicalness of the displacement operated here in the name of "thinking" and unconscious "representation"? By maintaining these terms, by continuing to use them in an unqualified fashion, do we not risk dismissing the entire problematics of subjecti(vi)ty, by heedlessly passing it off under the name of "unconscious"?

For unconscious desire is undoubtedly not (re)presented to consciousness, but it is presented to the unconscious, (re)presented ("fulfilled," "realized") in the unconscious. And this alone suffices to make the unconscious substantive, to institute it as a subject: a subject positing itself in and through (re)presentation, a subject assuring itself of itself in and through thought—in short, *con-scientia*. To specify, as Freud does ("The Unconscious," *SE* 14: 170), that the unconscious is not a second *consciousness* (a "splitting of consciousness," a "subconsciousness," and so on) changes nothing: *con-scientia*, rigorously speaking, designates above all the *co*-position of the subject with its representations, and this co-position has no need, finally, for consciousness in the psychological sense.

It changes nothing, either, when Freud adds—in another refrain as familiar as the statement that the unconscious is intelligible—that unconscious thoughts are erratic, independent of each other, and governed by laws other than those of waking thought (p. 170). Beyond the fact that insane thought, which knows neither reality "nor negation, nor doubt, nor degree of certitude," is thought nonetheless,[9] the fact remains that all these irreconcilable representations are indeed referred to a *single subject*, however chaotic or "id-ic" it may be, and that they coexist within a single subject, according to the utopia and the achronicity of the "primary processes." All in all, there will always be something or someone "beneath" the representations, to which or to whom they will appear (in other words, there will always be an eye to see the spectacle that is offered it on the "other stage").[10] How then can we rid ourselves of the impression that the subject-conscious-of-itself, dislodged from its privileged and central position, is never dislodged except to the benefit of an *other* subject—one that is deeper, more subjacent, more subjectal?

All this, which might legitimately cause concern that we are attempting to sidestep the scandal of the unconscious, nevertheless entails a reversion to it. For we must add at once—and this is a way of reintroducing the scandal, and the enigma—that that other subject is simultaneously the *same* as the subject-of-consciousness. The otherness labeled "unconscious" is an intimate otherness, if only because the unconscious (or the unconsciousness) *of* the subject is at stake. "The unconscious—there the subject is at home." Lacan's statement may be read just as legitimately in the other direction: The subject—there the unconscious is at home. Perhaps the ego is not "master in its own house," in Freud's phrase; the fact remains that *its* house is haunted, *its* property inhabited by something entirely "other." Moreover, Freud never pretends otherwise, since he always introduces the hypothesis of the Unconscious in this way as well. The hypothesis means that the *same* subject has and does not have access to a given representation, remembers and does not remember a given "scene," experiences and does not experience a given pleasure. In this sense, the cleavage or division of the subject that psychoanalysis keeps talking about takes place against a background of unity, a *unitary* subject. Let us look, for example, at the following passage from the "Introductory Lectures on Psycho-Analysis," later incorporated into *The Interpretation of Dreams*:

No doubt a wish-fulfilment must bring pleasure; but the question then arises "To whom?" *To the person who has the wish, of course.* But, as we know, a dreamer's relation to his wishes is a quite peculiar one. He repudiates them and censors them—he has no liking for them, in short. So that their fulfilment will give him no pleasure, but just the opposite; and experience shows that this opposite appears in the form of anxiety, a fact which has still to be explained. Thus a dreamer in his relation to his dream-wishes can only be compared to *an amalgamation of two separate people who*

are linked by some important common element [eine starke Gemeinsamkeit].
[*Dreams*, pp. 580–81, n. 1][11]

Now a formulation of this sort obviously gives rise at once to a major difficulty—the difficulty of the unconscious, once again, in its disconcerting simplicity. For if two subjects (two "persons") are involved, it is quite conceivable that one may not know what the other is thinking, or that the first may be distressed by something that pleases the second. But what if the two are linked by a tenacious common element, a *starke Gemeinsamkeit*? What if they are one and the "same" person? In this case, how are we to understand that *the* subject knows nothing of what *it* desires, fantasizes, imagines, and so on? How are we to understand that it is other *to itself*? How are we to understand, in other words, that the unconscious is the unconscious *of the subject*, the repressed aspect *of the ego*? Does it suffice to invoke repressed representations or fantasies in this connection? Is not the real question whether the subject has ever represented its desire to itself? If the answer were yes, we would quickly find ourselves confronting the phenomenological objection that Sartre once addressed to the hypothesis of the unconscious: if the repressed is to be maintained outside the field of consciousness, the censorship that is charged with eliminating it must at the very least *represent it to itself* in some way, so it will know what it has to reject—and the unconscious, then, according to Sartre, is only a modality of "bad faith."[12]

This objection relied in vain on the postulate of "unity"—of a *simple* unity—of bad-faith consciousness,[13] and thus it misjudged the most incontrovertible contribution of psychoanalysis from the outset. Yet psychoanalysis could not fail to encounter this objection in its own path as long as it persisted in conceiving of the unconscious within the category of representation—that is to say, within the category of subject, of *identity* (the term "subject," *subjectum*, designates what remains identical with itself beneath its various attributes or—in the modern sense—its various representations). Clearly, this very difficulty—but taken, as it were, the other way around, with respect to Sartre: how can we explain that censorship, resistance, repression are *not* conscious?—is what motivates the introduction of narcissism, and later the revisions of the second topographical schema, by obliging Freud at last to take into consideration the "unconscious aspects of the ego" or, we may already say, a certain unconsciousness constitutive of the ego *itself*.

It is toward the ego—toward this "repressing agency," as the "New Introductory Lectures" will put it, this ego "which had seemed so self-evident" (*SE* 22: 58)—that most of the questioning will be directed, as if the "I" (the *Ich*, the ego) until now predicated of consciousness would turn out, finally, to be most opaque to consciousness. And the unconsciousness in question designates not repressed representations so much as—well in advance of any representation or repression—the ego's identity or, more precisely still, its *identification*. Which is quite a different thing, precisely because an identification with an other comes into play. In short, and pending clarification in what follows, the otherness called "unconscious" no longer designates, rigorously speaking, that part of myself about which I wish to remain ignorant; rather, it designates my identity or my very sameness *as that of another*—the *starke Gemeinsamkeit* that connects me with an other that I am "myself."

I should like to ask, then, in the essays that follow, *who* is the subject of the unconscious—if it is a subject. This question may seem to have detective-story overtones, as if it involved an objectionable fingerprinting procedure. And we are indeed seeking to attach a name to the unconscious: Who is "the dreamer," the dream "capitalist" (in Sigmund Freud's dream, for example)? Who is the subject of fantasy (of the fantasies revealed by Sigmund Freud in the course of his self-analysis, for example)? Who is the subject of desire? Sex? The narcissistic ego? The death instinct? Who makes a transference onto the analyst? What is the unconscious actually called? "Ucs"? "Id"? "Ego"? "Superego"? And so on. But the very formulation of these questions already suggests that the identity of the unconscious is multiple, rigorously speaking unnameable, *unverifiable*. This may be so quite simply because of a very general law making the unconscious "itself": identity, as such, is not susceptible to identification; *it does not identify itself*. (Similarly, the sections that follow have no unity, do not form a book or thesis or treatise: their "common" subject—the subject of psychoanalysis, however that may be understood—is unascribable, properly unidentifiable, because its identity is plural. Thus it has been called "dramatis personae." This "book" is a play.)

That is why, rather than being seen as a detective-story question, the question "who?" has to be seen as naive. Like every naive question, it asks the impossible—and it is of course the child's question par excellence, the endless, inexhaustible question of origins: "Where do babies come from?" "Who are you?" Such questions always really mean "Where do you come from?" "Where does your name come from?" "Where were you born?" "Who made you what you are?" At its most naive, the question "who?" directs questioning toward birth, and thus questions beyond the subject, toward a "beyond" of identity. In this it is infinitely disconcerting; in this it is also quite different from the question "what?," which always establishes what it wants to know in advance. For to say *what* I am is relatively easy—that is even how I assure myself of myself beyond all possible doubt: to paraphrase Descartes, I am what I think, wish, fantasize, feel, and so on.[14] But to say *who* I am—who thinks, who wishes, who fantasizes in me—is no longer in *my* power. That question draws me immediately beyond myself, beyond my representations, toward a point—we shall name it, further on, the "point of otherness"—where I am another, the other who gives me my identity.

That is, the other who gives birth to me. My identity connects me with my birth. Hypothesis: the unconscious is that umbilical cord.

"Dreams Are Completely Egoistic"

> Scholtz states: "In dreams is truth: in dreams we learn to know ourselves as we are in spite of all the disguises we wear to the world, whether they be ennobling or humiliating. . . . The common expression 'I wouldn't dream of such a thing' has a doubly correct significance when it refers to something which can have no lodgement in our hearts or mind." (Plato, on the contrary, thought that the best men are those who only *dream* what other men *do* in their waking life.)
>
> Pfaff . . . alters the wording of a familiar saying: "Tell me some of your dreams, and I will tell you about your inner self."
>
> Freud, *The Interpretation of Dreams*

Let us look at the dream usually known as "the dream of the abandoned supper-party."[1] Of all the dreams presented in the fourth chapter of *The Interpretation of Dreams* to substantiate his thesis that "the meaning of every dream is the fulfilment of a wish," Freud dwells on this one at greatest length (save for the "dream of Uncle Josef," the "uncle with the yellow beard," to which we shall return). It is an interesting dream on more than one account. On the one hand, it is a hysteric's dream: because of this, in analyzing it Freud establishes parallels between the dream process and the "psychical processes of hysteria." This parallelism makes up for the absence of the chapter "Dreams and Hysteria" that Freud had initially planned to incorporate into *The Interpretation of Dreams* and that was to have connected it with his work on the etiology and psychotherapy of neuroses. Thus the dream offers a good summary of the overall problematics of Freud's work to that date. In addition, it gives rise to the first systematic presentation of the psychoanalytic concept of identification.

Yet identification is not merely a "psychical mechanism" peculiar to hysteria, as Freud seems to be suggesting in his dream analysis. It is something much more significant: perhaps *the* fundamental concept, the *Grundbegriff*, of psychoanalysis, whose initial ambiguity sets this new science or theory of the subject on shaky ground from its very inception. In any event, identification is the concept that alone makes it possible to understand, at a level that is relatively in-accessible in a first reading, the precise nature of the wish fulfillment that Freud posits at the foundation of dreams. At least that is what I hope to show.

Appropriation

Freud's summary of the dream is concise:

I wanted [*ich will*] to give a supper-party, but [*aber*] I had nothing in the house but a little smoked salmon. I thought I would go out and buy some-thing, but [*aber*] remembered then that it was Sunday afternoon and all the shops would be shut. Next I tried [*ich will*] to ring up some caterers, but [*aber*] the telephone was out of order. So [*so*] I had to abandon my wish to give a supper-party. [*Dreams*, p. 147]

The whole problem, of course, is to discover how this dream—we might almost say "this demonstration" (*Ich will . . . , aber . . . , so*)—fulfills a wish. Freud proposes three types of interpretation, of increasing depth and complexity:

First, the dream fulfills the wish of making the analyst lie (for, as it happens, the analyst has been claiming that every dream fulfills a wish). Hence the tone of vindictive triumph with which the "clever woman patient" reports it to Freud: "Well, I'll tell you a dream whose subject was the exact opposite—a dream in which one of my wishes was *not* fulfilled. How do you fit that in with your theory?" We would have in this case a ruse that is quite characteristic of re-sistance to analysis: the patient takes exception to dream censorship so as to prevent its being lifted. But this first interpretation, which is both the most general of the three (since, taken to the extreme, it applies to every counter-wish-dream [*Gegenwunschtraum*] in the an-alytic context) and also the weakest (since it says nothing about the content of the dream itself), informs us only about the strictly re-active "desire" of the ego. We still have to find the assertion of desire that is proper to the dream itself.

According to the second explanation, the dream fulfills the wish *not* to give a supper-party. And indeed, analysis reveals that on the previous evening the patient had visited a friend of whom she was secretly jealous, for her husband praised this woman constantly, even though the friend was quite thin and the patient's husband, a wholesale butcher, usually preferred a "plumper figure." The friend had confided to the patient her desire to gain weight, adding that she was eager to be invited to dinner by the butcher's wife ("You always feed one so well"). Thus the whole dream seems to center on the dreamer's refusal to grant her friend's request, as if it came down to a simple matter of getting rid of a rival while preventing that rival from appearing more desirable in the husband's eyes (the friend will not gain weight). This interpretation is further supported by the fact that the smoked salmon represented in the dream content is the friend's favorite dish. As a result, the whole scene seems to fit the framework of a highly conventional triangle and to appeal quite transparently to feelings of the utmost banality.

There is a further problem, however, which sets the analytic process into motion again and leads Freud to propose a third interpretation. He calls this interpretation "subtler" and "more complicated," though he insists that it does not contradict the second interpretation. The latter did allow us to confirm the presence of a desire or wish at the origin of the dream (an erotic desire, ultimately), but it failed to account for the peculiar turn taken by the process of wish fulfillment in this instance. For if the dreamer only wished to prevent the fulfillment of her friend's wish (to gain weight, to eat smoked salmon), then why does the dream show the patient denying *herself* the fulfillment of that same wish? The solution is at once uneconomical (it would have sufficed to represent the nonsatisfaction of the other's desire) and quite inept (since by depriving herself of a meal the dreamer runs the risk of growing thinner and thus of displeasing her husband). The second interpretation somehow fails to account for the nonfulfillment of the desire that is present in the dream's manifest content.

At this point, a more thorough inquiry brings to light two supplementary elements that endow the dream with a new meaning, a meaning that is considerably removed from the one disclosed by the previous decoding (and we are already tempted to declare the new one incompatible with its predecessors). In the first place, the dream reproduces in almost unchanged form a behavior pattern from the dreamer's daily life, a bizarre pattern in which she forbids herself to satisfy her very strong desire to eat a caviar sandwich every morning, even though there is no reason not to do so. This pattern is, in a word, symptomatic, since the only reasons the patient can give for her behavior are incoherent and disconnected; in this respect her behavior is very like that of "one of Bernheim's hypnotized patients . . . [carrying] out a post-hypnotic suggestion" (*Dreams*, p. 148). The dream and the symptom manifest the same tendency to create unsatisfied desires, the same propensity for cultivating a luxurious craving (for salmon or caviar) only in order to curb it.

Then, too, the symptom is never anything but the repetition— here again in almost unmodified form—of a behavior pattern (a symptom?) characteristic of the friend. For if smoked salmon is indeed the friend's favorite dish, as Freud has already indicated, it is also true—and this changes everything—that her behavior with respect to this special treat is just like the patient's own: "the same was no doubt true of my patient and the caviare" (p. 148). The inverse, of course, is implied: by her symptom, the patient is copying her friend, imitating her, with just one small difference, the substitution of caviar for smoked salmon—a substitution or displacement that the dream disdains to keep on implementing, since it openly reveals at the level of its most manifest content what the symptom still feebly concealed from view.

What is it, then, that is revealed? Imitation of the friend and, by the same token, imitation of the friend's strange "wish" for salmon. For now the dream can no longer be said to fulfill the wish to thwart the friend's wish (to eat, to gain weight), since the dish whose enjoyment is at stake for the friend (salmon) is the very one that she stubbornly refuses to allow herself to touch. Thus it is necessary, in a first phase, to turn the explanation on its head: the dream fulfills (by thwarting it) the friend's desire. We might say that the dream obeys the other: the dreamer gives in, subjects herself to her rival's wish. But this is also because she conforms to this wish, because she makes it her own, quite literally, by appropriating it for herself. And this appropriation or assimilation (this obedience) is a form of murder. In fact, by desiring what the other desires, the dreamer puts herself in the other's place and in that sense kills her, annihilates her. This accounts for the friend's absence from the manifest content of

the dream: that absence doubtless stems not so much from censorship as from the very impetus of the wish—that is, in this case, of
identification:

Thus the dream will acquire a new interpretation if we suppose that the
person indicated in the dream was not herself but her friend, that she had
put herself in her friend's place, or, as we might say, that she had "identified" herself with her friend. I believe she had in fact done this; and the
circumstance of her having brought about a renounced wish in real life was
evidence of this identification. [p. 149]

We must proceed a little more cautiously, however, and stop to
spell out the relationship between wishes and identification. For
Freud, it is not precisely a relationship of identity. It is a relationship
of expression: the identification expresses the wish; it is not yet the
wish itself. Here we have to recognize that the identification in question is not simply another name for the phenomena of mimesis (or
mimetism) that we described earlier in speaking of "imitating,"
"copying," and so forth. Identification is a name for an interpretation
of these phenomena, and it has the status of a specific psychoanalytic
concept. Freud insists quite clearly on this point, in the course of a
lengthy digression intended to explain the difference (the "break,"
we might say) between "identification" according to psychoanalysis
and the notions of "imitation" (*Imitation, Nachahmung*), "simulation" (*Nachmachung*), "sympathy" (*Mitleid*), and even of "psychical
contagion" that had previously prevailed in explanations of hysterical mimesis. Let us postpone our analysis of this discussion for the
moment, though it is a crucial one (we shall come back to it later on).
For the time being, we shall simply cite its conclusion, which is unequivocal: "Thus identification is not simple imitation but *assimilation* [*Aneignung* = "appropriation"] on the basis of a similar aetiological pretension; it expresses a resemblance [*gleichwie* = "just
as"] and is derived from a common element [*Gemeinsames*] which
remains in the unconscious" (p. 150).[2]

To speak of mimetism or imitation would be to continue to say
nothing at all. From Freud's point of view, we would still be re-
stricting ourselves to the outward appearance of the wish. For why
would one imitate except, here again, to satisfy a desire, to obtain
some increase in pleasure? In this sense, identification is indeed mi-

mesis, with its disconcerting lack of differentiation between self and other; but it is mimesis included within the scope of the wish, re-situated within the perspective of an economy or strategy that extends beyond identification (which is only one of its components), and illuminated by the secret goal that it is intended to serve (a goal toward which identification is but one means). This explains why the hysteric, for example (but the example is a paradigm that is valid, at least in the historical period in question, for any instance of identification), never engages in identification without a reason—never, as it happens, without sexual reasons. The etiology of identification, according to Freud, is sexual:

Identification is most frequently used in hysteria to express a common *sexual* element [*einer sexuellen Gemeinsamkeit*]. A hysterical woman identifies herself in her symptoms most readily—though not exclusively—with people with whom she has had sexual relations or with people who have had sexual relations with the same people as herself. Linguistic usage takes this into account, for two lovers are spoken of as being "one." In hysterical phantasies, just as in dreams, it is enough for purposes of identification that the subject should have *thoughts* of sexual relations without their having necessarily taken place in reality. [p. 150]

We do not love because we identify, we identify because we love. Mimesis is articulated on—and grounded in—sexuality. And thus we have the definitive explanation of the dream of the butcher's beautiful wife. If the butcher's wife puts herself in her friend's place, in fantasy or dream, it is not through "simple imitation," it is not in order to take her friend's place; it is, rather, as Freud sees it, "because her friend was taking my patient's place with her husband and because she (my patient) wanted to take her friend's place in her husband's high opinion" (pp. 150–51).

The dream's meaning, then, is far from exhausted in the phenomenon of identification, which has to be decoded in terms of the double advantage it procures: by virtue of identification, the dreamer wins back her husband's love ("I am the object of his esteem, of his desire"), and at the same time she eliminates her rival ("I am in her place, I am replacing her, she no longer exists"). To be sure, we may find this last interpretation difficult to reconcile with the one proposed just a moment ago, given that the dreamer in the first instance was working to prevent her friend from gaining weight, whereas here we see her eager to assimilate her friend's thinness. What is important for Freud, however (and this is why he can declare the two interpretations compatible), is that each of them manifests—by dissimilar and even inverse means, to be sure—the unity of an intention and the consistency of a wish: the dreamer's wish to have full enjoyment of her husband's love once again. And it is this wish, as powerful as it is simple, that the dream is said to fulfill, by representing it as accomplished, satisfied.

The enigma of the unfulfilled wish in the dream (and in the symptom) is thereupon dispelled. When the patient chooses to identify with her friend precisely insofar as the latter fails to satisfy one of her own wishes, it is not—as Lacan suggests—in order to preserve the emptiness of the Desire by preventing it from being demolished, from being reduced to the demand of the other.[3] (Such an explanation, which amounts to making nonfulfillment of the wish the very mainspring of the dream, obviously never tempts Freud.) The dreamer chooses to identify with her friend in order to conceal the identification in which the wish is fulfilled, by focusing that identification on a single behavior pattern associated with her rival: a pattern so incidental, so small in scope that it will at first glance appear insignificant and thus will elude censorship; and one that is disagreeable enough, moreover, to punish the wish[4] and to allow the conversion of the underlying pleasure into a surface displeasure. It is an instance of deformation, of displacement, then, but one based on wish fulfillment in the fantasy of identification. That is what had to be demonstrated.

Dramaturgies

> The transformation of ideas into hallucinations is not the only respect in which dreams differ from corresponding thoughts in waking life. Dreams construct a *situation* out of these images; they represent an event which is actually happening; . . . they "dramatize" an idea.
>
> Freud, *The Interpretation of Dreams*

Still, the peculiar status of identification in this instance is quite clear. On the one hand, it sets up a scenario in which the wish is presented as fulfilled: on this basis, identification is indeed the satisfaction of the desire as such, the very mainspring of wish fulfillment (and furthermore, that is why it has to be distorted in symptoms and in the manifest content of dreams). On the other hand, identification is by no means the object of the wish; it is not what is desired by the desire. Freud clearly designates the object of the wish, along with the (passive) goal of the instinct, as the husband, by whom the patient seeks to be loved. Thus from this vantage point the fantasy of identification is never anything but a stratagem aimed at wish fulfillment: as a stratagem, it is particularly shrewd, particularly oblique, since instead of representing the object of the wish directly, it represents the dreamer herself taking the place of another person who is positioned so as to enjoy that object. This ambiguity of identification—which is at once the last element disclosed by the dream analysis and the first of the dream's distortions—would not be particularly difficult to deal with, all things considered, if it were simply a matter of carrying the interpretation a little further in order to find, behind the scene of the patient's identification with a friend, a deeper wish-fantasy in which the object of the wish is finally to be represented in person, without dissimulation or distortion. Yet this is by no means the case, and for several reasons.

First of all, and even though Freud himself sometimes fails to go beyond this explanation, it would be a complete misunderstanding of the nature of fantasy—and thus of wish fulfillment[5]—to suppose that fantasy is content merely to hallucinate the object of satisfaction.[6] In fact, even in its crudest, most stereotyped forms (as in his "A Child Is Being Beaten," for example), a fantasy unfailingly calls up an entire scene complete with protagonists—dramatis personae—and plot. This minimal dramatization is simply amplified in dreams that rework the material of unconscious fantasy,[7] in the fantastic genealogies of "family romance," in the stories of daydreams, and also in literary fiction, which originates, according to Freud, in fantasy. Starting with the simplest fantasy, we are on a level with the potentially proliferating order of fable (*muthos*): we are already far removed from the drab imagination of satisfaction.

Furthermore, and this is no doubt what matters most, the subject (or the ego, as Freud would say) is always implicated in the scenario, either because it intervenes directly and in the "first person"—this is the case with most dreams and also with daydreams, which are, as Laplanche and Pontalis write, "filled to overflowing by the ego"[8]—or because it turns out to animate one fantasmatic character or another from within, as in those popular novels whose protagonist, as Freud notes, is a cover for "His Majesty the Ego, the hero alike of every day-dream and of every story" ("Creative Writers," p. 150). It is as if some obscure law compelled desire to follow a particular line—not a straight line that would lead it more economically to the object of enjoyment (or at least to the image of that object), but rather a broken line passing through the apex of a triangle in which the ego is represented in the position of enjoyment. In other words, it is as if wish fulfillment did not so much consist in *having* the object as in *being* the one who possesses it: a slight difference, an initially imperceptible nuance that liberates the fabulous space of fantasy in which a whole world of heroes is already stirring and around which pivots, quite unmistakably, the whole order of desire.

In this situation we can anticipate the crucial importance of identification, for identification is hardly a mechanism peculiar to the dream of the abandoned supper-party and that dream alone; it is not even a feature exclusive to hysteria, although it was initially described by Freud in relation to hysterical fantasy. It is required, in a much more general and much more necessary way, by every instance of fantasmatic wish fulfillment, as long as wishes have the dramatic structure we have just observed.[9] It goes without saying that the subject will derive pleasure from the fantasmatic scene only if he or she identifies with one or another of the drama's protagonists, by enjoying as the protagonist does, in the protagonist's place. In this sense, saying that wishes are fulfilled fantasmatically and that enjoyment is based on identification amounts to saying the same thing. This is what accounts for the fact that the subject's place in fantasy is always the place of another, and that statement holds true even when the ego is present in person (so to speak) in the scenario. Indeed, we might suppose that there is identification in an instance of fantasy only when its cast includes another person to whom the subject is covertly assimilated while remaining concealed by that "cover person." But it is no less true that identification occurs in the inverse case (doubtless the more basic case; we shall come back to it later) in which the subject seems to be alone on center stage: this is because he, in turn, is functioning as "cover" for another person, who is routinely revealed in the course of a more thorough analysis.

We have seen one example of this with the "dream of the abandoned supper-party," but there are many others. Thus in the "dream of the uncle with the yellow beard," in which Freud pitilessly eliminates two rivals for the post of *professor extraordinarius*, he puts himself in the place of the minister on whom their nomination depends, satisfying at the same time what he does not hesitate to represent as his tenacious, infantile megalomania (*Dreams*, pp. 136–40, 191–93, 322–23). The same desire and the same device appear once again in the "Otto" dream: here the analysis uncovers an implicit identification with one of the models Freud envied, the *professor extraordinarius*, R. (pp. 269–71, 555–56).[10]

As for the famous dream of the "botanical monograph," the associations that it arouses in Freud show clearly enough that the "I" of its manifest content ("*I* had written a monograph on a certain plant. The book lay before me, and *I* was at the moment turning over a folded coloured plate . . ." [p. 169]) occupies at least two clandestine positions: on the one hand that of Dr. Koller, who, by being the first to note the analgesic properties of cocaine, had unduly taken credit for a discovery that Freud himself had outlined in a monograph on the same theme (thus the dream signifies "I am the man who has done some valuable work on cocaine, some fruitful work"); on the other hand that of Fliess, who had written Freud the day before that he could already see the book (*The Interpretation of Dreams*, at that point still unfinished) in front of him (thus the dream signifies "I have written the Book, there it is spread before my eyes," but also, and especially, although Freud says nothing of the sort, "I am the *Seher*, Wilhelm Fliess, the double rival through whom I am at present anticipating my own glory" [pp. 171ff., 191, 282–84]).

It would be easy enough to accumulate examples, to move from dreams to hysterical fantasies, to invoke daydreams or literary fiction: everywhere we would encounter this play of ego identification, always this enigmatic shifting of wish fulfillment toward another subject's pleasure. Yet what is essential here is not the fact that the fantasmatic structure of dreams (or symptoms, or works of art) in some instances exhibits the ego although remaining silent about the identity that it usurps, while in other instances it presents an apocryphal character that the ego secretly inhabits. What is essential is, rather, the fact that in every instance the ego blends its characteristics with those of an outsider, and that in this indistinction of the "I" and the "he" lies the necessary condition of every wish fulfillment. For one must then ask who desires in dreams. Who is, in fact, the "subject" of the dream or fantasy? Who is enjoying, in such an instance? Who, then, is fulfilling a wish? Is it I, ego? Or is it the other?

We may reformulate these questions by asking: What is the egoism of the dream? In fact, as Freud tirelessly repeats throughout *The Interpretation of Dreams*, dreams are "completely egoistic":

I have spoken above of the egoism of children's minds, and I may now add, with a hint at a possible connection between the two facts, that dreams have the same characteristic. All of them are completely egoistic [*absolut egoistisch*]: the beloved ego appears in all of them, even though it may be disguised. The wishes that are fulfilled in them are invariably the ego's wishes, and if a dream seems to have been provoked by an altruistic interest, we are only being deceived by appearances. [p. 267]

Freud surely means to stress here that the wishes giving rise to the dream are hardly "altruistic"; indeed, if we may say so, they are profoundly *altruicidal*. Behind the egoism of dreams, he says, we regularly find the child's death wishes directed toward his Oedipal rivals.[11] But by adding that the ego appears disguised in dreams, he introduces a completely different motif (although it is closely linked to the preceding one, as we shall see). This is, once again, the motif of identification:

Every dream deals with the dreamer himself. Dreams are completely egoistical [*Traüme sind absolut egoistisch*]. Whenever my own ego does not appear in the content of the dream, but only some extraneous person, I may safely assume that my own ego lies concealed, by identification, behind this other person; I can insert my ego into the context. On other occasions, when my own ego *does* appear in the dream, the situation in which it occurs may teach me that some other person lies concealed, by identification, behind my ego. In that case the dream should warn me to transfer on to myself, when I am interpreting the dream, the concealed common element attached to this other person. There are also dreams in which my ego appears along with other people who, when the identification is resolved, are revealed once again as my ego. These identifications should then make it possible for me to bring into contact with my ego certain ideas whose acceptance has been forbidden by the censorship. Thus my ego may be represented in a dream several times over, now directly and now through identification with extraneous persons. [pp. 322–23]

This "egoism" is clearly rather peculiar. For though the *ego* is everywhere in the dream, though it can even diffract itself into several "part-egos,"[12] we still have to recognize that it is nowhere properly itself, given that it never avoids yielding to an identification and always confuses itself in some way with another (an alter ego—but one that is neither other nor self). This egoism can thus in no case be reduced to the frank and brutal affirmation of an ego that would refuse to give in where its own pleasure is concerned. To achieve its own pleasure, the ego has to take a detour, one that causes its own pleasure to pass through that of another. And this detour is identification (*mimesis*), resemblance (*homoïosis*). One only enjoys, in fantasy, as another: tell me whom you are miming and I'll tell you who you are, what you desire, and how you enjoy.

Here, no doubt, is the reason why the "logic" of dreams is defined essentially, according to Freud, as a logic of similitude. Let us recall the argument for the benefit of those who may have been rather too quickly turned away from the vertigo of resemblance (called the Imaginary) by the imputation to dreams of a logic of the signifier (called the Symbolic):

One and one only of these logical relations is very highly favoured by the mechanism of dream-formation; namely, the relation of similarity, consonance or approximation—the relation of "just as." This relation, unlike any other, is capable of being represented in dreams in a variety of ways. Parallels or instances of "just as" inherent in the material of the dream-thoughts constitute the first foundations for the construction of a dream; and no inconsiderable part of the dream-work consists in creating fresh parallels where those which are already present cannot find their way into the dream owing to the censorship imposed by resistance. The representation [*Darstellung*] of the relation of similarity is assisted by the tendency of the dream-work towards condensation.

Similarity, consonance, the possession of common attributes—all these are represented in dreams by unification, which may either be present already in the material of the dream-thoughts or may be freshly constructed. The first of these possibilities may be described as "identification" and the second as *composition*. [pp. 319–20]

Now if the dream-work is oriented in this fashion, if it is exclusively preoccupied with the relation of likeness, it is perhaps not simply, as Freud seems to say, because the very special grammar of the dream "language" into which the dream thoughts are "translated"[13] encompasses virtually no other relation. Between desire and resemblance there may well be a more essential, more fundamental complicity, for the following reason: by selecting from among all the logical relations included in the material of the dream those that express similarity and identification, the dream-work specifically chooses to retain those very relations that serve to fulfill the wish in the fantasy that inhabits the dream-thoughts ("I am like this or that person"). The result is that between the dream-thoughts and the manifest content, the dream-work is not solely the distorting (and therefore censoring) grid that Freud often seems to see: on the contrary, if only because of its enigmatic preference for resemblance, the dream-like representation rediscovers a fundamental feature of fantasy that is ensconced in the heart of the dream.

Thus we shall doubtless have to challenge the overly simple schema of a "translation" (which would be at the same time a betrayal) of the straightforward utterance of the dream-thoughts into the foreign, opaque, and at first glance undecipherable medium of dream language. There is, instead, a fundamental continuity in the order of the wish-fantasy, which is always already dissimulatory, because it is always "worked" by resemblance. In just the same way there is identity between the "grammar" of fantasy—the fantasy that weaves the dream-thoughts together from the start, according to Freud—and the grammar of dreams, since they both appeal to the same mode of dramatic enunciation, to the same ambiguous *lexis* in which the "I" speaks (and desires, and enjoys) in the name and in the place of another, without our knowing for certain whether that "I" has ever been located anywhere except in resemblance, where it plays all roles and simulates all identities. This argument can be restated as follows: the *lexis* of fantasy is *mimesis*—at least if we are willing to restore to this word the specific meaning that Plato gave it in the *Republic*, Book 3.[14]

All this has some very important consequences. For if a fantasy is indeed the complex drama that we have just described, and if mimesis is the indispensable mainspring for wish fulfillment, it is obvious why Freud's analyses never reach a clear formulation of the wish or a simple unveiling of its object: wish fulfillment takes place nowhere but on this displaced stage, this *andere Schauplatz* where "I" is always another, nowhere but in that fabulous (utopian) space of metamorphoses and visible changes in which resembling is equivalent to being and affinity is instantly transformed into identity. At the same time, it is obvious why the analysis of the dream of the abandoned supper-party was tripped up, as it were, by the fantasy of identification with the dreamer's friend. Above and beyond the fantasy, it was apparently necessary to present a finding concerning the wish that was being fulfilled, as Freud saw it, in the dream; but then we must already have exited from precisely the stage on which it was being fulfilled.

This is a strange situation, and one that calls for renewed questioning. For we are coming into contact with the blind spot in the entire problematics of wish fulfillment, or at least with its point of greatest obscurity. How, indeed, can we suppose that identification (mimesis) is at once what opens up the possibility of wish fulfillment as Freud consistently describes it to us and what moves, right from the start, to conceal the wish within the fable of the fantasy by subjecting it to the fundamental dramatization that confuses it with another's wish and another's pleasure? If our account is accurate, we are obliged to suppose that the wish is fulfilled only by disguising itself, and that wish fulfillment coincides with distortion from the outset. In other words, we are obliged to appeal to an original dissimulation, to a primordial opacity, and we must then conclude that the subject of the wish—that egoistic "I" which Freud describes—has no property, no identity prior to fantasy, since it is only in fantasy that the wish is granted, and since in fantasy the wish never manifests itself in the first person.

It is clear that Freud is more inclined to sidestep this difficulty than to deal with its rigorous necessity: hence the unstable coexistence, in his text, of two approaches that are ultimately incompatible. The first controls the concrete analyses of a given dream, a given symptom. This first thrust consists in plunging further and further into the order of the wish-fantasy, in being carried away by the multiple, fragmented drama in which the ego is simultaneously figured and disfigured, in which the ego is pluralized—and finally lost, owing to its being everywhere and everyone at once. Here Freud is following unmarked paths, pursuing free associations in the course of which he is not necessarily determined to have the last word, the definitive word on the wish. Thus he invites us to believe that the wish, too, is well served by the obscurity that surrounds the navel of the dream: "There is often a passage in even the most thoroughly interpreted dream which has to be left obscure; this is because we become aware during the work of interpretation that at that point there is a tangle of dream-thoughts which cannot be unraveled and which moreover adds nothing to our knowledge of the content of the dream. This is the dream's navel, the spot where it reaches down into the unknown" (p. 525).

The second thrust, a theoretical one, keeps up the pressure until the wish has been properly named, authenticated, identified. The characters of the fantasy are unmasked, the identification is "resolved," in order to rediscover the "I" hidden in it, the egoistic ego— in short, the desiring *subject*. Consequently, identification is conceived only as a simple vicissitude of distortion, as a disguise particularly apt to deceive the censoring agency; and correlatively, the fantasmatic wish fulfillment becomes the vassal of a rather banal theory of the "identity of perception," in which its sole remaining function is the hallucinatory restoration of the object of satisfaction.[15]

As a result, there is a split, or at least a tension, a discrepancy, between what one might for convenience call the description of wish fulfillment and its theorization. It is easy to see why things could not have been otherwise, given Freud's premises. Inscribing identification *within* desire (inscribing distortion within wish fulfillment) would amount to saying that disguise is the work of the wish itself, and not the effect of an exogenous censorship; it would mean destroying the idea of a disguise provoked by repression, and thereby unraveling all the binary, oppositional (dualist) logic that maintains the wish and the interdiction in a position of exteriority; finally, and especially, since the identificatory dissimulation is from this point on inextricably intertwined with the wish, it would mean challenging the very core of the movement of analytic interpretation that claims to be able to restore the wish to the clarity of a first-person utterance. It is no accident that the ambiguity we are speaking of is maintained: far too much depends on it.

Are these ambiguities necessarily overcome when, following Lacan, we invoke an original repression, a constitutive Law of desire? Is it enough to imagine—as Laplanche and Pontalis do, for example—a situation in which wish and interdiction would emerge together in fantasy?

To the extent that desire is not a pure eruption of instinct, but is articulated in propositions formed by fantasies, fantasy is the privileged site of the most primitive defensive operations, such as turning against oneself, switching to the opposite position, projection, denegation; these defenses are even indissociably linked with the primary function of fantasy—the staging of desire—if it is true that desire itself is constituted as a prohibition, that the conflict is a primordial conflict.[16]

We may begin to have our doubts about this. For if desire is linked to repression in a much more complex and radical way than Freud first imagined, we understand why it is hardly manifested in fantasy except in distorted form, why it never presents *itself*; but we have not yet explained why distortion so often, so consistently, takes an identificatory turn. And, if desire is always already "staged" in fantasy, it is doubtless understandable that its object will be forever elided from that stage where it is (only) represented, in absentia. But how are we to account for the dramatization, precisely, of the constant inflection that inclines fantasy toward the figure of the "subject" (and not at all toward the object) of the wish? This is a matter on which Laplanche and Pontalis themselves insist strongly:

The fantasy is not the object of desire, it is a scene. In fantasy, indeed, the subject is not seeking after the object or its sign, it figures itself caught up in the sequences of images. It does not represent the desired object to itself, but it is represented as participating in the scene, without any possibility, in the forms that are the closest to the original fantasy, of a place being assigned to it.[17]

How does it happen, in other words, that fantasy, far from merely dissimulating the object, consists above all in a dissimulation (or perhaps in a *simulation*) of the desiring subject? Why is it that in fantasy this subject has to be dispossessed, struck dumb within a role? In short, why is it that the wish has to be *mimed*?

The Point of Otherness

To try to answer these questions, we shall have to face up to a certain number of issues that psychoanalysis is tacitly evading even today. We shall have to connect desire with mimesis, instead of tying it first to interdiction (to the Imaginary instead of the Symbolic, one might say, except that in my view the distinction is no longer pertinent). We shall have to reconsider the idea that desire has a connection, however minor, with an *object* (even if the object is always already lacking, because it is articulated by way of a verbal demand), and at the same time we shall have to reconsider the idea of a *subject* of desire (even if it is the subject of original representation, language and repression, always already inadequate to itself). Finally, we shall have to abandon, or at least subject to a thoroughgoing reinterpretation, certain metaphors on which Freud and his successors depended heavily: metaphors of "scene," "stage," and "staging"—in other words, all the "representative theatricality" that persistently subtends the psychoanalytic theory of desire.

Desire bound to mimesis, without reference to a desired object: there in a nutshell is the basic hypothesis of René Girard's analyses:[18] desire has no object, at least not before some mediator—teacher, friend, books, fashion, culture, etc.—intervenes to tell it what is desirable. Thus we must not imagine some essential bond between desire and its object: the desire for an object is a desire-effect; it is *induced*,[19] or at least secondary, with respect to the imitation—the mimesis—of the desire of others. In other words, desire is mimetic before it is anything else. It is first mobilized by a "model" to which it conforms (with which it identifies), not so much because there is some sort of desire to imitate, some sort of "imitative instinct" (that would still be conceding a great deal to the idea that desire has aims of its own), but rather because mimesis informs desire, directs it, and, more broadly speaking, incites it. Mimesis is thus the matrix of desire and, by the same token, the matrix of rivalry, hatred, and (in the social order) violence: "I want what my brother, my model, my idol wants—and I want it in his place." And, consequently, "I want to kill him, to eliminate him." From the outset indissolubly bound to the other—the *petit autre*, one's "fellow-man," as Lacan would doubtless have it[20]—desire would be from the outset altruicidal: *philia* and *neikos*.

Equipped with this provisional hypothesis (and prepared to modify the often reductive terms in which Girard formulates it), let us go back to the Freudian theory of desire and fantasy and look briefly at the revisions our hypothesis may be able to offer.

The first of these revisions concerns the primacy Freud grants to sexuality, at least if we are talking about object-oriented sexuality. If desire is mimetic, it has no object, or at least no specific object of its own.

To be sure, when I desire what the other desires, I also desire the objects he desires: a given sexual object, for example (here is the banal "three-some" to which Girard limits his attention for the most part); but I desire this object only because it is one of the desirable attributes of the mimetic "model," one of its numerous appendages (in the sense in which Melanie Klein sometimes speaks of the Oedipal father as a simple appendage of the mother envied by the little girl).[21] In this sense, nothing predestines the sexual object to be desirable par excellence.

This observation is not exactly new, we shall be told; Freud himself had already succeeded in separating desire from the image of an instinct tending straight toward its *own* goal, when he insisted on the inherently substitutive, delegative nature of desire with respect to the needed object on which it "leans." And we may be advised to reread the "Three Essays on the Theory of Sexuality," where the sexual object is neither "sexual" in the ordinary sense of the term (it is the represented, fantasized object) nor properly an "object" (since it is fundamentally lost, irremediably absent, lacking, missing in representation). To be sure. Still, according to the theory of attachment (*Anlehnung*), the reason desire separates, deviates from need from the start is that it first takes need as a support, a prop, and "mimics" it, as Jean Laplanche says.[22] And if this erotic simulacrum of instinct theoretically implies the absence of an object, the fact remains that the aim of desire is still and always object-oriented, even though that aim may be indefinitely thwarted.

Now it is precisely the object orientation of desire—a major concession on the part of the theory of sexuality to the theory of need—that the "mimetic" hypothesis ought to allow us to get around. What triggers desire is not the empty space hollowed out by the representation of the object—by the hallucination that is vainly attempting to locate the object (as Freud sees it) or by the verbal demand in which the object would be at once formulated and annihilated (in Lacan's terms);[23] what triggers desire is mimetic assimilation, identification with a model of desire. Furthermore, this "model" may well coincide with what psychoanalysis identifies as an "object" (and we have already moved far beyond Girard's triangle). As Melanie Klein has shown, the properties of the "good" maternal breast (the "good object") may be *envied* by the nursling from the start; the breast then functions much more as an inductor than as an object of desire ("I want to have what the breast has, because I want to be the breast"). Desire, in other words, does not aim essentially at acquiring, possessing, or enjoying an object; it aims (if it *aims* at anything at all) at a subjective identity. Its basic verb is "to be" (to be like), not "to have" (to enjoy). On this point, let us look at a note Freud wrote shortly before he died:

"Having" and "being" in children. Children like expressing an object-relation by an identification: "I am the object." "Having" is the later of the two; after loss of the object it relapses into "being." Example: the breast. "The breast is a part of me, I am the breast." Only later: "I have it," that is, "I am not it." ["Findings, Ideas, Problems," SE 23: 299]

The result is that what we should expect to find, inexhaustibly, at the root of fantasies, dreams, and symptoms is not sexuality but something quite different: jealousy, for example, or envy, or rivalry, or ambition, all of which are passions aroused by the mimesis of another whom one wishes to equal, to replace, to *be*. Freud showed how well he understood this, in his way, when he produced his admirable descriptions of the ambitious and megalomanic content of his own dreams—descriptions in which his felicitous modesty kept him from confronting their sexual meaning[24]—or when he described the invariably "heroic," self-glorifying nature of daydreams or the neurotic's family romance. Better still, he linked the origin of fantasy quite explicitly with a desire (the desire for greatness) and an unquestionably mimetic activity (play). Thus he writes, in "Family Romance": "For a small child, his parents are at first the only authority and the source of all belief. The child's most intense and most momentous wish during these early years is to be like his parents (that is, the parent of his own sex) and to be big like his father and mother" (*SE* 9: 237).[25]

It follows that the form giving rise to fantasy is not, according to "Creative Writers and Day-Dreaming," imagination (hallucination, representation) of an object, but *play*, during which the child imitates grown-ups, heroes: "A child's play is determined by wishes: in point of fact by a single wish—one that helps in his upbringing—the wish to be big and grown up. He is always playing at being 'grown up,' and in his games he imitates what he knows about the lives of his elders" ("Creative Writers," p. 146).[26]

Only in a second phase—the phase of representation, of *Vorstellung*—does play (*Spiel*) give way to the fantasmatic scene, properly speaking, and later to literary fiction, of which the theatrical spectacle (*Schauspiel*) provides the paradigm, for Freud:

The growing child, when he stops playing, gives up nothing but the link with real objects; instead of *playing*, he now *phantasies*. [p. 145]

Language has preserved this relationship between children's play and poetic creation. It gives [in German] the name of *Spiel* ["play"] to those forms of imaginative writing which require to be linked to tangible objects and which are capable of representation. It speaks of a *Lustspiel* or *Trauerspiel* ["comedy" or "tragedy": literally, "pleasure play" or "mourning play"] and describes those who carry out the representation as *Schauspieler* ["players": literally, "show-players"]. [p. 144]

Now as mimesis passes through these successive forms, it may well undergo a change of status (from ludic mimetism, it becomes artistic imitation in the traditional sense: representation, scenic reproduction); nevertheless, according to Freud, what is being fulfilled is still a desire for greatness. How? By *identification*:

Being present as an interested spectator in a spectacle or play [*Schau-Spiel*] does for the adult what play does for children, whose hesitant hopes of being able to do what grown-up people do are in that way gratified. The spectator is a person who experiences too little, who feels that he is a "poor wretch to whom nothing of importance can happen," who has long been obliged to damp down, or rather displace, his ambition to stand in his own person at the hub of world affairs; he longs to feel and to act and to arrange things according to his own desires—in short, to be a hero. And the play- wright and actor enable him to do this by allowing him *to identify himself* with a hero. ["Psychopathic Characters on the Stage," *SE* 7: 305][27]

Freud's occasional success in removing desire and fantasy from the imperious dominion of the sexual is to be admired; the passages cited contain important notations that can serve as signposts. But such breakthroughs are few and far between. Indeed, the moment when desire is once again laden with sexuality, shifted back toward the object, is never far away. The Freudian paradigm of the Hero, as we know, is Oedipus, the parricide. This means that the only rea- son to identify with Oedipus is to possess the Mother: one would like to *be* Oedipus because one would like to *have* Jocasta, not the other way around. Beneath the mimetico-heroic ambition, beneath all the mythico-social proliferation of fantasy, we have to look for woman, the Object: "If . . . day-dreams are carefully examined, they are found to serve as the fulfilment of wishes and as a correction of ac- tual life. They have two principal aims, an erotic and an ambitious one—though an erotic aim is usually concealed behind the latter too" ("Family Romance," *SE* 9: 238).

Or, in another passage:

These motivating wishes [of phantasies] vary according to the sex, character and circumstances of the person who is having the phantasy; but they fall naturally into two main groups. They are either ambitious wishes, which serve to elevate the subject's personality; or they are erotic ones. . . . But we will not lay stress on the opposition between the two trends; we would rather emphasize the fact that they are often united. Just as, in many altar- pieces, the portrait of the donor is to be seen in a corner of the picture, so, in the majority of ambitious phantasies, we can discover in some corner or other the lady for whom the creator of the phantasy performs all his heroic deeds and at whose feet all his triumphs are laid. ["Creative Writers," pp. 146–47]

And there is the heart of the problem. For why should we not hold the opposite view? Why should I not desire the Lady to the extent of my "ambition," in other words, to the extent that I desire to accede to the place from which she is to be possessed? (Oedipus's desire, after all, is triggered by others: first by the oracle, who predicts, or prescribes, incest; then by the Thebans, who designate Jocasta as the prize for heroic prowess).

A second and no less telling consequence of the mimetic hypothesis involves the postulate of a desire governed by the pleasure principle. Freud's position on this point is well-defined, at least up to "Beyond the Pleasure Principle": desire is not only "object-seeking" (to borrow Fairbarn's terminology), it is also, and especially, "pleasure-seeking." Thus an instinct seeks an object only in order to attain its goal (*Ziel*), which is to obtain pleasure by suppressing the state of tension at the instinctual source, either by adopting the long, arduous, obstacle-ridden path of an appropriate transformation of reality (the path of the ego instincts) or by following the short, hurried, unsettling path of hallucination and the primary processes (the path of the sexual instincts, which resist the test of reality). All this finally brings us back to a hypothesis that Freud sometimes characterizes as a "theoretical fiction," sometimes as a "biological presupposition," but that he relies on everywhere: the hypothesis of a psychical apparatus governed by a tendency to ward off excitation or reduce it to as low a level as possible:

The accumulation of excitation (brought about in various ways that need not concern us) is felt as unpleasure and . . . it sets the apparatus in action with a view to repeating the experience of satisfaction, which involved a diminution of excitation and was felt as pleasure. A current of this kind in the apparatus, starting from unpleasure and aiming at pleasure, we have termed a "wish." [*Dreams*, p. 598]

In this sense, "the fulfillment of a wish" or a desire is strictly synonymous, for Freud, with "pleasure" or "enjoyment." This accounts for his insistence on holding interdiction and repression responsible for neurotic pain, for example, or for painful dreams; for the genealogy of unpleasure has to be *external* to desire, given the fact that desire, left to itself, is understood to tend only toward pleasure. But the association between desire and pleasure also accounts for the seriousness of the problem raised by phenomena such as masochism (in which one enjoys suffering), the "negative therapeutic reaction" (in which one refuses to get well), and the repetition compulsion (in which one repeats the experience of pain)—in short, by all that lies "beyond" the pleasure principle and that confronts Freud with increasing insistence—for are we not invited to construe, now, an *internal* articulation of desire and suffering?

It is possible, and even necessary, to show how these phenomena—behind which Freud detects the silent workings of a death instinct that tends toward a complete absence of tension (that is, toward absolute enjoyment)—stem from mimesis, from the *ambivalence* of the identification with the other, and, especially, from the reversibility of that identification. But even before undertaking these analyses, we can see that what is an obstacle in the way of a problematics of desire-pleasure is no longer an obstacle for a problematics of mimetic desire. The fact that desire is oriented toward unpleasant, painful, even death-dealing experiences is no doubt astonishing and requires additional explanation; but this fact no longer rightfully constitutes a theoretical scandal, once we recognize that desire is not governed *above all* by the obtaining of pleasure, but by an identificatory model. Mimesis, having no goal (*Ziel*) of its own, is indifferent with respect to pleasure and unpleasure—it lies "beyond" the pleasure principle, and "before" unpleasure.

We need only consider the example (the paradigm) of the baby with the wooden spool ("Beyond Pleasure," Chap. 2). Freud's astonished reaction to his grandson's game is well known: the child has gotten in the habit of throwing his toys away (*o-o-o-o, Fort*), especially a wooden spool or "reel" that he was perfectly capable of retrieving (*Da*), by pulling on the string that was attached; yet he chose to make it disappear over and over again. We should note that Freud's perplexity stems directly from the interpretation in which he associates the spool with a desired object, in this case the mother (who of course often leaves, "disappears"). Given this association, what accounts for the child's desire to repeat the painful experience (absence of the Object) much more often than the satisfying one (presence of the Object)? Why—in view of what "increase in plea-sure"—does the child "stage" the "first act" (departure) much more readily than the "second act" (return)?[28] Of Freud's various expla-nations for this, only the first is usually noted, because it appears to point "beyond" the pleasure principle. By reproducing the painful situation, the child would achieve active mastery of it, rather than allowing himself to be passively overcome by it. In short, by *desiring* to repeat the painful experience, he would not suffer or be subjected to it. (By sacrificing myself freely to the law or the destiny that de-termines me from the outside, I make it mine and thus I determine myself: this well-known schema of speculative dialectics no doubt counts for something in the fascination that this text has held for certain French psychoanalysts.)

But have the implications of the passage from passivity to activity, the *passage to the (ludic) act*, received adequate scrutiny? Instead of seeing it as the effect of a deliberate decision (whether conscious or unconscious), might we not do better to speak of an identification (a forced, passive identification) with the active pole of the scene, that is, with the mother? It ought to be obvious, indeed, that when the child abandons his toys (what he "has"), he is treating them the way his mother treats him. In this sense, by throwing his toys away he is not so much sacrificing the mother as himself: he himself is drawing away from himself by playing the mother's role (the "active role"). Thus we must take another look at Freud's still overly "economic" interpretation: the child is not playing at losing an object of enjoy-ment, with all the cunning and self-interest and calculation that such a staging may entail (the child pretends to lose in order to win: Georges Bataille would have called this situation "comic").[29] The child is playing at being his mother, and in so doing, *identifying* with her; he loses himself in the very gesture through which he is at-tempting to constitute himself as a proper subject, an autonomous, free, independent, and active subject.

Freud even suggests such an interpretation himself, just when he is forcefully asserting that "there is no need to assume the existence of a special imitative instinct in order to provide a motive for play" ("Beyond Pleasure," p. 17). On the one hand, he notes that the child sometimes made *himself* disappear from a mirror ("Baby o-o-o-o"), so it was not necessarily the mother (the maternal object, represented by the spool) that he was dismissing. On the other hand, Freud sets forth the idea of a sort of vengeful reciprocity, of an aggressive intrigue directed at the mother ("All right, then, go away! I don't need you. I'm sending you away myself" [p.16]): the child was indeed putting himself in his mother's place. Finally, and most importantly, Freud again advances the hypothesis of a game of the megalomaniac type, through which the child attempts to appropriate parental omnipotence (mastery, "greatness") for himself, mimetically:

It is clear that in their play children repeat everything that has made a great impression on them in real life, and that in doing so they abreact the strength of the impression and, as one might put it, make themselves master of the situation. But on the other hand it is obvious that all their play is influenced by a wish that dominates them the whole time—the wish to be grown-up and to be able to do what grown-up people do. [pp.16–17]

To be sure, Freud takes this as an argument in favor of an "economic" interpretation of the game, that is, one governed by the pleasure principle: playing at being Mother, Father, or Doctor is a way of accomplishing the desire to be grown up, and thus of obtaining an increase in pleasure, notwithstanding the unpleasures involved in the game. But this conclusion has to be viewed as suspect in its turn, since the "desire" to be grown up has nothing to do with pleasure or unpleasure. Its aim is not hedonistic: first of all, it has no *proper* aim. It does not *precede* ludic mimetism; it does not use play as a means to an end. Rather, it is formed in play: the child wants to be like grown-ups, to have what they have, only to the extent that he has first identified with them, prior to any desire. By that very token he moves forward blindly toward his goal: he anticipates nothing, aims at nothing, progresses in view of nothing, until he is "en-roled," so to speak, by identification. There is no goal orientation here, no calculation, no economy, at least not at first: desire is not oriented by pleasure, it is (dis)oriented by mimesis—and thus it lies beyond the pleasure principle.

The most important consequences of the mimetic hypothesis bear directly upon the theory of fantasy and wish fulfillment, and they are crucial for our purposes on this account. In the first place, if identification rather than an object is what orients desire, it is easy to understand why fantasy so often gives rise to dramatization. To appear in the place of another (by identifying with him, taking on his features, adopting his position within a structure, and so on) is precisely to play—in the sense in which one plays a role. Here is the justification for the connection Freud establishes between fantasy, child's play, and theatrical play properly speaking:[30] the "subject" of the fantasy is the actor (and not the spectator), the mime (and not the director). Far from standing aside, outside the drama, the "subject" is actively involved in the scene. He puts himself into play, as did the child with the wooden reel (he exposes himself, in every sense of the word). Thus in her fantasy, the hysteric *is* some girl who is seduced, seducing, seductive; the agoraphobe *is* some prostitute walking the streets; the hystero-epileptic *is* a dead man.[31] The fantasmatic identification is total, no holds barred. Hence we need to note at once that the "actor" of a fantasy is not the actor described (dreamed?) by playwrights: the playwright bases his actor on an "ideal imagined model," we are told (by Diderot), but he takes care not to enter into the skin of the character whom he merely "quotes," in the last analysis (as Brecht shows). The one who acts in the fantasy is mad, however, because he merges with the mimetic model (which is henceforth no longer a model). He is *caught* in the scene of the fantasy, as Laplanche and Pontalis write; by this we are to understand that he takes himself for one or another of the protagonists. A mime through and through, he is thus literally possessed by his role.

The numerous cases in which the subject occupies the position of spectator, third-party witness, or voyeur with respect to the fantasy may well be cited in objection. This objection may be supported by the evidence (which is to say, etymologically, by *sight*); it still may not stand up under examination, however. This at least is what I shall attempt to show here, by considering at somewhat greater length Freud's 1919 article devoted to feminine fantasy, "A Child Is Being Beaten."

The subject definitely does not appear in the terminal phase of the fantasy (the third phase, in Freud's chronology), from which the article takes its title. In this scene, we see a child (another child) being beaten, with no intervention in the scene on the subject's part. Freud notes that "in reply to pressing enquiries the patients only declare:

'I am probably looking on'" ("Child," p. 186). The subject therefore watches the performance, the *Schau-Spiel*, from the vantage point of the audience. However, it is noteworthy that Freud is intent on showing that the patient's expulsion into the position of a spectator counting the blows is an *alibi*, an effect of the repression of the second, "masochistic" phase in which she herself received the blows from the father ("I am being beaten by my father" [p. 185]). In fact, it is again "she" who gets beaten in the guise of a boy, Freud declares in 1919, just as it is "her" penis, he adds in 1925,[32] which is "beaten-caressed" from then on—hence the onanistic voluptuousness procured by the fantasy, which is enough to confirm her involvement in the scene.

Appearances notwithstanding, this involvement is just as clear in the first phase of the fantasy as Freud describes it ("[The] father is beating the child" [p. 185]). However, Freud himself does not suggest such a possibility in his article, for he is bent on referring the scene back to the classic Oedipal trio: the father is supposed to represent the incestuous object who proves to the subject the exclusiveness of his love by punishing a third-party interloper, a *terzo incommodo* (a brother or a sister). This entails the hallucinatory satisfaction of a desire for an object, then, and one that seemingly leaves the subject outside the action. But when Freud suggests, six years later, that the jealousy that directs the blows to the other child is rooted in penis envy, he opens the way to an entirely different understanding of the rivalrous situation, and thus of the fantasy. For as the Kleinian school has shown,[33] envy is inscribed in a two-sided relation, not a triangle. It does not arise out of competition for the object (the loved, desired object); it focuses instead on a double (and not a third party), an interloper who is increasingly hated as the subject puts herself in the other's place and finds herself deprived of what then becomes *her* place. To go from here to conceiving of envy (penis envy, even) as rivalry of the mimetic type requires just one short step, which we shall take: the child who was punished in the first phase of the fantasy is indeed the subject herself (if we may still say so), just as the boys who are "beaten-caressed" in the third phase are the subject herself.

This enraged identification with the mimetic rival results in the blows administered to that rival on the spot: such is the "sadism" of the first phase, which thus does not depend (as Freud hypothesizes) so much on a buried sadistic instinct joining forces with the Oedipal impulse as on the aggressiveness that the Double inevitably arouses (as Hoffmann, Poe, and Dostoevski understood so well). By the same token, we see the close connivance between this "sadism" and the "masochism" of the second phase, for if the "other" is beaten to the extent that I identify with him or her, it goes without saying that I "myself" will also be the beaten one. Sadism instantly becomes masochism in the timelessness of fantasy (for the unconscious, there is no such thing as time). Thus it is no doubt superfluous to imagine, after Freud's fashion, a chronological succession between the two phases, in the present case a *secondary* reversal of sadism toward the person involved and a pregenital *regression* subsequent to the Oedipal repression. In fact, we find ourselves in the order of "transitivism" that child psychologists have described (and that Merleau-Ponty and Lacan, in their day, found so fascinating):[34] the "masochistic" passion is not, here, a mark of Oedipal guilt, but the necessary obverse of the "sadistic" action, one that does not allow the subject to be pinned down as "the one who is doing the beating" rather than as "the one who is beaten," since he is both at once (for the unconscious, there is no such thing as contradiction). Freud must have assumed such a reversibility between self and other, for in 1925 he demonstrated that the child who was thrashed because of penis envy also represented—and "from the beginning," he said—the beaten-caressed penis of the subject, who held out his rod, as it were, so as to be beaten.

Thus from this point on we may contend that the subject is never in a simple face-to-face position with respect to the fantasy: it is still the subject her/himself who is gesticulating up there on stage. But there is a more important issue here. For, even if the subject identifies with the spectacle, and even if this identification is so upsetting that it keeps the subject from recognizing the representative framework and incites her to enter into the scene (somewhat like Don Quixote at Master Peter's marionette theater), a *spectacle* still remains, or so it seems. With the "transitivist" or "dual" relation, we remain within the order of the specular: the other, even if he is an *alter ego*, is seen;

he is not acted out. Thus we have to turn to what Freud identifies as the second phase of the fantasy. This time the subject is unquestionably the actor of the fantasy. First because the fantasy is assumed in the first person: "I am being beaten by my father." Then because this "I" is apocryphal, as is fitting when one is playing a role: the "I" appears here in the place of the mimetic rival, as we have just seen; it speaks, or it is spoken from the place of another (note that I am not saying "of the Other").

Now this phase of the fantasy is noteworthy on two counts. On the one hand, Freud tells us, it is the most decisive of the three, "the most important and the most momentous of all" (p. 185). It continues to work, in one direction, in the fantasy "a child is being beaten," which draws from this phase its deep ("masochistic") "meaning." On the other hand—in the other direction—this phase gives meaning to the *memory* that "the father is beating the child." Freud shows a quite significant reluctance to grant this "preliminary" phase the status of fantasy: "One may hesitate to say whether the characteristics of a 'phantasy' can yet be ascribed to this first step towards the later beating-phantasy. It is perhaps rather a question of recollections of events which have been witnessed, or of desires which have arisen on various occasions" (p. 185).[35]

The scenes observed provide an *occasion* for the fantasy, which seizes on them and cathects them, but they are not the fantasy itself, properly speaking. This unmistakably suggests that Freud's "second" phase is actually preliminary to his "first" phase, if we think not in terms of a "masochistic" phase preceding a "sadistic" phase but rather of a transitivist indistinction of self and other (of action and passion/passivity) preceding any differentiation of roles.

The precedence is a peculiar one, however, for this phase does not appear, never presents itself, to the subject. Whereas the terminal phase is fully conscious, and whereas anamnesis brings forth the preliminary phase without too much difficulty, the one we are dealing with remains tenaciously concealed from the subject, who has no access to it. It remains unconscious, according to Freud. In fact, it becomes known to us not through the patient but through the analyst, who infers it, as a missing but logically necessary link, on the basis of the material at his disposal. And however the analyst may attempt to communicate this "construction" to the patient, he will not succeed in bringing about real adherence, or real conviction, on the latter's part—in short, there will be no *recollection*: "This second phase is the most important and the most momentous of all. But we may say of it in a certain sense that it has never had a real existence. It is never remembered, it has never succeeded in becoming conscious. It is a construction of analysis, but it is no less a necessity on that account" (p. 185).[36]

This point calls for our attention: the two scenes capable of acceding to consciousness and of being verbalized are those that are *observed*. Consequently, they imply spectacular distance (observer vs. observed, audience vs. stage) and specular spacing (ego vs. alter ego), no matter how tenuous and ambiguous. The representation is thus theatrical in nature (to go to the theater, we must recall, is to go see, *theorein*). Yet when the subject goes up onto the stage, enters the scene, *he no longer represents it to himself*. When he plays it, the scene is unconscious. That does not mean he has simply passed "beyond representation," in Lyotard's terms,[37] since he is still representing, miming (the "mimetic rival," as we said). On the contrary, he has passed, like Alice, "through the looking glass": the representation involved (or that does the involving) does not belong to the order of the specular, the visible, the theoretico-theatrical (it is not mimesis as mimesis has been understood since Plato and Aristotle).[38]

It follows that the phase we are concerned with constitutes the blind spot of the fantasy, for it is the spot or standpoint from which the subject sees—let us play with words and call it *the point of otherness* (since the other whose place is occupied by the subject is *not* apprehended as other). This point is invisible to the subject; it is not perceived. The subject cannot see himself miming another at the moment he is miming, just as he cannot say that he is playacting precisely while he is acting. In order to do that—in order to see the invisible, or say the unsayable—he would have to reflect himself, absent himself from the plane on which he is speaking, take himself as reference point for his own discourse; in short, he would have to arrive at the vantage point of the lucid spectator (philosopher, analyst, director) who sees both the model and its copy, who distinguishes what is imitated from what is imitating, and thus gives himself a way to denounce either the lie of the mimetician who is passing himself off as another (as Plato shows in the *Republic*, and Brecht) or the misrecognition of the Self that takes itself for another in the so-called specular relation (as Lacan argues). But then *he is no longer miming*. Then he has passed over into the order of theoretical doubling, where he can see himself, see himself see, and ultimately see himself not see.

Thus the subject either plays a part in the spectacle or is a spectator; either he merely sees or he sees *himself*, by presenting himself to himself, confronting himself, in the objectivity of the *Vor-stellung*; either he is in representation, here and now, *in* the scene on stage, or he is representing himself there, *on* the stage. This dilemma is implacable, insurmountable. The lack of distinction between self and other—the mimesis—has to be acted out; yet no sooner is it represented to the subject in the specular mode than it is betrayed. At that very moment the image in the mirror, the spectacle will have already opened up the space of adversity (note that I am not saying of alterity): hence the instantaneous rage that overcomes the child when she *sees* the other in *her* place, hence the blows she distributes so generously even as she receives them, mirrored. And no doubt the other will be at that moment scarcely different from me myself (almost myself); but this self, myself, being specular, will already be an adverse, adversary self, an enemy (almost another).

There is, consequently, a cleavage between the stage where one is playing—the "other stage," the "other place," Freud writes, doubtless meaning that it is unlocalizable, unplaceable, irreducible to any spatiality and to any visibility—and the stage that one sees, the stage about which one speaks. The former will always be invincibly inaccessible to the latter. (Orpheus can never look upon Eurydice. To do so would be to kill Eurydice in himself. For, of course, Orpheus *is* Eurydice.) In other words, mimesis is unrepresentable for the subject in the mode of *Vorstellung*: ungraspable, inconceivable, unmasterable, because unspecularizable (even if it is always already specularized). Thus we are beginning to have a sense of what "unconscious fantasy" may mean. If an unconscious fantasy does not accede to consciousness, it is not because it is conscious elsewhere, projected on another screen, represented in some "private theater" for the benefit of a hypothetical "subject-of-the-unconscious." It is time to give up all this *imagery* of subjects embedded in each other, once and for all. If the concept of an unconscious is to be retained, it needs to be definitively liberated from the phantom of the *other subject* and the *other consciousness* inherited from late-nineteenth-century psychology and psychiatry (Azam's "somnambulic" or "hypnotic consciousness," Binet's "personality alterations," Breuer's "hypnoid state," the early Freud's "dissociation of consciousness," and so on).

No, if there is nonconsciousness in this instance, it is because there is irrepresentability in the sense we have just indicated. What Freud attempts to pin down under the name of unconscious fantasy—the other's place, the point of otherness where "I" is the other—exceeds representation by way of objects as well as representation by way of words. It can be neither seen nor stated: as soon as patients test this, under pressure from Freud, they fall back upon views, upon scenes, to be sure: scenes about which they can then speak, as analysis urges them to do, but which by that very token betray the unsayable. And these scenes may well be ambiguous, their sadistic "form" envelop a masochistic "signification," the characters that evolve in them turn out to be "substitutes for the child itself" (as Freud remarks with reference to the boys beaten in the terminal fantasy): the theater has already been set up and "the others" are the ones who will appear on stage. The representation (of oneself) has already begun, along with speculation.

It is easy to see why Freud's proposed verbalization of the "unconscious" phase leaves patients indifferent, even when it seems to come very close to a properly mimetic utterance (that is, properly improper) from which, like so many orphans, the scenes observed proceed: "I (an other) am being beaten." The patients' indifference stems from the fact that the mode of utterance they are invited to adopt in the course of analysis is precisely not mimetic. What is the analyst asking of them, actually? He is asking them to recollect scenes, real or (and) fantasmatic. He is encouraging them to represent these scenes to themselves, to summon them up before consciousness, and to express them. In other words, he is committing his patients to diegesis, to narrative: they are to recount. In the present case, they are to recount themselves by distancing themselves from themselves and by observing themselves being beaten.

Now this specular doubling is precisely what does not take place in the other('s) place, on the other unconscious stage where the "subject" is playing: *mimesis is, in a wholly new sense, nonreflexive, prereflexive*. By that very token, it is unrecountable, inaccessible to analytic self-narration. Moreover, we may well ask where Freud has come by the idea that one sees oneself in fantasy (or in dreams) in the same way one sees oneself in a mirror. It is quite significant, in this regard, that in their effort to see the other stage Freud's patients finally arrive at fantasies in which *others* are beating, or being beaten. Only then do they see themselves in that other, in those others: the mimetic coalescence of self and other, thus projected into the adversity of the visible, will of course already have been lost; but at least it will have been approached, and in some sense maintained, in the identification with the specular others.

To see oneself, on the contrary, would be to distance oneself definitively from oneself, by suppressing all reference to mimetic identification. But in fact the "subject" (the mime) never sees himself in fantasies, any more than he does in dreams. When Freud tells us, in *The Interpretation of Dreams*, that he sees a book lying before him (the dream of the botanical monograph), he is already under the regimen of reflection, has already passed into the second (secondary) order of the "dream narrative" in which he sees himself see, thus opening the way to the interpretation that will see him in the place of the "seer," Fliess; but when he dreams, he merely sees, without any possibility of stepping back for perspective, for he is in the grip of the primary process (that is, of mimesis): there, he *is* Fliess, "himself." Similarly, Freud's patients have never seen themselves being beaten; they *are* beaten, they *are* the one whom they are beating (beaters-beaten, observers-observed, active-passive: on the other stage, these distinctions are still entirely irrelevant, which is what makes them so difficult to think about).

It follows that this "phase" is not recollected on the couch: indeed, it has "never had a real existence." In other words, it has never been represented to consciousness, nor can it ever be so represented without being, by that very token, betrayed. This, however, in no way precludes the "phase" in question from exercising an effect, a very "real" one; quite the contrary. It will not be recollected, to be sure, but it will be *repeated*: not represented in the past, not recounted, but staged in the present, dramatized in symptomatic behaviors or in the analytic relation. It will not be recaptured in reflection; instead, it will be acted out in an analytic "letting go." In short, it will not be recognized on the analytic scene or stage, but rather played out in misrecognition. The other scene/stage is not elsewhere, inaccessible like a deeply buried treasure. It is here and now, in broad daylight, and all the more invisible for the one who is playing (on) it: a surface unconscious, as it were, and one that resembles point for point what is usually called consciousness. Here is what Freud has to say about it, even though, throughout "A Child Is Being Beaten," he has stressed the irreducibility of this "phase" to any conscious recollection:

[The second phase . . . is incomparably the more important.] This is not only because it continues to operate through the agency of the phase that takes its place; we can also detect effects upon the character, which are directly derived from its unconscious form. People who harbour phantasies of this kind develop a special sensitiveness and irritability towards anyone whom they can include in the class of fathers. They are easily offended by a person of this kind, and in that way (to their own sorrow and cost) bring about the realization of the imagined situation of being beaten by their father. [p. 195][39]

Here we can appreciate the full ambiguity of the notion of unconscious fantasy, the very notion that powerfully encumbers the Freudian concept of the unconscious, that is to say, unconscious *representation*. For in the passage we have just quoted, what is the meaning of "realization of the [unconscious] imagined situation"? Is it a question, in the *acting out*, of a re-presentation, in the order of so-called exterior reality, of what is already represented in the hallucinatory mode in an inner preserve, in the "reserve" of Phantasy? Is it a second staging, in the world, of that intimate scene that the subject, according to Freud, secretly carries around *within* himself? There is every reason to doubt it, at least if one is reluctant to conceive of the unconscious as a subject within the subject, and if one is also reluctant to impute to it any consciousness of this scene in which the subject would render itself blind.

In fact, nothing can prevent fantasy from being conscious (represented to a consciousness—even if that consciousness is christened "unconsciousness" for the purpose) as soon as it is seen, as soon as it appears to a subject. Under these conditions, can one continue to speak of unconscious *fantasy*? Whatever precautions may be taken in this respect, the origin of that word (*Phantasie, phantasma*) cannot fail to turn it irresistibly back into the order of luminous appearance, visible phenomenality, spectacular theatricality.[40] Now, as we have just noted, fantasy is (pre)conscious when it is seen. When it is unconscious, it is quite simply not seen: it is (en)acted by the "subject" who executes its scenario *blindly*—at the risk of bumping into all those "others," in the world, that he is playing on the other stage. At the risk of getting himself beaten by himself and of endlessly crashing into mirrors, with the "demonic" stubbornness that characterizes the repetition compulsion, according to Freud.

These remarks ought to apply to all fantasies. Fantasy, as we have amply demonstrated, can never be reduced to a mere hallucination of the object of desire. But neither is it enough to say, as Laplanche and Pontalis do, that fantasy is a "stage" and that the subject "himself makes his appearance on it in the sequence of images." The correction is crucial, to be sure, in that it makes it clear that the characters who evolve on the stage always function, in one way or another, as images, or rather *imagos* (models), of the subject, who is representing himself in them. But even with this correction we are left viewing fantasy as a spectacle represented to a subject who remains outside the drama, outside representation. Thus it is necessary to go further: we have to leave the visible (the imaginary, the specular) behind and dismantle the theater, we have to stop placing the subject in a position of exteriority (*sub-jacence*) with respect to representation. The fantasy, to be sure, is there in front of me, in the mode of *Vor-stellung*: I (re)present it to myself. Better still, I (re)present myself in it through some "other," some identificatory figure who enjoys in my place. But the point from which I contemplate the scene—the fantasy's "umbilical cord," we might say, through which it is linked with what is invisible for the subject—is not offstage. I am *in* the fantasy, there where I am the other "before" seeing him, there where I am the mimetic model even "before" he arises in front of me, there where I am acting out before any distancing, any drawing back: a nonspecular identification (blind mimesis) in which consists (if he/it consists) the entire "subject" of the fantasy. That is to say, unquestionably, the "subject," no more and no less.

And if we now ask where wish fulfillment is to be found in all this, the answer begins as follows: in identification, in mimesis. Identification is not a means for the fulfillment of desire, it is that "fulfillment" itself. This is so, first of all, because the desire that is fulfilled in fantasy and in dreams (but we shall have to abandon the idea of a desire that would precede its fulfillment, for reasons that will appear shortly) is a mimetic desire. Let us take, for example, the dream of Uncle Josef, "the uncle with the yellow beard," in Chapter 4 of *The Interpretation of Dreams*, the analysis of which directly precedes that of the dream of the smoked salmon or of "the abandoned supper-party."[41] Here we can watch Freud develop a whole dreamlike "argument" destined to keep his two colleagues and coreligionists R. and N. from the post of *professor extraordinarius*. What wish is this argument supposed to fulfill, according to Freud himself? The wish to be named professor in their place: the desire that is satisfied is concurrent with (identical to, like) a desire held by his two rivals. In short, it is a mimetic desire, an identificatory wish.

"What is new about that?" the reader may ask. "You have not progressed beyond a mere preconscious desire left over from the day before: ambition, social climbing, professional rivalry. We have to look deeper, toward infantile desire, toward the dream 'capitalist.'" All right, let us go "deeper," into hell. Drawing on the analysis of the dream *non vixit*, we may note, first of all, that the relationship Freud maintains here with his friend/rival R. was one of the most constant and, by his own account, one of the most important of his emotional life, replicating his close childhood relationship with his nephew (his "brother") John, a relationship characterized by transitivist reciprocity ("I hit him 'cos he hit me" [*Dreams*, p. 484]) and mimetic rivalry ("Ote-toi que je m'y mette!"—Get out of there so

I can get in!" [p. 484 and, more generally, pp. 421–25 and 479–86]).[42] Thus behind (*within*) the adult's professional rivalry, the child's "egoistic" and ambivalent identifications can readily be found. But even if we do not follow this path, it suffices to accompany Freud in his "deep" interpretation of the dream of the uncle to observe that his interpretation leads us in just the same way to a desire that is mimetic in nature. In fact, by "mishandling" his rivals (by "beating" them, as it were), Freud not only puts himself in their place, but also puts himself in the place, he tells us, of the anti-Semitic Minister who denied them, as he had denied Freud, the position of *professor extraordinarius*. And in so doing, Freud takes revenge on the Minister by taking his position and playing his role:[43] here is the mechanism of "identification with the aggressor" later described by Anna Freud.

"But this is still nothing but a defense mechanism," the reader will retort. "Where is desire, in all this? You are hovering at the dream's surface, you are not getting beyond its 'facade.'" Perhaps so, but then it is Freud himself who must be held accountable. The facade is for him the very basis of the dream (the mask is the face, the *persona*, of desire). For it is *in identification* and nowhere else, he tells us, that the archaic-infantile desire of the dream is fulfilled, a desire which is nothing other than a desire to be Minister:

In mishandling my two learned and eminent colleagues because they were Jews, and in treating the one as a simpleton and the other as a criminal, I was behaving as though I were the Minister, I had put myself in the Minister's place. Turning the tables on His Excellency with a vengeance! He had refused to appoint me *professor extraordinarius* and I had retaliated in the dream by stepping into his shoes. [p. 193]

In fact, we know where this desire—this desire to be—comes from: a double prophecy. When Freud was only eleven or twelve years old, in a café in the Prater where he had gone with his parents, a singer (Freud even says "a poet": everything begins in fiction) predicted that he would one day become a Cabinet Minister, just like the Jews who had recently entered the bourgeois ministry and whose portraits had been brought home by Freud's father. Here, then, is the source of the desire that is fulfilled in the dream. The first prophecy, to be sure, goes back no further than Freud's adolescence. The second, however, takes us back to a time that antedates "Sigmund Freud" himself: the immemorial eve of his desire.

What, then, could have been the origin of the ambitiousness which produced the dream in me? At that point I recalled an anecdote I had often heard repeated in my childhood. At the time of my birth an old peasant-woman had prophesied to my proud mother that with her first-born child she had brought a great man into the world. [p. 192]

And *that* is the source of Freud's tenacious megalomania, his undying thirst for greatness (*Grössensehnsucht*), which the second prediction only channeled in a secondary way.[44] This prophecy, then, was to be Freud's family romance, the myth of his birth, the legend of his desire. And this makes it clear, finally, that identification (here with the "great man," later with the Minister, with *professores extraordinarii*, and so on) induces—*predicts*—desire much more than it serves desire. In the beginning is mimesis: as far back as one goes in anamnesis (in self-analysis, we might say, if the *self* were not precisely what is in question here), one always finds the identification from which the "subject" dates (the "primary identification," as Freud later puts it). In the beginning is the apocryphal "subject" of fantasy as we have attempted, for better or for worse, to delimit it.

This is why the chronology Freud most frequently indicates has to be inverted. Desire (the desiring subject) does not come first, to be *followed* by an identification that would allow the desire to be fulfilled. What comes first is a tendency toward identification, a primordial tendency which then gives rise to a desire; and this desire is, from the outset, a (mimetic, rivalrous) desire to oust the incommodious other from the place the pseudo-subject already occupies in fantasy. That is why it is appropriate to spell out what I was saying a moment ago about wish fulfillment. If desire is satisfied in and through identification, it is not in the sense in which a desire somehow precedes its "gratification," since no desiring subject (no "I," no ego) precedes the mimetic identification: identification brings the desiring subject into being, and not the other way around.

"Desire is fulfilled in dreams": this statement now has to be understood as comparable to "the time has come." What was to happen, what was prescribed, predicted well before the birth of desire—namely, the subject "himself," in his undecidable identity—happens (if it ever happens) in the dream. *After a complete interpretation, every dream turns out to be the fulfillment of a destiny.*

We can thus reach a conclusion concerning the relation of identification to desire. Identification does not grow out of dissimulation, deformation, or dis-placement, it does not arise from distortion. To present things that way would mean continuing to assume that the subject of desire precedes his masks, precedes his fantasmatic places. It would mean presupposing the subject of representation (the *subjectum*, the *hupokeimenon*). And while repeating the most ineradicable problematics of subjectivity, we would also be assuaging anew the ineradicable megalomania of desire—which is, finally, nothing other than a will-to-be-a-subject (a will-to-be-present-to-oneself, a will-to-be-free, auto-nomous, ab-solute). We would be continuing to dream.

But no: if there is distortion, it comes first. The so-called subject of desire has no identity of its own prior to the identification that brings it, blindly, to occupy the point of otherness, the place of the other (who is thus not an other): an original alienation (which is thus not an alienation); and an original lure (which is thus not a lure, either). Before there are any falsehoods, before there is any dissimulation, desire goes by another name.

The Desire of Psychoanalysis

Let us return briefly, in conclusion, to the dream of the abandoned supper-party. In the light of what has just been said, it is clear that Freud might easily have taken his analysis in a very different direction. In the first place, he might have abandoned the idea of a sexual, object-oriented desire. After all, the butcher's wife's identification with her friend does not necessarily betray an *erotic* desire. Is her desire really, as Freud insists, a heterosexual desire for her husband? All the evidence suggests, on the contrary, that Freud was guilty of the same "technical error" he committed in his analysis of the Dora case. As he himself acknowledged later on,[45] in the Dora case he had failed to recognize the predominance of "homosexual tendencies" in neurotics—and these tendencies in turn are no doubt simply *homophilic*, that is, mimetic. If the butcher's wife identifies with her rival, it is not because she loves her husband with a hetero-sexual love (and indeed, would such love really require repression, censorship?); it is not even because she loves her friend with a *homo-sexual* love (if that were the case, why would she *identify* with the loved object?). It is much more probable that she loves herself in her friend, desires herself in the person of her friend, is fascinated with herself in the other: a movement of mimetic passion (of "narcissis-tic" love), which can of course bear sexuality in its wake (especially the form called homosexuality), but can by no means be reduced to sexuality.

Here is a first and important displacement of emphasis, then, that might have led Freud to a second displacement involving the rivalrous, "Oedipal" triangle.[46] He might have granted primary sta-tus to the bond between the butcher's wife and her friend, rather than to the bond between the wife and her husband. Once again we have to move beyond the self-evident or conformist aspect of the erotic trio. If jealousy so strongly motivates the butcher's wife's dream and her symptom, it is not because her friend is stealing away her husband's love, nor is it because an unconscious homosexuality is reinforcing a normal jealousy, or even producing it (as Freud later hypothesizes in speaking of delusions of jealousy);[47] there is actually no cause at all, since jealousy comes first. Before the *triangular* com-petition for an object, there is the *duel*, the rivalry "of pure prestige" with the hatefully loved double (the *odiosoamato*)—hence the wife's aggressiveness toward her friend, which is at once equated (via the symptom of the caviar, for example) with a self-directed aggressive-ness, an inhibition of desire "itself." And, before the specular duel, there is the pre-specular *union*. "Two lovers are 'one'"—hence the identification in which the desire of the butcher's wife is fulfilled (because it originates in that identification).

This interpretation, which amounts to putting mimesis before de-sire in every instance, is not Freud's own, as we need hardly insist. What must be added now is that in Freud's continual relegation of mimesis to a secondary position he is making a *deliberate* gesture— the very gesture that had made a properly psychoanalytic interpre-tation of hysterical symptoms possible, thus creating the possibility of psychoanalysis itself. Freud reminds us of this in a long digression on the "psychic processes of hysteria," which he places right in the middle of his analysis of the dream of the abandoned supper-party. This page speaks for itself:

What is the meaning of hysterical identification? It requires a somewhat lengthy explanation. Identification is a highly important factor in the mechanism of hysterical symptoms. It enables patients to express in their symptoms not only their own experiences but those of a large number of other people; it enables them, as it were, to suffer on behalf of a whole crowd of people and to act all the parts in a play single-handed. I shall be told that this is not more than the familiar hysterical imitation, the capacity of hysterics to imitate any symptoms in other people that may have struck their attention—sympathy, as it were, intensified to the point of reproduction. This, however, does no more than show us the path along which the psychical process in hysterical imitation proceeds. The path is something different from the mental act which proceeds along it. The latter is a little more complicated than the common picture of hysterical imitation; it consists in the unconscious drawing of an inference, as an example will make clear. Supposing a physician is treating a woman patient, who is subject to a particular kind of spasm, in a hospital ward among a number of other patients. He will show no surprise if he finds one morning that this particular kind of hysterical attack has found imitators. He will merely say: "The other patients have seen it and copied it; it's a case of psychical infection." That is true; but the psychical infection has occurred along some such lines as these. As a rule, patients know more about one another than the doctor does about any of them; and after the doctor's visit is over they turn their attention to one another. Let us imagine that this patient had her attack on a particular day; then the others will quickly discover that it was caused by a letter from home, the revival of some unhappy love-affair, or some such thing. Their sympathy is aroused and they draw the following inference, though it fails to penetrate into consciousness: "If a cause like this can produce an attack like this, I may have the same kind of attack since I have the same grounds for having it." If this inference were capable of entering consciousness, it might possibly give rise to a *fear* of having the same kind of attack. But in fact the inference is made in a different psychical region, and consequently results in the actual realization of the dreaded symptom. Thus identification is not simple imitation but *assimilation* [or appropriation, *Aneignung*] on the basis of a similar aetiological pretension; it expresses a resemblance and is derived from a common element which remains in the unconscious. [*Dreams*, pp. 149–50]

Thus mimesis (imitation, simulation, contagion) is indeed found in hysteria, but it can never take the place of an explanatory principle; it has to be explained itself, that is, criticized as an appearance, as a surface phenomenon. The mimetic "way" is one thing; the "mental act"—the syllogism of desire, the reason of unreason—is quite another. There, as Lacan will repeat, is

what Freud grasps in one of those sidelong looks with which he surprises the true, shattering on his way the abstractions to which positivist minds so readily lend themselves as an explanation for everything: what we have here is the imitation dear to Tarde. In each particular case one must activate the mainspring that he provides there—namely, hysterical identification. If our patient identifies with her friend, it is because she is inimitable in her unsatisfied desire for this goddamned salmon.[48]

Desire does not imitate (or it is inimitable, which doubtless amounts to the same thing): here we have an absolutely essential proposition, one that unmistakably marks a limit or boundary of psychoanalysis.

This boundary line corresponds first of all to the "break" that separates Freud from his predecessors. The passage we have just quoted is a clear allusion to all the half-"scientific," half-moral discourse that was being heard on hysterical mimetism ("imitation," "simulation," "theatricalism") at the time: the hysteric, it was often said, is a person who is particularly susceptible to the influence of others; she is malleable, "suggestible" (Bernheim), or else a pretender, an "actress"[49] — in every case an *improper* subject, unspecifiable, unidentifiable. Although we shall not explore further, here, the combined history of hystericism and mimetism (which is also the history of hypnotism, a topic to which we shall return), there is no doubt that the psychoanalytic "break" plays a large part in the gesture through which Freud himself *identifies* (authenticates) the hysteric: not as Charcot had done,[50] by objectifying hysteria in a symptomatology presumed to be fixed and not mimetic, but by imputing the hysterical mimesis, henceforth christened "identification," to a subject—that is, as we have just seen, to a desire. Which is to say, to a desire that is "proper," original, and authentic, anterior to mimesis: *the desire of/for psychoanalysis* (the relation is to be understood in both senses, subjective and objective) *is a desire of the subject*, not that of another—and therein lies, as it were, its full *originality*.

Now this boundary line that separates Freud from his prehistory is by the same token an internal limit or boundary of psychoanalysis, which psychoanalysis can cross only by abandoning *itself*; thus this limit prevents Freud from granting mimesis the status we have given it. This is what remains to be demonstrated: all the major revisions that lead to the "second topography"—the introduction of narcissism, the emphasis on the analysis of the ego, the identification of a repetition beyond the pleasure principle, and so on—are summoned up by the ever more pressing necessity to integrate the mimetic mechanisms, for better or for worse, into a problematics that is *allergic* to them. But this never leads Freud to sacrifice this problematics to them, that is, to sacrifice the originality of psychoanalysis, either as a science or as the Freudian Cause of desire. A desire is at stake here, and it belongs to "Freud" himself.

Let us analyze, then (if it is analyzable) this desire of and for psychoanalysis, this psychoanalytic desire.

Ecce Ego

> It seems to me above all necessary to declare here who and what I am. . . . It is a duty—and one against which my customary reserve, and to a still greater degree the pride of my instincts, rebel—to say: *Listen! for I am such and such a person. For Heaven's sake do not confound me with any one else.*
>
> Nietzsche, *Ecce homo*

Anyone attempting to follow the outlines of the mimetology that Freud's texts at once include and evade—anyone attempting, in other words, to follow the silent *work* of his work—cannot fail to come across the problematics of narcissism set forth in the well-known text, "On Narcissism: An Introduction" (1914). At first glance there is a paradox here. If we consider only the most overwhelmingly obvious thesis of Freud's essay, narcissism designates self-love, the self's desire for itself or the desire of and for the ego, as differentiated from object love, by which Freud means any desire oriented toward what is not the ego itself. Nothing in the hypothesis of narcissism, therefore, seems to announce or anticipate a theory that would be more attentive to mimetic mediation, to the phenomena of desiring identification, to all that separates the subject from "itself" and its "own" desire. Quite the contrary: the hypothesis of narcissism looks more like a stumbling block to such a theory, given that the hypothesis of narcissism continues to presuppose the subject, in its identity with itself, its unalienated propriety, its "primary" integrity, and so on. Moreover, preliminary evidence of this incompatibility between the theory of mimetism and the hypothesis of narcissism may be sought in the fact that "On Narcissism" makes no room for the concept of identification, as if the problematics of narcissism had to entail a retreat from the problems left unresolved in Freud's research on hysteria, dreams, and fantasies. In view of all this, what keeps us from skipping over this essay and passing directly to texts like "Group Psychology and the Analysis of the Ego," or "The Ego and the Id," in which identification is one of Freud's central preoccupations and has wide-ranging implications?

There are several reasons for taking the essay on narcissism into account. First of all, we have to keep in mind that we were able to begin to decipher the mimetic nature of desire on the basis of the sort of "egoism" it manifests. The singular egocentricity of dreams and fantasy had no doubt already pointed the way to an always already eccentric, always already distorted (displaced, dissimulated) subject in all sorts of identificatory roles and figures, and, as such, a fundamentally *improbable* subject. Strangely enough, the self-exhibition of the ego never stops motivating desire; it is as if the process of identification were regularly transformed into a claim of identity ("I am so-and-so"), or as if mimesis (of the desire) of someone else led automatically to a declaration of ego autonomy—in other words, to a protest that is antimimetic in form ("Don't mistake me for another"). Something presumably produces a firm bond between desire and the dissimulation (or the misrecognition) of its mimetic origin, between desire and a tenacious "ego-ic" infatuation— something that may as well be called narcissism.

Indeed, we cannot fail to note that Freud does introduce the question of narcissism as a question of the ego, the desire of and for the ego. Up to this point, his concern with "egoistic" desires has been quite marginal; now it is abruptly amplified in such a way as to throw the earlier problematics completely out of kilter, so that the libido theory is affected as well as the topographical representation of the psyche.[1] The sentence with which Freud concludes his two introductory paragraphs makes his new orientation quite clear: "Narcissism . . . [is] not a perversion, but the libidinal complement to the egoism of the instinct of self-preservation, a measure of which may justifiably be attributed to every living creature" ("On Narcissism," pp. 73–74).

This simple definition encompasses the whole problem on which Freud's essay hinges. We shall attempt to pinpoint it, as dryly and formally as possible, first of all at the point where it disturbs the apparatus of the first topographical schema. In fact, to say that the libido (or the sexual instinct, as Freud had been calling it) converges with the egoistic instinct for self-preservation (the ego instinct) is also to say that the ego can no longer enjoy the same status as before. On the one hand, the ego is no longer *only* a repressive instance of censorship: far from being opposed to desire, it is itself overcome (cathected, Freud says) by libido; and egoism stems correlatively from a sort of erotic passion. On the other hand, it is no longer only an instance of adaptation to reality, an ego-reality: the rest of "On Narcissism" will demonstrate that the ego loves itself sometimes quite madly, to the point of megalomanic delusion. If narcissism is the libidinal complement of the self-preservative instinct, this peculiar complement (or supplement, *Ergänzung*) can perfectly well go against the interests of the ego (the *Ichinteresse*), and even lead it to suicide and self-destruction, at least if we can believe the fable that prescribes from afar the writing of this essay. The ego in love, the deranged ego, the suicidal ego—this is where the ego begins to pose a problem for analytic theory. From here on it will continue to be a thorny issue. And we can understand nothing about the second topographical schema and the "turning point" of the 1920's if we fail to take into account this slippage from the analysis of desire toward what Freud soon comes to call "the analysis of the ego." For this reason, if for no other, it is essential to linger over "On Narcissism."

But there is more. The topological transformations are accompanied, conversely and necessarily, by a revision of the libido theory. It is easy to see why: to speak of libidinal egoism amounts to expanding not only the concept of the ego but also that of the libido. Quite clearly, the latter can no longer be contained within a unilaterally sexual, erotic definition. To love or desire *oneself* in the narcissistic sense is not the same thing, for example, as loving the *body proper* in the autoerotic mode (by stroking it, caressing it, and so forth). Otherwise there would be no reason for Freud to distinguish narcissism so carefully from the sexual perversion that the sexologists (Näcke, Ellis) identified by the same name. In particular, there would be no reason for him to feel impelled to bring forth a new libido ("ego libido," "narcissistic libido") in this context, when he had been perfectly satisfied thus far with the *libido sexualis* alone. Moreover, no matter how clearly Freud may differentiate this ego libido from ego instincts, the fact remains that the former is added to or combined with the latter as a "complement," and that it consequently collaborates with forces that Freud had always characterized as *opposed to sexuality*.

Indeed, the third section of "On Narcissism" is essentially devoted to the implications of narcissism in the "psychology of repression": there we learn, among other things, that "for the ego the formation of an ideal would be the conditioning factor of repression," and that this ideal "demands" the sublimation of the libidinal instincts (p. 94). Hence if narcissism names a desire (and not a need or an "interest": once again, Freud is speaking of the narcissistic *libido*, and it is no coincidence), we have to add that this desire is no longer of the erotic type, since it contributes in one way or another to all that may inhibit sexuality—idealization, repression, sublimation. Let us not ask again what the meaning is of this aporia of the theory of instincts, this strange conjugation of desire with the forbidden, with authority, with the sublime, and so on. Let us be content for the moment with the observation that the hypothesis of narcissism does appear to imply a tacit revision of the sexual (object-oriented) schema that seemed to weigh so heavily upon the theory of desire. This gives it a further claim on our attention.

Correspondence

> I am immensely grateful that you are making me the gift of an Other. . . . I cannot write if I have no public at all, but I can be quite content to write for you alone.
>
> Freud, Letter to Fliess, May 18, 1898

Are we to conclude that "On Narcissism" simply dismisses the sexual problematics? Not at all, especially since the essay was written during a critical period for Freud (critical in "theoretical," "politico-institutional," and "affective" terms)—a period that was wholly dominated by his break with Jung. In his *Psychology of the Unconscious*,[2] C. G. Jung had just proposed "expanding" the concept of the libido and diluting the opposition (that is, the conflict) between sexual instincts and ego instincts in a vague monism of "psychic interest in general." It had thus become necessary to take a stand, to break with the Zurich school, to regroup the "savage horde" around the scandalous theory of sexuality, to establish psychoanalysis—as a "science" and as a "movement"—on the basis of fidelity to Freud's name alone (let us recall the episode of the "secret committee"), and so on.

In fact, the first section of "On Narcissism" fits directly into this polemical, agonistic context. Freud vigorously denounces the speculative nature of Jung's theories and reaffirms the need to retain the opposition between sexual instincts and ego instincts, pending further research. The entire discussion is organized as a forceful response to Jung, and it cannot be understood properly if the stakes are not made clear. Freud is manifestly concerned here with maintaining the gains of psychoanalysis: he is seeking to preserve its originality, in other words, to establish differences—between dualism and monism, between psychoanalysis and non-psychoanalysis, between Freud himself (as science, Cause, or Freudian "thing") and Jung. Anything that might attenuate or blur this difference, therefore, must be kept out of sight.

And yet what does Freud actually do in this text? As we look more closely, we find him doing exactly what he criticizes Jung for doing. Like Jung, Freud speculates freely (about a "primary narcissism"). What is more, he, too, "expands" the concept of the libido, by advancing the hypothesis of an ego libido—inevitably raising the question, at the time, of whether this hypothesis did not tend to rescind the dualism between the sexual instincts and the ego instincts.[3] Not only are all these developments dictated, then, by the pressure of the adversary (I would have been glad to dispense with it, Freud says), they are rigorously modeled according to that pressure as well. The implacable law of strategy is such that it requires one to espouse the opponent's viewpoint, to fight using the opponent's strategy, and this holds true for the strategies of thought, like any others: difference is established only on the basis of a fundamental likeness. Freud eventually acknowledges this himself, for he does not hesitate to admit later on that, in "On Narcissism", he had come very close to Jung's theories, "as though the slow process of psycho-analytic research was following in the steps of Jung's speculations about a primal libido, especially because the transformation of object-libido into narcissism necessarily carried along with it a certain degree of desexualization" ("The Libido Theory," in "Two Encyclopedia Articles," *SE* 18: 257).

Certain heirs bound to the proper name of Freud will argue that Freud is being quite unfair to himself here: Freud is *not* Jung, and he is tendentiously "reinterpreting" his own thought.[4] But is this really so clear? Freud's avowal stands, and it attests to the fact that, in 1914, something had, after all, been conceded to Jung, something that took the form of a "certain degree of desexualization." We have yet to learn just what that means. Thus we shall have to follow the discussion with Jung somewhat more closely, by means of the Freud-Jung correspondence. This correspondence has them responding to each other, through the intermediary of letters and books, according to the laws of a certain affinity or conflictual symmetry. Appearances notwithstanding, our attention to this correspondence will not deflect our attention from the question of narcissism; quite the opposite is true.

This is so, first of all, because the Freud-Jung correspondence deals, above all, with insanity. There is no doubt, in fact, that Freud's focus on psychosis, much more than his attention to perversion,[5] was what motivated the introduction of narcissism. "Normal" narcissism had first been inferred on the basis of the "pathological" narcissism of the insane, as Freud reminds us at the beginning of "On Narcissism": "A pressing motive for occupying ourselves with the conception of a primary and normal narcissism arose when the attempt was made to subsume what we know of *dementia praecox* (Kraepelin) or schizophrenia (Bleuler) under the hypothesis of the libido theory" (p. 74).

Now this "idea" or hypothesis cannot be separated from the correspondence in question. It was Jung who had gotten Freud to read Senate-President Schreber's *Memoirs*, in connection with which he first explored the "idea" in a text written for publication. It was *with* Jung (that is, by arguing against him) that Freud had elaborated the "idea," in the course of an exchange that went on for several years. And it is again with (against) Jung that he now has to amplify, support, and justify the idea:

The libido theory has already come to grief in the attempt to explain the latter disease [schizophrenia]. This has been asserted by C. G. Jung (1912) and it is on this account that I have been obliged to enter upon this last discussion, which I would gladly have been spared. I should have preferred to follow to its end the course embarked upon in the analysis of the Schreber case without any discussion of its premisses. [p. 79]

Indeed, we must not forget that the terrain of madness was the arena where Freud and Jung first met, in 1906. Jung already held a position of eminence in the psychiatric world. And when Freud first established contact, he had a very specific purpose, which was both "political" and theoretical in nature. For one thing, he meant to use Jung as a sort of ambassador to official psychiatry, in order to bring psychoanalysis out of its ghetto (the scientific ghetto, but also the Jewish ghetto: Freud wrote to Abraham that Jung must be spared, for he alone could see to it that psychoanalysis did not remain "a Jewish nationalist affair"). It was crucial to return to the institutional fold, to be recognized by the scientific community, and for this Freud was ready to form an alliance with a "German," setting him up as his "successor" and heir (*Letters*, pp. 167–97). (Later, after the break, he decided it was necessary to return to the ghetto and institute another type of alliance, this time a secret, quasi-religious Jewish alliance.)

From this point of view, Jung was already an intermediary, a mediator, a go-between. But he had an even stronger claim to these roles, for Freud intended to make a *theoretical* conquest of the domain of psychosis (to bring psychoanalysis out of the ghetto of neurosis, as it were), again using Jung as a means: by trying out his hypotheses on him (Jung, as a psychiatrist, had the clinical material that Freud lacked); by building on his objections (for Jung, from the beginning, "resisted," hung back); and also, more insidiously, by installing himself in that ambiguous, mimetic zone of *thinking in the other*, crediting Jung with his own theories and stealing Jung's theories from him at the same time. Shortly after their first meeting, Freud made Jung the following proposition:

In regard to Dem[entia] Pr[aecox] I have a proposal to make to you. Since your departure I have jotted down a few ideas on the subject we discussed. I should like to let you have them unless—for two reasons—you would prefer not to see them. First, because you might hit on them yourself, and second because it may be distasteful to you to accept anything whatsoever.

I must say that I regard a kind of intellectual communism, in which neither party takes anxious note of what he has given and what received, as a highly estimable arrangement. [p. 28]

The proposed "contract" is clear, and it resembles the one Freud had made earlier with Fliess, in another well-known correspondence. It is not simply a matter of exchanging working drafts (we know that Freud had sent several such to Fliess, the most important being the famous "Project for a Scientific Psychology" of 1895). It is also, much more fundamentally, a matter of thinking and speculating together (in this instance, on delusion), with each partner having the right to appropriate the other's thoughts, so that the other becomes by that very token a double, another self, and/or a different— an other—self.

Let us note, prematurely, that this amounts to a continual flirtation with delusion. Fliess, it seems, had succumbed to delusion at the end of his relationship with Freud, and the outcome of that earlier correspondence must have had an impact on the Freud-Jung exchange. In fact, as François Roustang has so aptly noted,[6] this latter correspondence is literally haunted by the "Fliess affair," at two levels:

1. Fliess is constantly being taken as a "case," that is, as an exemplary example or paradigm of paranoia (pp. 121, 124). He is thus the *object* of a theoretical discourse on paranoia sustained by both correspondents. From the point of view of the pragmatics of the Freud-Jung communication, he may be said to function as an absent or excluded third.

2. Next, both correspondents obsessively compare their own correspondence to the exchange between Freud and Fliess (pp. 122, 209, 212, 216). Fliess's name comes to signify not only the object mentioned in the discourse (its utterance, or *logos*) but also the way in which it is mentioned (its enunciation, or *lexis*)—that is, the way in which the *subjects* Freud and Jung implicate themselves and correspond. From a pragmatic point of view, the name "Fliess" may be said to designate, by analogy, the relation of communication itself, which is a relation of communion (Freud speaks of "communism") between doubles. Because these two levels are inevitably intertwined, we find ourselves confronting a discourse on madness whose very

form threatens to lead to madness. Furthermore, the way in which the two correspondents invoke Fliess's ghost leaves no doubt on the subject. They threaten each other with it between the lines, they frighten each other with it, and they do so because they know (but with a secret, esoteric knowledge that never goes beyond the bounds of the private correspondence) that Fliess had "gone mad" owing to his correspondence with Freud. This knowledge ultimately proves useless, wholly impotent, since it fails to prevent the reproduction of the same "deadly" scenario: like so many others after him, Jung broke with Freud, and he is even said to have suffered a "psychiatric episode" in the process.[7]

As a result, there is a close proximity between knowledge of paranoia and paranoic knowledge, between knowing of delusion and the delusion of knowing, which we shall now have to investigate.[8] The matter is of both practical and theoretical importance (the two are inseparable). The peculiar psychoanalytic "theory-practice," and the peculiar implication of the subjects "themselves" in this theory of the subject, are such that the failure of the empirical relationship with Jung (or Fliess, and others) also marks a failure of the *analysis* of that relationship. To simplify the question, we may reduce it to a question of the value of a theory of madness (Fliess's madness, for example, but also Jung's, and so on), when everything about that theory suggests that it has been developed within a relationship or correspondence that has contributed to bringing about the phenomenon being addressed (in Fliess's case, for example, but also Jung's, and so on). Can the theory account for something in which it is, in some sense, a concerned party? Is there not, here, a fragment of self-analysis (as it has been called) all the more unterminated and interminable in that it interferes with its own position as *subject* of (self-)analytic theory and collides with its own narcissism?

We must remember, too, that all Freud's statements on the subject of madness—and especially those concerning narcissism, the ego, and so forth—are inscribed within the framework of this correspondence, of this theoretical duo or duel with Jung, and they are all marked by it. This mark, let us hasten to add, is not trivially biographic, in the sense in which we might say, for example, that the personal circumstances of the empirical subjects "Freud" and

"Jung" weighed heavily in their writings. Although that is also part of the picture, the relation between "subject" and "theory" that concerns us here is of another sort, if only because, under the circumstances, we can no longer tell *who* is theorizing what. Thought or speculation, here less solitary than ever, cannot be summed up under proper names—"Freud" *or* "Jung," for example. This does not mean, however, that it is purely anonymous. It is, rather, *countersigned*: signed *with* another, *against* the other, in intimate opposition to the other. (And what are the implications, then, for the Freudian heritage, for the whole movement that lays claim to the proper name of Freud and returns to it untiringly, by virtue of the supposedly "self-analytic" institution of psychoanalysis? The question will be pursued.)

For the time being, let us proceed as though we are exclusively concerned with what is said in the correspondence, what is communicated in this communication. We shall therefore read the speculative manuscript that Freud sent to Jung in accordance with their contract. The content of these "Theoretical Opinions on Paranoia," and of the two letters that follow (pp. 38–43, 46–48), is not entirely new. Freud condenses and systematizes ideas that already have a long history; they concern the role of projection, rejection (*Verwerfung*), and autoerotism in paranoia.[9] Projection, he writes, must be seen as the type of repression proper to psychosis. Contrary to what happens in neurosis, the "content of the desire" appears here in the most manifest fashion; but it appears *projected*, in the distorted form of perceptions (visual hallucinations, voices) that come from the outside and that the subject at once experiences as an undeniable reality (everything that comes from "the P[erception-Consciousness] extremity meets immediately with *belief*") and rejects (*verwift*) with the greatest indignation. An example: "People say that I love coitus. That is what they say, but it's not *true*" (p. 46). Instead of repressing the content of the desire (shoving it back inside), then, one projects it onto—and rejects it as—an outside, an exterior.

But Freud makes it clear at once, in response to one of Jung's remarks, that this projection of desire onto external reality has nothing to do with a hallucinatory realization of the desire. Delusional hallucinations are not fantasmatic hallucinations. If it were only a question of "a fantasy copy of reality," as Jung suggested (p. 44), we would remain within the horizon of neurosis. Delusion would appear basically as a triumph of fantasy, as a victory on the part of the repressed. Now delusional hallucinations are indeed products of repression, and even of a radical repression. Far from being the effect of a "desire for reality" (Jung again), they must be conceived as anemic specters left behind by desire when the latter retreats absolutely from the object—from the real object, of course, but also and especially from its fantasmatic representation: "I believe, rather, that the libido departs from the object-image, which is thereby divested of the cathexis that has characterized it as internal and can now be projected outward and, as it were, perceived" (p. 46).[10]

This projection is thus neither a projection of the "content of desire" on the internal screen of fantasy nor, as is often supposed, the attribution to another person of feelings that have been internally repressed. It is, rather, a matter of an abjection, of a total refusal (and this "repression" is consequently something more, or something other, than repression properly speaking). The desire for the object is challenged to such an extent that the subject can no longer even represent it to *himself*, can no longer assume it in the first person, *even in the unconscious*, and that is why it appears in the form of an external, foreign, other voice (*they say* about me that I like coitus). Freud says this again quite clearly in "Psycho-Analytic Notes on an Autobiographical Account of a Case of Paranoia (Dementia Paranoides)" (the Schreber case): "It was incorrect to say that the perception which was suppressed internally is projected outwards"; in fact, it is because the feeling for the object has been "suppressed within" that it resurfaces, terribly and incomprehensibly, "from without" (p. 71).[11]

But let us proceed cautiously here. What is this rejected "object," from which the libido withdraws, which resurfaces, and so on? It is, first of all and quite obviously, an object of desire. We need to recall one important thing: whether it is total or partial (breast, feces, penis), real and/or fantasmatic, autoerotic or alloerotic, the *Objekt* always designates, for Freud, the object of the drive—that owing to which the drive reaches its goal, its *Ziel*. However, Freud often uses the term in a more specific (and more classical) sense; this second meaning is superimposed on the first without contradicting it. Everything that is op-posed to the subject, everything that confronts it—in short, everything that is "not-ego"—is, then, an "object." It is in this second sense that autoerotism, for example, is said to be "deprived of an object" (even though this is not true in the first sense).[12] And when the context does not specify that a partial object (such as the breast, primordial object) is in question, the term designates, finally, the "other person," the "other [of the] ego" inasmuch as it is chosen as love object. That is the case here. The loss of reality in psychosis is a vicissitude of desire, one of the "vicissitudes of the libido" (*Letters*, p. 48): it is what happens when the libido abandons the object (in both meanings of the term) and returns to the ego itself (which is the object in the first sense but not in the second) .

Let us say, more simply, that the relation to the other is the key to the relation to external reality, and that madness begins where commerce with the other breaks off. This is how we have to understand the use of the concept of autoerotism at this point in Freud's argument:

In paranoia, the libido is withdrawn from the object. . . . Where the libido has gone is indicated by the *hostility to the object*, found in paranoia. This is an endogenous perception of libido withdrawal. In view of the relation of compensation between object-cathexis and ego-cathexis, it seems likely that the cathexis withdrawn from the object has returned to the ego, i.e., has become autoerotic. [p. 39]

When this autoerotic withdrawal succeeds (from the point of view of "repression"), the result, Freud adds, is the picture of dementia praecox (autism, schizophrenia) favored by Jung. When it fails, the resulting picture is one of paranoia properly speaking, a domain in which Freud seems to move much more easily: the libido returns, then, in part toward the object that "has turned into a perception" (p. 47), and comes back to inhabit delusions (by plotting against the patient, assailing him with voices, blatantly spying on him, and so forth).

This is the heart of the matter. The schema established here is roughly the one that Freud adopted four years later when he drafted the theoretical portion of his study of the Schreber case ("On the Mechanism of Paranoia"). But we must also note that two essential components are still missing from the picture: on the one hand, *narcissism*, in which Freud comes to see the "stage" to which the libido regresses when it withdraws; and, on the other hand, *homosexuality*, which Freud comes to view as what is at stake in the paranoic "repression." We shall have to examine these two points to understand what motivates their introduction.

Narcissism

The absence of narcissism in the manuscript addressed to Jung is all the more remarkable in that, in 1911, it occupied precisely the place of the autoerotism of 1907. A quick comparison leaves no doubt on the subject: everything that Freud had said earlier about the autoerotic "ego" is repeated, in "Psycho-Analytic Notes," in connection with the narcissistic ego. Correlatively, autoerotism does not entirely disappear in the second version, but it retreats somewhat in the "history" of the libido, since it is said to come *before* the narcissistic stage. In particular, where Freud had earlier posited the same withdrawal of the libido at the origin of both major psychoses (a successful withdrawal in the case of dementia praecox and a partially unsuccessful withdrawal in paranoia), room now has to be made for two regressions of varying amplitude. Thus, in dementia praecox,

the regression extends not merely to narcissism (manifesting itself in the shape of megalomania) but to a complete abandonment of object-love and a return to infantile auto-erotism. The dispositional fixation must therefore be situated further back than in paranoia, and must lie somewhere at the beginning of the course of development from auto-erotism to object-love. ["Psycho-Analytic Notes," p. 77]

We must conclude that narcissism and autoerotism are not identical, and that the narcissistic ego is not identical with that autoerotic "ego" that Freud mentioned earlier: curiously enough, megalomania is a feature of the former and not the latter. Something has happened, then, in four years, to make Freud attentive to this difference.

Here is where the correspondence has to be brought into play. Let us go back to it, then, and stop ignoring the fact that Freud does indeed send Jung his theses on paranoia, despite the possibility that he is sending them to "himself," since Jung, he says, may well have "come across them." Who knows? Perhaps Jung thinks *as he does*.

Does he think, as Freud does, that psychosis stems from a decathexis of the object to the benefit of the autoerotic "ego"? Yes, Jung seems to reply, and perhaps he even believes it. (How can we weigh the contributions of good manners, strategy, and sincerity in this correspondence?) In any event, did not the contract consist in sharing their thoughts? Thus Jung absorbs Freud's ideas. He identifies himself with them, and them with himself, by thinking *in Freud's place*, with the same words. But at the same time, by making them his own, he turns them to his own benefit:

Your views on paranoia have not lain fallow. I have been able to confirm them many times over. Only the thing is not yet ripe. I have therefore kept silent about it so far. The detachment of libido, its regression to autoerotic forms, is probably well explained by the self-assertion, the psychological self-preservation of the individual. Hysteria keeps to the plane of "preservation of the species," paranoia (Dem. pr.) to the plane of self-preservation, i.e., autoerotism. . . . The psychoses (the incurable ones) should probably be regarded as defensive encapsulations that have misfired, or rather, have been carried to extremes. The Fliess case bears this out. [*Letters*, pp. 123–24]

The "Fliess case"? Or the Jung case? Is not Jung, too, beginning to isolate himself, to protect, preserve, and assert himself when confronted with his correspondent, his other self? This "affirmation of self" (an affirmation of independence, autonomy, difference, originality, and so forth) here takes the twisted, duplicitous form of a misunderstanding of the word "autoerotism," a misuse that allows Jung to say the opposite of what Freud says, even as he appears to be saying the same thing.

Indeed, when one knows (and Jung of course did know) how rigorously Freud associated self-preservation with the ego instincts, as opposed to the sexual instincts, which were devoted to the "preservation of the species," it is clear that a formula such as "the plane of self-preservation, i.e., autoerotism" stems from the purest sort of provocation. It does so first of all because it amounts to associating autoerotism, an essential component of the theory of sexuality, with the "psychological self-preservation of the individual," in other words, with the sphere of the ego instincts. Second, by that very token it authorizes an amalgam between the "paranoid ego" Freud had been talking about and the ego-agency: the delusional affirmation of the self would not result from a process unfolding at the level of the libido (disinvestment of the object, reinvestment of the body itself) but, on the contrary, from a sort of egoistic crispation or stiffening up, from a "protective isolation" of the ego. And Jung, at the end of his headlong plunge into misunderstanding, all the stages of which can be followed in the first volume of the *Letters*, goes so far as to see in self-affirmation a defense of the ego against the libido (or more precisely against erotic *dependency*). As the "constitutional basis of the neuroses," he says, one would find

the imbalance between libido and resistance (self-assertion). If, at the start, the libido displayed too strong an attraction or need for love, hate would soon appear by way of compensation . . . I think this is the basis for the immense self-assertion that appears later on in obsessional neurosis: the patient is always afraid of losing his ego, must take revenge for every act of love, and gives up the sexually destructive obsessional system only with the greatest reluctance. . . . Obviously the self-assertion in obsessional neurosis is far exceeded in D. pr. [p. 275]

To this Freud finally offers a trenchant, cutting response, in terms that already hint at the break to come. Jung is accused of going over to the enemy, of betraying the Freudian Cause:

Oddly enough, it is very hard for us with our human minds to fix our attention equally on these two instinctual camps and to carry over the opposition between ego and libido into our observation, so as to embrace them both without bias. Thus far, it is true, I have concentrated on the repressed material, because it is new and unknown; I have been a Cato championing the *causa victa*. I hope I have not forgotten that there is also a *victrix*. Adler's psychology takes account only of the repressive factor; consequently, he describes "sensitivity," this attitude of the ego in opposition to the libido, as the fundamental condition of neurosis. And now I find you taking the same line and using almost the same word: i.e., by concentrating on the ego, which I have not adequately studied, you run the risk of neglecting the libido, to which I have done full justice. [pp. 277–78]

Libido contra Ego, then, and Freud contra Jung. Let us nevertheless try to move beyond these slightly paranoid accents ("paranoepic," to echo Roustang), beyond any Manichaeism or militant "dualism" that would split the world into good and bad forces, allies and adversaries, disciples and renegades. What is important in this discussion is not what stands out at first glance—the misunderstanding, then the disagreement, and soon the open struggle between the two men. What counts is, rather, what unites them, paradoxically, in their difference, a factor from which Freud will manage to profit fully as soon as the game of communistic thought-sharing has reached its fateful conclusion: their reciprocal hatred.

First of all, we have to recognize that Jung's "misunderstanding" is favored from the outset by a certain indeterminacy in Freud's thesis on paranoia. On the one hand, Freud uses the same word to designate the paranoid, autoerotic *Ich* and the topographical *Ich*. On the other hand, the context that ought to have made it possible to differentiate them is slippery or at least ambiguous. For when Freud speaks of the libido's withdrawal with respect to the ego, he is obviously thinking of the degradation of relations with others ("hostility towards the object," misanthropy, the persecution delusion, and so on), and especially of the megalomanic delusion. But why would such a turning in on oneself be characterized as auto*erotic*? Could Freud seriously have deemed it equivalent to the instinct's turning back toward its organic source (which is the strict definition of autoerotism)? No doubt megalomaniacs are fascinated by their own "ego," to the detriment of "objects" (and that is why they so often write "auto"-biographies: *Confessions*, *Ecce homo*, *Memoirs of My Nervous Illness*, and so on); but this is in order to proclaim their unheard-of uniqueness, their incomparable solitude, their absolute autonomy. This "ego" is not the body proper of autoerotism, as Freud surely knew. All this suggests that he is playing with indeterminacy at least as much as Jung is.

Furthermore, the "communism" of the correspondence is such as to preclude lifting the indeterminacy. In the face of Jung's misinterpretation, Freud might have—and, under normal circumstances, should have—criticized, pointed out the difference, and broken the contract (this is yours, that is mine). Yet he does nothing of the sort. On the contrary, he stakes out his position within the misreading, claiming not to understand that Jung does not want to understand. Is he being blindly "transferential"? Or is this a clear-sighted strategy? Probably neither one. Freud is behaving lucidly *as if* Jung thinks the way he himself thinks; in return, blindly, he begins to think *like* Jung. For if it is true that Jung appropriates Freud's thoughts for himself (the contract said not to keep track of "what one has given and what received"), the converse is equally true: in exactly the same way, Freud appropriates Jung's thoughts for himself, makes them his own, assimilates them, "incorporates" and "digests" them, and so on.

It is this double identification, doubly appropriating, which accounts for the final break between them (and its passionate, even "delusional" nature) much more plausibly than some initial disagreement that would have ripened slowly before bursting out in the open. The contract Freud proposed—a phony contract, a mimetic contract without a safety net—could lead to no other outcome: as each of the correspondents was appropriating the other's thoughts, the latter of necessity had to appear as a double who was dispossessing the former of his "own" thought—hence the quarrels over who was first, the claims to originality, the accusations of ill will (one step further and we have the paranoic plot, thought-stealing, persecution, and delusional interpretation, as the "Fliess case" confirms). Contrary to expectations (but quite logically), the correspondents' intellectual communism ends up exacerbating, paroxyzing, the proprietary impulse. This is the classical schema of mimetic rivalry: similarity leads to disagreement and the claim of difference; mimesis of the other leads to propriation.

All this precludes our being astonished, then, at the substitution of "narcissism" for "autoeroticism" in the theory of paranoia proposed in "Psycho-Analytic Notes." Resituated within the framework of the correspondence, this displacement of emphasis (or conceptual shift) clearly indicates that Freud has now arrived at Jung's positions, at least as far as the difference between autoerotism and delusional megalomania is concerned. If the latter is from here on attributed to narcissism, this is because delusional megalomania is not autoerotic but something else. Something other—but what? Jung, as we have seen, proposed to identify the "affirmation of self" with an egoistic—and therefore nonsexual—affirmation. But Freud, at the very moment when he is walking in Jung's footsteps and embarking, in

Jung's place, on the study or analysis of the ego, does all he can to prevent this identification (of the narcissistic ego with the ego-agency, but also—however we may wish to understand this—of the Freudian ego with the Jungian ego). The narcissistic overestimation of the ego would be a *sexual* overestimation. Here, in fact, according to "Psycho-Analytic Notes," is the underlying "proposition" of delusions:

"I do not love at all—I do not love any one." And since, after all, one's libido must go somewhere, this proposition seems to be the psychological equivalent of the proposition: "I love only myself." So that this kind of contradiction would give us megalomania, which we may regard as a *sexual overestimation of the ego* and may thus set beside the overvaluation of the love-object with which we are already familiar. [p. 65]

A little further on:

The majority of cases of paranoia exhibit traces of megalomania, and . . . megalomania can by itself constitute a paranoia. From this it may be concluded that in paranoia the liberated libido becomes attached to the ego, and is used for the aggrandizement of the ego. A return is thus made to the stage of narcissism (known to us from the development of the libido), in which a person's only sexual object is his own ego. [p. 72]

This brings us back to the description of this "stage":

There comes a time in the development of the individual at which he unifies his sexual instincts (which have hitherto been engaged in autoerotic activities) in order to obtain a love-object; and he begins by taking himself, his own body, as his love-object, and only subsequently proceeds from this to the choice of some person other than himself as his object. . . . What is of chief importance in the subject's self [*Selbst*] thus chosen as a love-object may already be the genitals. [pp. 60–61]

It is obvious that all these discussions stress the sexual, sexualized nature of the narcissistic ego. It is the "body proper," taken as "sexual object." Not the autoerotic body—an anarchic body, parceled off into erogenous zones, shot through with component instincts, and so on—but the whole body, unified and identified as "individual," "self," "ego." So be it. But what is it, precisely, that assures this totalization, this unification, this identification? How is it that I may have a relation to my body as *my* body, my *own* body, if it is not by saying "I," "me," "ego," *Ich*? And is this "ego" that makes it possible to identify my body identical with that body? Are we not dealing, much more probably, with the ego-agency, with that ego which Freud admitted he had not "sufficiently studied"? Here is another way of putting the same question: Since the entire argument is designed to account for delusional megalomania, can this latter be identified with a "sexual overestimation of the ego proper"? What does that mean? That the megalomaniac overestimates his sexual power? In short, is it his body that he overestimates, or his ego? Are those the same thing?[13] Is it not rather his identity and the very possibility of saying "I," "me" that obsesses the victim of a delusion (Nietzsche: "I am Prado, I am Prado's father, . . . I am also Lesseps"; Artaud: "I am my son, my father, my mother, and myself")? And if such is the case, would we not find ourselves very close to the "affirmation of self" described by Jung?

Freud, of course, caught up as he was in the mimetic rivalry with Jung, could not or would not say this, so he says it without saying it, by playing once again on the indeterminacy of the concept(s) of the ego. Indeed, nothing makes it possible to establish a rigorous distinction, once and for all, between the narcissistic ego and the ego-agency, unless it is a dogmatic and self-interested assertion of the sexual nature of narcissism. Nothing, in other words, allows us to differentiate Freud's thesis sharply from Jung's.[14] Let us make no mistake about it: if Freud emphasizes sexuality so strongly, he does so in order to bring forth an otherwise undiscoverable difference. "Sexuality" functions here as a differential feature that makes it possible to find one's way around, like a shibboleth and, let us say, like a signature. By invoking sexuality, Freud is appropriating Jung's ego for himself, he says "I" (articulates the ego) in Jung's place, and thus he signs the entire correspondence with his own proper name: it is a matter of wiping out (or finishing off) the communism of thought-sharing while (re)instituting intellectual private property—that is to say, the narcissistic economy, the *oikonomia*. The elaboration of the concept of narcissism does not escape the effects of narcissism. (And we come back to our question: Can this concept, then, account for something of which it is the effect?)

Homosexuality

To the dossier of this more or less clandestine "desexualization," we still have to add all Freud's statements concerning the role of homosexuality in paranoia, strange as this may seem. To justify this move we shall retrace the path that leads from the hypotheses outlined in the Freud-Jung correspondence to the theory proposed in "Psycho-Analytic Notes." As we have already observed, homosexuality is absent from Freud's 1907 tableau: Freud is satisfied to find paranoia's roots in a decathexis of the libido to the benefit of the ego, without further specifying the nature of the object from which love is thus withdrawn. In 1911, however, he specifies that a homosexual object is involved. Why?

At first glance, this new hypothesis seems to come into play because it offers a better account of the clinical reality. In fact, we know that the "object" around which the persecution delusion gravitates is very often of the same sex as the patient, as the Schreber example shows, for the figures that tormented him were undeniably male.[15] The same holds true for the jealousy delusion: jealousy becomes properly delusional only from the moment when the jealous person becomes exclusively preoccupied with his rival and the rival's hateful conduct, losing all interest in the faithless party.[16] As for the erotomaniac, who might seem to bring a jarring note to this tableau, let us recall that the passion that she devotes (more precisely, that devotes her) to her Lover is purely platonic, impossible, and, in the extreme case, irrelevant to feminine attachments.[17] Consequently, as in the case of the jealousy delusion, the "heterosexual" relationship serves as pretext for, or screen to, a relationship that might well be called, in a first approximation, "homosexual."

This is in any case what Freud says, since he proposes to interpret each of the major types of delusion as a way of "contradicting" the proposition *I (a man) love him (a man)*: the persecution delusion reversing the verb (*I do not love him*, to which the "projection" must be added, *because he hates me*); the jealousy delusion permuting the subject (*it is she who loves him*); the erotomaniac challenging the direct object (*I love her*, "projected" into *because she loves me*); and megalomania, finally, rejecting the entire proposition (*I love no one,*

I love only myself; "Psycho-Analytic Notes," pp. 63–65). Let us note at once that these four statements are not on the same level, and they are not generated in the same way. The first three are matters of logic, as it were: Freud deduces them by exhausting the various ways of denying the homosexual proposition. But he bases the fourth statement on a sort of genetic hypothesis: If the delusion of grandeur also entails a negation of homosexuality (which is not logically obvious, since the megalomaniac disclaims *any* object), Freud believes this is because the narcissistic stage to which the megalomaniac regresses for the purpose of repression comes immediately before the homosexual stage in the normal development of the libido.

Let us recall that "what is of chief importance in the subject's self thus chosen as a love-object may already be the genitals" (p. 61). Freud added: "The line of development then leads on to the choice of an external object with similar genitals—that is, to homosexual object-choice—and thence to heterosexuality" (p. 61). In this view, then, object orientation is homosexual at the outset, and the libido at first cathects only doubles—objects (others) that resemble the narcissistic ego. The paranoiac accomplishes this evolution in reverse, regressively. In withdrawing from the homosexual object, the libido would have no way out except to return to narcissism—that is, to non-object orientation; hence the delusion of grandeur and the paranoic "end of the world." And it is only when the libido returns, as "repression" fails, toward objects (by the same path, that of *sameness*) that we would have the three other delusions, with their specific negations and projections.[18]

Let us interrupt the recollection of these familiar propositions to discuss a different question. Is the strange resemblance that binds the delusional ego to a double (and does so even while proclaiming its *incomparable* identity: "Do not mistake me for another") necessarily a *sexual* resemblance, a homo*sexuality*? Why must we postulate that the narcissistic ego and its "likeness" resemble each other in terms of "genital organs" alone? The ambiguity noted earlier with regard to narcissism is of such a nature as to alert us to this point. If the ego that asserts itself in megalomania is a "desexualized" ego, as has been suggested, can one not hypothesize that the same is true for the "object" that dominates the delusion? Let us note that Schreber's own doctrine differed markedly from Freud's in this regard, since he attributed his "nervous illness" to the plot concocted by Professor Flechsig to prevent him from becoming a "nerve specialist": that is (taking said projection into account), he attributed it to his "own" desire to occupy Flechsig's post.[19]

If we pursue this hypothesis (and why not? because Schreber was mad? did Freud not admire in Schreber the *theoretician* of madness?), Flechsig would not be a sexual double but a professional double, of the "rival" type. A delusional hypothesis? After all, what is more strangely similar than a rival, an enemy brother whose place one wishes to occupy, with whom one is competing for the same object, and so forth? The uncanniness of the Double is implied in the principle of all rivalry, be it professional, political, intellectual, or sexual,[20] and we have already caught a glimpse of this in connection with the Freud-Jung correspondence. Why not suppose, then, that this rivalrous resemblance, as awkward as it is inevitable, is what the delusion rejects and at the same time aggravates to the point of absolute estrangement? And why was Freud so strangely blind to the hate-filled rivalry that poisons the delusional patient's relations with his double?[21]

Jung was much more sensitive to the effects of rivalry on "mental illness." Let us go back once more to the correspondence, since a brief episode included there confirms our view. On August 19, 1907, Jung wrote the following to Freud: "I would now like to ask you for an explanation: Do you regard sexuality as the mother of all feelings? . . . Are there not hysterical symptoms which, though codetermined by the sexual complex, are predominantly conditioned by a sublimation or by a nonsexual complex (profession, job, etc.)?" (*Letters*, p. 79).

Jung is speaking here of hysteria in general, but also of the "hysteric" in himself. The question about the "nonsexual complex (profession, job, etc.)" is by no means coincidental. It concludes a letter in which there has been much talk of colleagues and counterparts, of professional tensions and rivalries. Jung has just admitted that he is "jealous" of Abraham, because Abraham was also corresponding with Freud. He has also just acknowledged that it was his own ambition that kept him from casting his lot decisively with Freud in the psychiatric community (Freud had reproached him for this): "as usual you have hit the nail on the head with your accusation that my ambition is the agent provocateur of my fits of despair" (p. 78).

"Agent provocateur" was the term Charcot had used to designate the factor that set off hysteria, and in his earlier letters Jung was quite prepared to describe himself as a hysteric. In his own question to Freud, then, he is clearly speaking of himself, figuring himself: Might it not be the case, most honored Professor, Sir, that neurosis (my "neurosis"), or hysteria (my "hysteria"), could have a great deal to do with my ambition, my confraternal rivalries? We might almost say that Jung is conducting a self-analysis (in somewhat the way Freud analyzes his own "dreams of grandeur" in *The Interpretation of Dreams*), were it not all too obvious that his self-analytic lucidity is at the service of a professional rivalry—as it happens, with Freud—which is itself left largely unanalyzed. As always, the theses and hypotheses set forth in this correspondence have to be resituated within their interactional, mimetic, and conflictual framework. Jung poses his question as a trap, attempting once again to draw Freud over to his *own* territory, that of the ego: if hysteria could be "predominantly conditioned" by a sublimation or by professional interests, its etiology would no longer be sexual, as Freud was arguing, but egoistic. The psychoneuroses would stem from an ego psychology, from an analysis of the ego's *social* interests.

Let us now read Freud's return mail, his "feedback":

I regard (for the present) the role of sexual complexes in hysteria merely as a theoretical necessity and do not infer it from their frequency and intensity. Proof, I believe, is not yet possible. When we see people made ill by their work, etc., that is not conclusive, for the sexual (in the male, homosexual) component can easily be demonstrated in analysis. I know that we somewhere encounter the conflict between ego-cathexis and object-cathexis, but without direct (clinical) observation I cannot even speculate. [p. 80]

The benefit of this appeal to homo*sexuality* is readily apparent. It allows the instant translation of the egoistic into the erotic, of sociality into sexuality. Freud does not deny that one may fall ill because of one's work: from a conflict over prestige, for example, or over a disappointed ambition. But no professional illness would arise without the intervention of a deeper conflict (Freud accuses Jung of practicing "surface psychology"), without an unconscious conflict (accessible only to psychoanalysis) that puts a homosexual component into play.

Next—and this is by no means a secondary benefit of this simultaneous interpretation or translation—Freud surreptitiously allows himself the luxury of analyzing Jung's resistances: If, dear colleague, there is any professional conflict between us (on the subject of the sexual or nonsexual nature of professional conflicts), it is not for the reason *you* invoke (self-affirmation of the ego, nonsexual complex), but for the one that *I* am evoking (homosexual complex, resistance of the ego). Our interpretations are not *equally* competitive: mine is more powerful because it accounts for yours. (So Freud "says": but might not the opposite be said just as well?)

So far so good; it is less clear, however, why Freud appeals specifically to *homo*sexuality. Is it because jobs, professions, sublimations—the "political" zone, let us say—would be essentially a masculine affair, so that every conflict that arises in this arena would involve people of the same sex? (The restriction is indeed strange: "the . . . [in the male, homosexual] component"—not in woman? The question does not even come up.) But Freud might very well have related this type of conflict to an Oedipal conflict, to the paternal complex, and he does not hesitate to do so elsewhere. If he does not do so here, it is no doubt because the Oedipal conflict is produced within a fundamental inequality or dissymmetry (father vs. son), whereas the conflict he is imagining in this instance points him irresistibly toward the idea of similarity or identity between the protagonists (of the brother vs. brother type, if we must remain within a familial schema).

Still, the rapidity and ease with which Freud passes from Jung's professional complex to the homosexual complex remain inexplicable as long as the intermediary link that surreptitiously authorizes the translation is not reestablished. Let us reconstruct it here. Where Jung speaks of a pathology proper to professional or social relations, Freud thinks immediately about rivalry among colleagues—aggressive rivalry, ambitious jealousy (but he does not say so, any more than Jung does: "colleagues understand each other"). And where he is thinking "rivalry," he is thinking no less immediately—but no doubt more obscurely—"resemblance," "sameness," "identity" (as for the question about *whom* he is thinking, we shall learn the answer in a moment). This is where the theme of *homoïosis* comes in, the theme of *homo*sexuality, which points toward a resemblance that is much more rivalrous than sexual. But Freud does not say this, for colleagues understand each other too well; they resemble each other too closely. Thus it was necessary to stress the difference, displace the accent, inflect the resemblance from one of rivalry to one of gender.

Perhaps we seem to be lingering too long over a perfectly anodyne, quite marginal remark (it is in parentheses) within a private correspondence that is itself marginal in the eyes of the public. But the correspondence, as we keep discovering, intervenes actively in the content of this crisscrossed work, and the "theoretical" can never be separated from the "biographical" or even the "autobiographical." As for Freud's parenthetical remark, it supplies the model for all the "responses" that he will address to Jung from this point on, concerning not hysteria but paranoia. Freud suddenly observes that the "homosexual component" plays a major role:

I have been in contact with a few paranoia cases in my practice and can tell you a secret. . . . The paranoid form [of psychosis] is probably conditioned by restriction to the homosexual component. . . . My one-time friend Fliess developed a dreadful case of paranoia after throwing off his affection for me, which was undoubtedly considerable. I owe this idea to him, i.e., to his behaviour. One must try to learn something from every experience. The breaking down of sublimations in paranoia belongs to the same context. [p. 121][22]

One must try to learn something from every experience, indeed. Just as Jung earlier claimed to be speaking of hysteria in general in order to raise his very personal question, Freud begins by looking for guarantees of objectivity on the side of practice, and ends up admitting that he is speaking out of his own experience: speaking of himself or of Fliess, of his relations with Fliess and thus equally of his relations with Jung.[23] All this is very "subjective," first because it is autobiographical, then because the autobiography is not without some narcissistic bias or auto-apology. It amounts to saying, finally:

I, Freud, have succeeded (I have enlarged my ego) where Fliess failed; he is the paranoid one (or you are, Jung), not I. Or else: I am not the one who loves him, he is the one who loves me, because he hates me (or else: I do not love you, and so on).

Or perhaps: I am not competing with him (I do not hate him), he is competing with me, since he hates me (or I am not competing with you, and so on). In fact, once we have learned to what extent the friendship (or the correspondence) between Freud and Fliess was confused with their "common" theoretical and professional preoccupations—once we have learned, too, that their relations terminated over a question of priority—we can no longer mistake the very particular character of the "homosexuality" Freud is thinking of here. Quite clearly it is a matter once again of a *homosociality*, a *rivalrous* homosociality. The same translation schema is in effect, this time concerning paranoia, and we may thus conclude that the latter has a great deal to do with a "nonsexual complex (profession, job, etc.)." Moreover, that is why Freud needs to mention, "in the same context," the problem of sublimations in paranoia. For if these are "back-formations" in delusion (by which Freud means that they are reconstructed in the form of grandiose speculative systems, religious or political in nature), it is because the starting point of the paranoic regression was already situated in the sphere of sublimations[24]—that is, in orthodox Freudian doctrine, in the sphere of instincts that are inhibited as to their sexual aim and that are redirected toward socially (homosexually?) valorized objects (Art, Science, Power, Holiness, and so forth).

All this can be read, finally, in "Psycho-Analytic Notes," an open letter that leads to the correspondence. In this text, homosexuality is characterized, significantly, as "social," "sublimated," "inhibited as to its aim":

Paranoia is precisely a disorder in which a sexual aetiology is by no means obvious; far from this, the strikingly prominent features in the causation of paranoia, *especially among males*, are social humiliations and slights. But if we go into the matter only a little more deeply, we shall be able to see that the really operative factor in these social injuries lies in the part played in them by the homosexual components of emotional life. So long as the individual is functioning normally and it is consequently impossible to see into the depths of his mental life, we may doubt whether his emotional relations to his neighbours in society have anything to do with sexuality, either actually or in their genesis. But delusions never fail to uncover these relations and to trace back the social feelings [*das soziale Gefühl*] to their roots in a directly sensual erotic wish. [p. 60; emphasis added]

How large a contribution is in fact derived from erotic sources (with the sexual aim inhibited) could scarcely be guessed from the normal social relations of mankind. [p. 61]

We can assert that the length of *the step back from sublimated homosexuality to narcissism* is a measure of the amount of *regression* characteristic of paranoia. [p. 72]

It is apparent that not just any homosexuality gives rise to the paranoic conflict, and that this conflict does not appear just anywhere. The conflict mobilizes a very desexualized homosexuality, one that is very sublimated, very ethereal, and it begins by creating a disturbance precisely in a field—the social field—where sexuality is not evident at all. Here we have a zone of fragility particularly vulnerable to psychotic rupture. Just as the neuroses could be included within an intrapsychic conflict between the sexual instincts and the social interests of the ego, it appears that psychosis requires us to take into account a pathology of the social bond, a pathology of the ego in its social relationships with others.

Is that not what Jung was already saying? Of course, and it is unnecessary to insist on this further. The entire thesis on paranoia in "Psycho-Analytic Notes" is summed up in the parenthesis of the Freud-Jung correspondence. Here Freud repeats and amplifies his "translation" of Jung's "nonsexual complex." And if the translation is provided to establish the difference with the double, the repetition attests, on the contrary, to the identity, the ever-deeper identification with the adversary. This is an implacable law of strategy, as we have noted already: duplicity of thought, double-thought (thought of the double) cannot be practiced with impunity. And there is an implacable irony, too, in the following prophecy written by Freud to Jung (just before Jung acquired his "nonsexual complex"):

What you call the hysterical element in your personality, your need to impress and influence people, the very quality that so eminently equips you to be a teacher and guide, will come into its own even if you make no concessions to the current fashions in opinion. And when you have injected your own personal leaven into the fermenting mass of my ideas in still more generous measure, there will be no further difference between your achievement and mine. [*Letters*, p. 77]

"Self, the Gloomy Tyrant"

In "Psycho-Analytic Notes," this theoretical duplicity is marked, or re-marked, by the peculiar position assigned to homosexuality. This phenomenon is twofold, doubly marked.

First of all, homosexuality is *social*. To be more precise, we may say that it opens up the possibility of social relations in general. At this point, Freud cannot be satisfied with appeals to actual practice in order to justify his translation of social relations into homosexual ones. If analysis *consistently* discovers the presence of a homosexual component in social relations with others, the reason this is always the case has to be explained. Hence Freud's outline of what has to be called a genesis (ontogenesis) of social relations, an outline designed to shore up the aforementioned translation by linking it with the history of the libido.

Let us retrace this history starting with the phase immediately preceding the emergence of sociality. As we know, this is the narcissistic phase: the individual takes himself as his own love object, and so on. It is therefore not yet a "social" phase, even if the individual passing through it is already quite interested in the genitals. We may even call it the asocial phase, in which one loves oneself too much to love anyone else. This is why sociality, viewed as a relation with an other, presupposes the *sacrifice* of the Narcissus complex, of the megalomanic ego:

We are justified in assuming that megalomania is essentially of an infantile nature and that, as development proceeds, it is sacrificed to social considerations. Similarly, an individual's megalomania is never so vehemently suppressed as when he is in the grip of an overpowering love [*Verliebtheit*].

> Denn wo die Lieb' erwachet, stirbt
> das Ich, der finstere Despot.

> [For when the flames of love arise,
> Then Self, the gloomy tyrant, dies.]
> ["Psycho-Analytic Notes," p. 65]

At the highest level of generality, the social bond is love—love as object love, or love of an other; more precisely, love as self-sacrifice or gift of self. At this point we may begin to suspect why the phase immediately following narcissism—the first object-oriented phase, and thus the first social phase—is a homosexual phase: the other is not entirely other, but bears a likeness to the self, so one does not lose oneself entirely by the gift of self to that other, and for that reason the sacrifice is easier to make. Let us reread the following passage:

> The line of development then leads on to the choice of an external object with similar genitals—that is, to homosexual object-choice—and thence to heterosexuality. . . . The infantile sexual theories which attribute the same kind of genitals to both sexes exert much influence. [As we know, these theories are phallocentric, so we have to conclude once again that homosexuality—and, by the same token sociality—exists only on the male, masculine side.]
>
> After the stage of heterosexual object-choice has been reached, the homosexual aspirations are not, as might be supposed, done away with or brought to a stop; they are merely deflected from their sexual aim and applied to fresh uses. They now combine with portions of the ego-instincts and, as "attached" components ["*angelehnte" Komponenten*], help to constitute the social instincts, thus contributing an erotic factor to friendship and comradeship, to *esprit de corps* and to the love of mankind in general. [p. 61]

Homosexuality is thus doubly social, and at two different levels. In the first place, it is social because it opens the way to object orientation in general. Without that first narcissistic wound or break, no relation to the other as such could come about, nor—consequently—any social relations at all. On this account, homosexuality is an archisociality, or the primary "social instinct." Homosexuality can also become social in the strict or narrow sense of the term, when it is combined with the ego instincts. This is where it would seem to be distinguished from heterosexuality. Although it is object-oriented, and thus social, in the broad sense, heterosexuality is not social in the narrow sense. Why is this? Quite simply because "sociality" has come to mean *nonsexual* relation with an other." Whereas Freud earlier seemed to be committing himself to a libidinal genesis of the social relation, he now needs to assert the non-libidinal (egoistic) nature of that relation. Thus homosexuality would become properly social only on the condition that it is sublimated. And it would transform itself into a social instinct only by *combining with* or *attaching itself to* the ego instincts, which is a way of saying that these instincts exist prior to such a combination and are not libidinal in and of themselves. Homosexuality is only a *contribution* (*Beitrag*) of eroticism to sociality, just as narcissism will be a libidinal *complement* (*Ergänzung*) of the ego instincts. The libidinal genesis of sociality is thus aborted, in a manner of speaking, and the dualism of instincts is maintained.

The fact remains (and this is what makes the whole argument so strange) that something seems to predestine homosexuality in particular—and homosexuality alone—to social sublimation. Why? Because homosexuality is a little less sexual than heterosexuality, because it is *already* somewhat desexualized? Because, by opening up the relation to the other in general, it is already opening up the properly social relation to the other? Or is it because sublimation, conversely, would *always* bear upon homosexuality? In the last analysis, we have no basis for deciding, and to make matters worse, Freud is not very forthcoming (here or elsewhere) about the enigmatic operation of sublimation. How can the (homo)sexual instinct be inhibited? How can it turn into its own opposite? (Sublimation is different from repression, as Freud frequently insists.) How does it lift itself up? (The sexual is *lowly*: groundwork or material base; the sublime is *elevated*: spirituality, ideality, and so on.) How is it transformed? (Sublimation is also chemical transmutation—one is tempted to say transubstantiation.) About all this we are kept in the dark.

What is certain, however, is that this very ambiguity supplies the transitional element between the sexual and the social. It serves to transfer erotism onto egoism; it helps slip in, surreptitiously, the dualism of instincts. For of course this is what *must* be demonstrated, in the confrontation with Jung: if it is true that there is a pathology proper to sociality (and Freud does not contest this), it is necessary to show that there is something sexual underneath or, more precisely, inside. But that, too, is what must *not* be demonstrated: by insisting too strongly on the cathexis of libido in the social relation, one runs the risk of doing away with all differences, all oppositions between desire and its others (ego, prohibition, society, and so on).

By "eroticizing" the social relation, one runs the risk of "desexu-alizing" libido at the same time, and this would bring about a pe-culiar resemblance between Freud's dualism and Jung's monism, the monism of the double. Freud's entire argument is henceforth swal-lowed up in this dilemma, oscillating between contradictory require-ments according to an ambiguity that only increases in "On Narcis-sism" and later texts.

That is why homosexuality, if it is stamped with the seal of so-ciality on the one hand, is also stamped with the seal of *nonsociality* on the other. This is true first of sublimated homosexuality, which is at once social and nonsocial; Freud's reasoning here moves very rapidly, and almost imperceptibly, from one statement to the other. On the one hand, the homosexual eroticization of the social bond is considered to be the energizing force behind sociality itself, the force that transforms the simple interest of the ego into a social instinct; that is why, as Freud adds here (clearly thinking of Leonardo da Vinci), manifest homosexuals who sublimate their "sensuality" take "a particularly active share in the general interests of humanity" (p. 61). But on the other hand, this eroticization is supposed to pose a constant threat to the social bond in the capacity of its internal ex-teriority. It is a matter of threshold, or intensity: when the homo-sexual impulse becomes *too* strong, "unusually intense," the social instincts become, as it were, too instinctual and not social enough. One must then defend oneself against the social *instinct* with one's *social* drives, and that is what happens in paranoia: paranoiacs *"en-deavour to protect themselves against any such sexualization of their so-cial instinctual cathexes"* (p. 62). Freud is certainly not saying that they defend themselves against their homosexuality as such: that sort of repression would give rise to a neurosis, not a psychosis (it might well be called just one more repression). No, according to Freud they are protecting themselves against an over-eroticization of their *social* in-stinctual cathexes, that is, their *sublimated homosexuality*.

Sublimation, in short, is what ails paranoiacs; this explains why, for them, the path of neurotic repression remains blocked: the "re-pressed" adheres too closely, in this instance, to the "repressor," since what it has to protect itself against is invading the defense mecha-nism itself, the egoic sphere. Here we have an inextricable *double bind*, which would thus leave the paranoiac no way out except to reject both sociality in the narrow sense (the social interests of the ego) and sociality in the broad sense (homosexuality as opening up the possibility of object love), by turning back toward a pure and simple a-sociality (narcissism).

All this can be understood only if we acknowledge that homo-sexuality is simultaneously a threat to sociality from without (since it is an instinct which has to be repressed when it is too powerful) and from within (since the defense against it has to repress itself, in a way). And is that not what we have just observed? At any level, in any "phase," homosexuality condenses within itself the most con-tradictory predicates, and this allows it to keep on transgressing all the dualistic prohibitions set forth by Freud. It may be erotic and hardly erotic at all, direct and indirect (sublimated), libidinal and (almost) egoic, external and internal to sociality—all these at once. And this means that homosexuality is not simply "other" with re-spect to egoic sociality, but also, in a way, the same.

In fact, it is time to observe that the value of *sameness* (sameness as resemblance) is what brings about the transition between oppo-sites. This history of the libido (or of desire) is a history of the Same, inasmuch as it is a *history of the subject*, a narcissistic history.

Once again, we have to back up. In the beginning, then, is the ego. (In the beginning? Not quite, to tell the truth. The ego comes after autoerotism, and this leads to the conclusion that it begins somewhere, that it has a beginning older than itself. Freud says this quite clearly in "On Narcissism," without venturing into the abyss of that beginning, however: the ego's unity is not present at the out-set, and something, "a new psychical action," has to be "added to auto-erotism" for narcissism to take [a] shape ["On Narcissism," p. 77]. But Freud does not say this in "Psycho-Analytic Notes," and by not saying it he takes for granted a subject that is already constituted, already formed and identified, without raising a single question about the enigma of its birth. We shall come back to this problem.)

In the beginning, then, is the ego. The ego? Yes, but also, and especially, the Self. This *Ich* is a *Selbst* (*autos*, *idem*, and *ipse*), and this substantial identity or *Einheit* is indeed that of a subject, of a consciousness of self—as it happens, a desiring or loving consciousness of self: the narcissistic ego loves itself, desires itself. (Had not Hegel already said the same thing? "Self-consciousness is Desire in general.")[25] What does this mean, if not that the ego desires to present itself to itself, to exhibit itself to itself, and that it must consequently get outside itself, posit itself as other than itself before returning to itself, beside itself? This line of thinking has an inescapable logic: the *Selbst* can relate to itself (and desire itself) only if it is penetrated by an internal difference, an intimate exteriority— only if there is difference, a difference produced within the element of the Same. This difference, in other words, must pass between me and myself: I must be other than myself, and that other must be another myself. I must, let us say, resemble myself.

This logic—which will be called speculative-dialectic, except for the mimetic motif that we have just introduced—is not made explicit by Freud, of course (he speaks somewhere of the "abstruse Hegelian philosophy"). All the same, he allows himself to be obscurely and implacably ruled by it as soon as he uses the word *Selbst*, as soon as he invokes the myth of Narcissus (that is, specular reflections, mirrors, and so on). This accounts for the fact that in the *Selbst* the genitals already (*bereits*) constitute the primary attraction: the narcissistic ego is already homosexual (already "object-oriented"), it already loves itself as it is going to love the other myself (it loves itself similar to itself). And that is what explains, too, the fact that the first object—the first other—is once again a (my)self (is once again "narcissistic"). As suggested earlier, the homosexual object is not really an alter ego (another *self* as *other* self), since it is similar or analogous to the ego. This theme of analogic apprehension of others in no way serves to point toward the irreducible otherness of the *alter* (as it does for Husserl in the fifth *Cartesian Meditation*, for example); on the contrary, it serves (and in a much more classical fashion) to reduce that otherness, by making the other into a modification of the (my)self. The alter ego is here the other me, the other self, so that the opening toward the other stems much less from a break than from a continuity. By loving that other who resembles me like a brother, I am still loving myself in him, I love him as I have already loved myself.

May one speak, under these conditions, of a sacrifice of the Narcissus complex destined to institute sociality as such? Narcissus in fact does not die, and what we are confronting, as Bataille would have said, is, rather, a "comedy"—a dialectic and speculative comedy, of course. Self-sacrifice, as always, is an economical sacrifice, since it is a narcissistic sacrifice: by giving myself to the other, I am still giving myself to myself. This gift entails no loss, inasmuch as it speculates on a self-donation, inasmuch as this cathexis of the libido outside itself brings immediate returns, returns as reappropriation.

This reappropriation is, of course, a reappropriation of *self*, for it must be apparent that the entire process is one of propriation, much more than of appropriation. What is at issue here is not so much having or possessing objects in order to enjoy them as not losing *oneself* in "objects," finding *oneself* in them, enjoying *oneself*, and so on. As for the desire that animates the process, it has to be called "subject-oriented" rather than "object-oriented" (or perhaps egoistic rather than sexual), in the sense that the subject moves toward objects only to the extent that they are like him and that he can be like himself and can collect himself in them. However strongly Freud may insist on the sexual character of that resemblance, it is clear that the motif of likeness lies behind the introduction of homosexuality into his discourse. The homosexual object is not chosen as primary object because the ego wishes to have it (why, after all, would the ego feel a need to go outside itself?), but rather because it is the (self-)same, the ego itself—in other words, because *it is not an object in the Freudian sense(s) of the term*.

Yet if *Objekt*, up to now, has meant (1) object of enjoyment in the form of *having* and, more specifically, (2) the *other* person as nonego, then we have to recognize that the homosexual object referred to here is, appearances notwithstanding, neither one nor the other. On the one hand, the ego *has* the object only to the extent that it *is* that object, and it enjoys the object as itself. On the other hand, and for the same reason, that other is not (entirely) another, since it is the other *of* the ego, since the ego itself becomes an object in order to experience enjoyment *of* itself (these genitives float more freely than ever between objectivity and subjectivity). That quasi-object arises from what, in a formula that sums up the logic at work here, Freud calls the "narcissistic object choice": the object is the ego, myself.

Does the passage from homosexual archisociality to sociality proper introduce any sort of break in this story of the self-Same, of (my)self? It does not seem to, and the ambiguity we noted earlier was made to order to facilitate the transition. Lacking any precise indication about the process of sublimation of homosexuality, we are obliged to describe things as follows: just as narcissism was already a homosexual relation to oneself and as homosexuality was still a narcissistic relation to the other (myself) and sociality is still a homosexual relation to (another) myself. Narcissus is always already dead and always already in the process of rebirth, Narcissus sacrificing himself in order to find himself in his other.

And is this not, for Freud, a definition of sublimation: the self-sacrifice of desire? Perhaps it is clearer now why homosexuality is sublimation's target of choice: because this desire is narcissistic, it is potentially its other (the other as law, prohibition, and so on) and can be identified with, can identify itself with, that other. It is clearer, too, why homosexuality is combined so easily with the ego instincts: the "homosexual" relation to the other is already an egoic relation, in the sense that what interests me in the other—brother, colleague, comrade—is myself. What difference is there, then, between the narcissistic ego and the ego-agency? Between narcissistic (homosexual) desire and the ego's interest? Are we not in fact in that zone where Freud seemed to refuse to follow Jung?

Let us suppose that all the oppositions, all the dualities have been established only to be immediately transgressed and dissolved. Narcissistic asociality, homosexual archisociality, egoic sociality—all these are the Same (which is not the identical), and all these "phases" merge imperceptibly into each other. The Same makes a bond, and it is the bonding element or the "social" bond in general that opens up the possibility of *relations* as such: of me with myself, of myself with the other (my)self, and so on (later, in the context of the third theory of instincts, Freud will speak of binding, *Bindung*, as a unification, *Vereinigung*).

Very well. But why, then, is homosexuality so threatening? For here is the irony of this process of homogenization: taken to the extreme, it leads straight to paranoia—that is, to what has to be described as a process of desocialization, of unbonding, of redifferentiation. Is not the paranoiac, according to Freud himself, the one who relieves himself of any social bond, of any relation to the other—and by precisely the same token relieves himself of an overly insistent sociality, of an excessive proximity to his neighbor? Is that not what needs to be explained? We rediscover the dilemma stressed earlier: either we set up homosexuality as the energizing force behind the social relation to the other—and then we cannot expect to understand how homosexuality endangers sociality, why it must be warded off with paranoia—or we consider that homosexuality comes to sociality from without—and then we can no longer account for the undeniably social nature of paranoic "homosexuality." Either homosexuality is the *likeness* of sociality or it is its *other*. Since Freud maintains both positions simultaneously, his text finally precludes the alternative, inviting us thus to conceive of homosexuality—homosociality—as (a)sociality: sociality and non-sociality, relation and non-relation to the other, factor of social assimilation and deassimilation. Double bond, double bind.

This situation becomes considerably clearer if we recall the context that leads Freud to advance these arguments concerning social homosexuality. The recourse to homosexuality, as we have seen, allows Freud to "translate" phenomena of mimetic rivalry that he apprehends first of all—and very concretely, in his own professional relations—at the level of a highly conflictual, even pathological, sociality. Behind this homosexual history or genesis of sociality, we therefore have to read the *other history*—the very same one that had just been weaving a web of hatred between Freud and his doubles, the one that led in the end to derangement and madness. This history is a history of mimetic desire, which means that it is also a bearer of violence.

Thus by projecting homosexuality—but we now know what that means—at the basis of the opening toward the other, Freud in no way accounts for the social bond, *if by that is meant the principle of a pacific sociality*. On the contrary, by inferring what is normal (archisociality) from what is pathological (rivalrous, paranoid sociality), he inscribes the pathological within the normal in spite of himself, as it were; he inscribes excess within the norm and the state of war within the state of law—a gesture that can be written off as inconsequential only if one continues to move, with Freud, within an ethico-political conceptuality that opposes the law or forbids it to its other. But Freud brings us back to a point prior to that opposition and makes the opposition conceivable.

In fact, if the primary relation to the other is a mimetic relation to the other myself (and how could it be otherwise? how could any sort of *relation* to the other be instituted anywhere except in the element of sameness?), it is also a question of a non-relation to the other. The otherness of the other *as such* is not respected. The term "respect" indicates this at once: this experience of the other is not a moral experience, it cannot yet be situated in the ethico-political register. The relation to the other myself is in no way "altruistic," as Freud seems to want to say, it is not opposed to the "egoism" of the narcissistic ego, and there is the problem in a nutshell. The opening of the possibility of relation to others, as it is described here, is at the same time the opening of the possibility of violence. The notions of peace and war, love and hatred, are on this point equally relevant—that is, irrelevant. No doubt the double is loved, since I love myself in him; but that is also why he provokes hatred and hostility, precisely inasmuch as he is close to me, too close.

This has to be maintained against conventional wisdom: to "love one's neighbor as oneself" is no doubt the shortest route to cutting his throat. And there is no need to invoke in this connection, as Freud does later in "Civilization and Its Discontents," an obscure "tendency towards aggressiveness" that would interfere with and in some way poison peaceful relations with one's neighbors (*SE* 21: 111–115), nor even to call—as Girard too often does, in our view—on a mimesis of appropriation that would cause me to desire the same object as the mimetic double and *as a result* to compete with him in hatred.[26] No, the hostility arises straight out of the relation to one's neighbor from the very moment the latter is loved as (a) myself, from the very moment he presents himself to me as an adverse "I"—an outsider—who is infinitely dispossessing me of myself, since he is at once what is nearest to me and what is farthest away: he is what moves of its own accord in my place (the double is always an automaton), lives unduly in my place (the double is always of the living dead), enjoys my place (the double is always hateful), and so on. The rage that overwhelms me at the sight of him does not come from the fact that he is dispossessing me of something, but from the fact that he is robbing me, inexplicably, of and from myself. Hence the total, totalitarian character of the war that is begun then and that no satisfaction can appease: "Either him or me."

How, indeed, could I not want to get rid of *him*, in order to be simply *myself*? Consciousness of self, as Hegel had seen, begins by splitting in two and warring with itself. It appears to itself as (the) other, and this means that the experience of consciousness (phenomenology) is inaugurated in internal violence, in a duel unto death. There is a violence inherent in the very *appearing* of the other, a violence to which all empirical violence bears witness, and it has no "reason" other than desire (that is, *consciousness of self*), which seeks itself in the other and wants to be for-itself, independent, beside itself in its property. Desire is violence because it is a desire to be proper, a desire for propriation, and, as such, a hostile, murderous desire.

To this we need only add—positioning ourselves as close to, and as far from, Hegel (and Freud) as we can—that this desire is all the more violent in that it is not a desire of any subject properly speaking; it is all the more mad in that it makes a desperate attempt to eradicate the naive impropriety that makes the subject appear to itself *as* the other. There would be no specularization of self in the other if the *other* were not lodged in the Same, and the specular is consequently just as much the condition of possibility as the condition of impossibility of speculative dialectics—that is, the condition of possibility and impossibility of a desire (of and for the) proper. Desire is an improper desire of the proper—a *mimesis of propriation*.

Desire is a violent mimesis, then. What does that mean, if not that the relation to the other that seems most respectful of the other's otherness—for example, the social relation—will always presuppose this assimilation to and of the other? And that the experience of the other is always capable of turning into a hostile experience of the double? It is clearer now why Freud had to situate homosexuality both within sociality and without, for if the social bond is always a "homosexual" relation to the other myself, and if there is access to the other only on this condition, then this condition is also, from the very outset, what ruins sociality as ethical or political sociality, what opens it *of its own accord* onto what is naively taken to be its *outside*—discord, violence, or even madness. In this sense, it is no coincidence that Freud discovers madness at the very core of the most sublimated social relationships. Paranoia perpetually haunts sociality, not as an external threat but as its most intimate exterior. And when it bursts forth, we can say, *with and against Freud*, that it lays bare its intolerable truth, the very truth that the *socius* must perpetually, tirelessly exclude from itself in order to institute ethical or political peace: the truth that the other is a same, and by that very token gives rise to desire—that is, to violence.

This allows us to note that hostility toward the double—always present in one way or another in paranoia, even in erotomania[27]—does not arise in love (or, therefore, in peace), as Freud hypothesizes. Because "homosexual" love for the other myself is at the same time hatred, the latter is indeed first, "primary." The statement "I hate him," for example, in no way represses the statement "I love him": delusions, far from concealing desire, reveal it as clearly as possible, and it is rather Freud's interpretation that occupies a position of repression here. The same must be said of the persecutional statement "he hates me": this does not hide the hate-filled love that "I" feel for him; on the contrary, it declares straightforwardly that that "he" is an "I," and that to hate *him* is equally to hate *me* in him, to persecute *myself*. Since the relation to the double is perfectly symmetrical, all that "I" do (to him), "he" does just as well (to me).

Indeed, that is why "it was incorrect to say that the perception which was suppressed internally is projected outwards" ("Psycho-Analytic Notes," p. 71). For that to be possible, there would first have to be a subject capable of experiencing feelings properly speaking, within himself, even before projecting them outward onto the other. Now what delusions make clear—and there is no reason not to believe them on this point—is that a feeling is by its nature responsive, a justified *reaction* to the hateful maneuvers on the part of the rival or the persecutor, a generous (overly generous) *response* to the advances of the Lover, and so on. As Clérambault said of erotomaniacs, it is always the other one who starts things. If we now propose to subscribe to this "postulate" of delirium, it is not, of course, in the sense in which we ought to believe in the objective reality of paranoic accusations. It is all too clear, too obvious, that these visions or voices that the subject attributes to the other are "his" (and psychiatrists will show, for example, that he silently articulates the curses that he claims are being hurled at him, in other words, that he *hears* himself speak).

Yet if we failed to go beyond this level of evidence, we would miss the heart of the matter, namely, that the "subject" in such a case experiences himself and relates to himself as (the) other, prior to any normal, normed division between interiority and exteriority, selfhood and otherness, auto-affection and hetero-affection, and so on—and thus prior to any projection. What "returns from without" (Freud) or "turns back in the real" (Lacan) is nothing that would have been projected or rejected by a prior subject (or that would have remained foreclosed to it). It is the subject "itself," presenting itself to itself from without, in the inevitable internal dissension produced by mimetic doubling: primary return or reappearance that turns the subject over, in the most immediate and the most peculiar certainty, to that hallucination in which the subject sees itself or hears itself as (the) other.

That is, the subject sees or hears itself as an enemy, as we have said—and then, too, at the extreme point of delirium, as *dead*. For to kill the double is of course to kill oneself. We must not forget that Schreber had read his own obituary.[28] This was at the time when he was absorbing the "rays" of God Flechsig in his head, provoking the well-known "end of the world." By incorporating the double murderously, he had committed suicide—except that he would see himself rise up again, inevitably, like a walking cadaver, like the living dead: "I am the first leper corpse and I lead a leper corpse," the voices made him say.[29]

Inevitably. The double, in fact, insists in "demoniacal" fashion, and he is never as crushing or mocking (as Girard would say) as when one is attempting to get rid of him. Put another way, the struggle unto death *repeats itself*, gives rise (does not give rise) to dialectics, to (re-ap)propriation. Desire—that is, the subject—does not go back on its mimetic "mediation." On the contrary, the more it attempts to (re)turn to itself—the more it attempts, in other words, to make itself absolute, to relieve itself of every bond—the more it comes back to itself, in the adverse form of an absolute double.[30] In this sense, madness is not only the caricatural truth of the social bond (the other is an other myself), but also bears witness to the caricatural truth of narcissism (myself is the other). Since the subject has no relation to self except as relation to the other, the question of narcissism, as question of "oneself," cannot be separated from the question of the social or homosocial bond, as question of the "other myself."

In this connection, we must not let ourselves be misled by Freud's genetic presentation of the concept of narcissism: narcissism does not *precede* the relation to the other, and likewise the delusion of grandeur in narcissism is not a return to the original solitude of a monad walled in upon itself. There is only one "stage," and it is that of the primary opening (the narcissistic wound), which opens me to myself as (the) other. So let us not dream, with Freud, of an ego whose existence would precede sociality (or—and it is the same thing—a sociality that would relate already-constituted subjects to each other). This would be to theorize with delusion, to speculate in line with desire. For narcissism is precisely that: the violent affirmation of the ego, the violent desire to annul that primitive alteration that makes me desire (myself) as the mimetic double. Here we find a sort of instantaneous undertow that makes desire forgetful of its own origin, as Girard sees quite clearly: desire is mimetic and *by the same token* narcissistic, and that means that it launches headlong into a systematic, unreflective forgetfulness of what institutes it.

It follows that desire is love of oneself, as Freud writes: self-love, love of the proper. It follows too that it is organized as a vehement rejection of all resemblance, all mimesis. To recognize that I resemble the other, that I resemble myself in him even in my own desire, would be tantamount to admitting the inadmissible: that I am not myself and that my most proper being is over there, in that double who enrages me. It is that resemblance that paranoia "represses" to the point of delusion, as each protestation of autonomy on the part of the ego inevitably hurls itself against an ever more obsessive, ever more autonomous, and ever more similar double—since it is (the) ego.

It follows, finally, that narcissism is violence and that the ego, as Freud says through an interpolated quotation, is a "gloomy tyrant." It is no coincidence that metaphors of tyranny (that is, of private appropriation of political power) abound in Freud's writing whenever he deals directly or indirectly with narcissism,[31] even where they are least expected (after all, if Narcissus is a-social, he is not involved in politics). Nor is it coincidental that delusions develop so readily in the realm of politics on the broad scale (plots, projects for social reform, and so on). Narcissism is in profound collusion with power—by which we mean tyrannical power or, put another way, political madness—by virtue of its mimetic, rivalrous, (a)social origin. Since the struggle with the double has no other object, no other stake but the struggle itself, it necessarily exhausts itself in a fratricidal struggle for power—"power" being in this instance the name of that place from which I must forcibly remove the double in order to be myself.

Narcissistic desire is, by definition, a desire for power:[32] assimilation and thus subjection of the other to His Majesty My Ego. A gloomy tyranny indeed, and all the gloomier in that it can only be exacerbated as it encounters a fundamental powerlessness. A gloomy economic violence (in all senses of the term, and first of all in the Greek sense), which would be rediscovered at the "collective" as well as the "individual" level: the totalitarianism and the imperialism of the "we" are never anything but the supreme phase of the absolutism of the ego, the "I," and they are implied in even the most solitary, most pacific meditations on the *ego cogito*.

On Love

She took my heart from me,	*Tristan:* Tristan thou,
she took me, she took my	I Isolda,
world, then she took herself;	no more Tristan!
she left me only my desire and	*Isolde:* Thou Isolda,
my thirsting heart!	Tristan I,
Bernart de Ventadour,	no more Isolda!
Chansons d'amour	Wagner, *Tristan und Isolde*

After that lengthy detour, we are now ready to confront the essay "On Narcissism: An Introduction." In a way, it has nothing new to tell us. It merely expands on the problematics outlined in the correspondence with Jung and in the Schreber case; that is why it seemed appropriate to retrace this problematics in some detail, as an introduction to the introduction of narcissism. The difficulties with which Freud is grappling are the same ones, and thus they are already somewhat familiar.

These difficulties become more intense and more serious, however, when they are raised to the metapsychological level. In Freud's discussion of the Schreber case, the term "narcissism" still designates merely a libidinal *phase*, a phase that is abandoned or "sacrificed" in normal libidinal development, whereas the abnormal regression of the paranoiac leads back to it. Freud begins his new discussion by reminding us that the study of psychosis had given rise to the idea of "a primary and normal narcissism" ("On Narcissism," p. 74); he adds that paranoid megalomania would be a secondary narcissism, "superimposed upon a primary narcissism that is obscured by a number of different influences" (p. 75). However, it is more than a coincidence that he refrains from speaking of the "narcissistic phase" and prefers to use the term "primary narcissism," for "primary" here does not mean simply "first" in chronological terms. The primary status of narcissism is also a primacy, and primary narcissism has to be understood as a *fundamental* narcissism. In this sense, narcissism no longer designates one libidinal phase among others, but rather the general regime of the libido: *any* libidinal cathexis is henceforth considered narcissistic in its foundation (or, as we can already say, in its re-sources).

Hence there is no discontinuity, no irreducible opposition, between the narcissistic cathexis and the object cathexis, so it is clear that this new theory of the instincts confirms the "homogenizing" logic that we uncovered in discussing the homosexual genesis of object orientation described in Freud's presentation of the Schreber case. We learn this now from Freud himself—narcissism is *never* abandoned:

We form the idea of there being an original libidinal cathexis of the ego, from which some is later given off to objects, but which fundamentally persists and is related to the object-cathexes much as the body of an amoeba is related to the pseudopodia which it puts out. In our researches, taking, as they did, neurotic symptoms for their starting-point, this part of the allocation of libido necessarily remained hidden from us at the outset. All that we noticed were the emanations of this libido—the object-cathexes, which can be sent out and drawn back again. We see also, broadly speaking, an antithesis [*Gegensatz*] between ego-libido and object-libido. The more of the one is employed, the more the other becomes depleted. The highest phase of development of which object-libido is capable is seen in the state of being in love [*Verliebtheit*], when the subject seems to give up his own personality in favour of an object-cathexis; while we have the opposite condition [*Gegensatz*] in the paranoic's phantasy (or self-perception) of "the end of the world." [pp. 75–76]

On the one hand, then, narcissism persists *alongside* object love: the quantity of libido cathected (invested, stockpiled, capitalized) in the ego may certainly vary, but it is never null. On the other hand, and this is even more important, narcissism persists *within* object love. The economic problematics that Freud mobilizes leaves no room for doubt on this point: the ego functions as a sort of libidinal bank (elsewhere the term "reservoir" is used) which releases libido, *while the libido in question never ceases to be an ego libido, even when it is cathected in objects.* The ego, in keeping with narcissistic circularity, is not only the (cathected) object of the libido, it is also the (cathecting, cathector) subject of the libido or, better yet, the proprietor. The libido belongs to the ego, is the exclusive property of the ego alone, to such an extent that it is difficult to imagine how the two might be differentiated.

It follows that the release of libido is a "yielding," even an "impoverishment." This statement is obviously made from the ego's point of view, for the libido itself loses nothing, lacks nothing (however it may be distributed, we must suppose that its global quantity remains constant). It follows, likewise (and conversely), that the release of libido is not a gift (that is, a loss), but rather a loan: the cathexes may at any moment be withdrawn from objects by the ego, which is always free to insist on its proprietary rights, to withdraw *its* cathexis, to withdraw *itself*. The comparison with amoebic pseudopodia makes the point all the more clearly: object cathexes are like extensions of the ego itself (of the "body of an amoeba"), which is tantamount to saying that this libidinal substance is (the) subject and, furthermore, that it literally appropriates objects to itself (as pseudopodia "capture" other microorganisms).

We are thus obliged to remark that there is not a straightforward opposition between narcissism and object orientation, between ego libido and object libido. The latter is continuous with the former, and the *Gegensatz* that Freud mentions arises less from a difference in nature than from a difference in dominion: the more the one absorbs, the more the other is impoverished, given that the same egoistic wealth, as it were, is being distributed on both sides. We shall have the opportunity to confirm this with the example of *Verliebtheit*—an extreme case of object love, according to Freud—for there is no doubt that here the object appears to come into opposition with the ego (the lover alienates himself in favor of the object of his passion, he forgets himself, depreciates himself to the very extent that he is overvaluing the Lady, and so on). But the logic of erotic self-sacrifice quickly transcends opposition: the lover loves himself in the object, and if there is difference or opposition in the situation, it is self-differentiation or auto-(op)position. The image of "yielding" libido expresses just this, and economics functions aptly here as a dialectics. Object libido is never anything but a vicissitude of ego libido, within a certain economy of the (my)self.

The metapsychological originality of "On Narcissism" therefore does not reside, as Laplanche and Pontalis state in their *Vocabulary of Psychoanalysis*, in the adjunction of an ego libido alongside object libido, within sexual instincts in general:[33]

The distinction that Freud introduces later appears at first glance to be a subdivision of the sexual instincts according to which object they cathect:

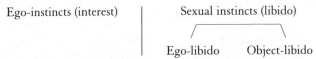

Ego-instincts (interest)	Sexual instincts (libido)	
	Ego-libido	Object-libido

Taken literally, this schema greatly oversimplifies a situation that is quite complex. The dichotomy between ego libido and object libido, in particular, does not take sufficient account of the ambiguity of the genitive construction in the expression "ego-libido."[34] Since the ego is understood not only as object of the libido but also as subject or "source," the *libido sexualis* is not specified as ego libido or object libido; rather, the latter is derived from the former, for Freud's gesture consists in extending narcissism to the libidinal realm as a whole. As for the barrier separating ego instincts from ego libido (inasmuch as ego libido is a sexual instinct), it can certainly be justified by the passages in which Freud pursues his polemics with Jung and persists in maintaining the dualism of instincts, although by the same token, in terms of dogma, this barrier cuts right into the ambiguity of the Freudian *Ich*. Is it indeed legitimate to make such a sharp distinction between the narcissistic ego, conceived as object of the sexual instinct, and the ego-agency, conceived as representative of "interest"? It is time to cite the passage that concludes the introduction of the concept of ego libido:

Finally, as regards the differentiation of psychical energies, we are led to the conclusion that to begin with, during the state of narcissism, they exist together and that our analysis is too coarse to distinguish between them [*ununterscheidbar*]; not until there is object-cathexis is it possible to discriminate a sexual energy—the libido [*eine Sexualenergie, die Libido*]—from an energy of the ego-instincts. ["On Narcissism," p. 76]

This sentence unquestionably carries the ambiguity to its peak, rendering Freud's reasoning wholly enigmatic. That is no reason to avoid it—quite the contrary, especially since the statement is repeated elsewhere in virtually identical terms.[35] What does it say?

First of all, it says that *in the state of narcissism* it is not appropriate to distinguish between ego instincts and libidinal instincts. If the sentence means anything, it means that in the beginning the narcissistic ego and the ego-agency are one and the same, the same "source" releasing the same psychic energy. Since ego instincts and ego libido are inextricably mixed, it is just as legitimate to speak of an originally nonsexual "state" of the libido as of an absence of sexual libido at the outset. Freud is visibly speaking both languages at once. On the one hand, he characterizes the undifferentiated "state" as "narcissistic," which is clearly a way of designating it as the primary state *of the libido*. On the other hand, he proceeds by claiming to reserve the term "libido" *for "sexual energy" alone* (*eine Sexualenergie, die Libido*), which is itself identified with *object libido alone* (it is only with object cathexis that the libido appears as such)—a gesture quite obviously incompatible with the previous one, since it amounts to canceling out the very possibility of an ego *libido*!

A contradiction as flagrant as this one is no longer a contradiction but a confession. It bears witness, by a reductio ad absurdum, as it were, to the fact that the concept of "libido" is no longer equivalent to that of "sexual instinct" and can no longer be enclosed within the framework of the first theory of the instincts. The reason is simple, and it stands out in the peculiarity (we are almost tempted to say the bad faith) of Freud's reasoning. It is this: up to now, the term libido has designated the sexual instinct *understood as desire for an object*; this stops being the case once a place is set aside for egoistic desire (libido) and, in addition, as soon as object-oriented desire (libido) is *also* conceived as narcissistic.

Thus a "desexualization" of the libido is inherent in the advancement of narcissism, not because the term "libido" would cease to designate, among other things, the energy of object sexuality, but because object sexuality is henceforth understood in a different way. In other words, it is not a matter of denying that there is such a thing as object love, that is, sexuality; rather, it is a matter of recognizing that sexual desire for an object refers back to something deeper than itself, which Freud continues to call "libido" (meaning by this that it is still a desire), but without being able to distinguish it clearly from the ego instincts (since that desire is no longer sexual). In short, the concept of the object has changed, in conjunction with the concept of desire. At this point, even when I desire an object, it is myself that I desire in it. The object is a *narcissistic object*.

But that is not all, for the strangeness of this passage is by no means dissipated by being imputed to a disparity between a conceptual framework inherited from the first theory of the instincts and the new problematics of the libido. It is one thing to remark that Freud contradicts himself by identifying the libido with object libido alone, just as he is introducing the notion of ego libido; it is something else again to understand why the narcissistic libido *appears only in the form of object libido*. Freud is not satisfied to state that he had been deceived by appearances when he neglected the narcissistic libido "hidden" in object love, "masked" in object libido.[36] By adding that this libido becomes accessible to observation only after it has been cathected in objects, he continues to imply that this appearance is the *very coming-into-being* of narcissism. Moreover, there is no reason to doubt that this is just what he means, since

he returns to the point a year later, and with no ambiguity whatsoever, in a chapter added to a new edition of "Three Essays on the
Theory of Sexuality":

We thus reach the idea of a quantity of libido, to the mental representation
of which we give the name of "ego-libido." . . . This ego-libido is, however,
only conveniently accessible to analytic study when it has been put to the
use of cathecting sexual objects, that is, when it has become object-libido.
We can then perceive it concentrating upon objects, becoming fixed upon
them or abandoning them, moving from one object to another and, from
these situations, directing the subject's sexual activity. ["Three Essays,"
p. 217]

The situation of narcissism is peculiar from this point on: narcissism is everywhere (in objects: it is the ego libido that "directs
sexual activity") and nowhere (since it is not accessible anywhere
except in objects). Given that it presents itself as always already
"masked," one must conclude that it never presents *itself*, or rather
that it presents itself *by* concealing itself. As we have just seen, it is
only "then" that we can "perceive" ego libido—that is, without per-
ceiving it.

What does this mean, if not that this theory of narcissism must
be groping its way in the dark, constantly dazzled by what is presented to it? Translated into Freudian language (that is, in this instance, Kantian-positivist language), it means that the paths of such
a theory will be necessarily *speculative*. It is all very well for Freud
to defend himself against such a charge at length in "On Narcissism," by appealing to experience and empirical observation as
against Jungian "speculation"; it is clear that he is violating his own
principles here. To say that ego libido manifests itself only by trans-
forming itself into object libido is also to say that it can only be posited as transgressing the limits of the experience in which it is concealing itself from the start. And speculation is precisely the transgressive gesture that exceeds the observable evidence.

But does this not also make the very concept of narcissism profoundly problematic? Appearances notwithstanding (and even
though Freud himself is taken in by them), the speculative movement does not consist in positing narcissism as situated on one side
of experience or the other, as a "state" that may be inaccessible but

is nevertheless assignable. In a manner of speaking, primary narcissism is introduced only in a crossed-out form, and this is where we find the full originality of Freud's speculation.[37] No sooner has narcissism been identified at the origin and foundation of object libido than it literally fades away into object libido, inasmuch as it never presents itself anywhere else. This is tantamount to eradicating its primary character, at least if one insists on conceiving of the origin in the form of presence or, more precisely still, in the form of presence to self.

In the last analysis, narcissism begins in the phase of object orientation, that is, in its second stage. Because the ego presents itself to itself only "exorbited," outside of itself, lost in objects, it is necessary to conceive of this "impoverishment" as *preceding* any "wealth" and to reformulate the narcissistic economy from top to bottom. This is not easy, especially since Freud gives us very little help. For over his gesture of moving back to a point prior to the first theory of instincts and establishing it on a new footing by "narcissizing" the whole domain of object orientation, we are now obliged to superimpose that other, apparently inverse, gesture through which he takes the ground out from under the theory and suspends it in the air, as it were, by "objectalizing" the entire narcissistic realm. And *this* contradiction cannot be resolved. Should we therefore avoid it? We shall doubtless do better to take the impasse as an invitation to rethink the contradiction in different terms—in the case at hand, to conceive of "narcissistic" and "object-oriented" as the Same, beyond the logic of identity and also beyond their opposition (which is, here, op-position itself: of subject and object, self and other, and so on).

As a result, we must do more than merely recognize that Freud dissolves object orientation in general in narcissism, to the point of making it a modification of the (my)self. We must also recognize the peculiar necessity that compels him to dissolve narcissism in object orientation, at the risk of undermining the self-evidence (the presence as presence to self) of the ego *itself*, and thus of proceeding, step by speculative step, into the void.

The analysis of the concept of "narcissistic object choice" ought to help us in this task, or so it would seem. After all, does not the aporia that is already obvious in the terminology (narcissistic object orientation vs. object-oriented narcissism) sum up the whole problem we are facing here? Let us take a closer look. The concept is introduced by way of a discussion of the "erotic life of the sexes." After acknowledging once again the impossibility of *direct* access to narcissism ("certain special difficulties seem to me to lie in the way of a direct study of narcissism" ["On Narcissism," p. 82]) at the beginning of the second section of the article, Freud goes on to list the *indirect* approaches that make it possible, as he sees it, to establish a conjecture. Beyond the study of psychosis (paraphrenias)—"our chief means of access"—some "other means of approach remain open to us . . . : the study of organic disease, of hypochrondria and of the erotic life of the sexes" (p. 82).

The third approach is the only one that will concern us here.[38] Freud pursues it in the second part of the second section of "On Narcissism," as well as in the third section, which is devoted to the ego ideal (to the extent that this ideal is the object of a narcissistic love, as we shall see). It concerns "erotic life"—in other words, object love in general or the object orientation of the libido. In keeping with the theory of the libido presented in the first section, the various object choices might *all* be expected to appear as narcissistic object choices, or perhaps as modalities of the "yielding" of ego libido to objects. For example, the distinction between homosexuality (in which the chosen object is like the ego) and heterosexuality (in which the object is different, other) ought to turn out to be relatively secondary in relation to a fundamental likeness.

However, this is not the case. Far from establishing a typology of choices of narcissistic objects, Freud distinguishes between object choices of the narcissistic type (*Narzissmustypus*) and object choices of the "attachment" type (*Anlehnungstypus*). Thus "a person may love:—"

I. According to the narcissistic type:
    a. what he himself is (i.e., himself),
    b. what he himself was,
    c. what he himself would like to be,
    d. someone who was once part of himself.
II. According to the anaclitic (attachment) type:

a. the woman who feeds him,
b. the man who protects him, and the succession of substitutes who take their place. [p. 90]

Does this imply that certain object choices are more narcissistic than others, given that all object choices are ultimately narcissistic? Not at all, for two reasons.

First, type II is not *less* narcissistic than type I; it is not narcissistic *at all*. Let us recall that the notion of attachment served, in the "Three Essays" of 1905, to account for the "marginal" or "supplementary" emergence of the sexual instincts out of the self-preservation instincts, the former "attached" to the latter even as they detached themselves little by little. We shall not be concerned here with the intrinsic problems raised by this genesis of the libido, nor with the numerous changes that Freud deemed it necessary to offer later on.[39] We shall merely emphasize its nature, which is object-oriented from the outset: however sharply the object (substitutable, fantasmatic, and so on) of the sexual instinct may be distinguished from the object of need on which it is modeled, it remains an object. This is to say, as well, that libido is object-oriented *from the outset*— an implication that is of course incompatible with the hypothesis of a narcissism yielded *after the fact* to objects.

Thus we find ourselves once again facing an exasperating discrepancy between the first libido theory and the second. By maintaining the possibility of an object choice of the attachment type, Freud throws his whole argument out of kilter, inasmuch as such a choice, by definition, could not be narcissistic. The two examples with which he introduces the distinction between the two types of object choice provide clear evidence of this. The example he gives of object love of the attachment type is the mother. Hardly an example at all, then, but rather a paradigm: here we have the primordial object in relation to which all other objects will be only substitutes or copies. The example of a love object of the narcissistic type, however, is the homosexual object: homosexuals take "as a model not their mother but their own selves" (p. 88). In the one case, consequently, objects are chosen according to the model of a primary object (one loves its representatives); in the other case, objects are chosen according to the model of the ego (one loves oneself represented—and one loves to represent oneself—in them). These two examples, quite obviously, cannot coexist in the same picture. They involve two different theories both of libido and of object orientation.

Second, we are not through expressing our astonishment at this section of Freud's text; for in it, oddly enough, Freud describes virtually no narcissistic object choice. There is, of course, the homosexual object choice (which we shall classify as type I.b.). Instead of lingering over this example, however, Freud focuses on the example of female object choice. As he sees it, the difference between the two types of object choice parallels sexual difference: men love according to type II, women according to type I. A woman's erotic life thus provides an excellent example of narcissistic object choice:

A comparison of the male and female sexes then shows that there are fundamental differences between them in respect of their type of object-choice, although these differences are of course not universal. Complete object-love of the attachment type is, properly speaking, characteristic of the male. . . . A different course is followed in the type of female most frequently met with, which is probably the purest and truest one. With the onset of puberty the maturing of the female sexual organs, which up till then have been in a condition of latency, seems to bring about an intensification of the original narcissism, and this is unfavourable to the development of a true object-choice with its accompanying sexual overvaluation [*Sexualüberschätzung*]. . . . Strictly speaking, it is only themselves that such women love with an intensity comparable to that of the man's love for them. [pp. 88–89]

Woman—the properly feminine, womanly woman—thus loves herself, like a child or like "certain animals which seem not to concern themselves about us" (p. 89). This, moreover, is what makes men unhappy: the "incongruity between the types of object-choice" is such that men love women, whereas women do not love men. The two types are not complementary; they do not form a pair, and now we see why: it is because the feminine type, contrary to all expectations, *is not a type of object choice*. The example that is intended to illustrate the narcissistic type of object is a typical example of non-object-oriented narcissism. Women love no one, and they must therefore be classified under I.a.—in other words, in the category of non-choice of object. To be sure, women still take themselves as love object; furthermore, Freud states that "a human being has originally two sexual objects—himself and the woman who nurses him" (p. 88). Nevertheless, and even beyond the fact that these observations simply obscure the concept of narcissism once again, the fact remains that self-love does not stem from an "object choice" in the sense in which Freud himself uses the term. In Freud's sense, to choose an *object* is to love another person (an *other*). And that is not the case here.

Let us try to sort out these peculiar operations. We can hardly fail to see that Freud, under the pretext of distinguishing two types of object choice, ends up differentiating between an object choice and a non-choice of object, that is, between an object-oriented libidinal cathexis and a narcissistic cathexis. The distinction between types I and II is by no means internal to object libido, for the good reason that it surreptitiously reproduces the distinction—which thus tends to become an opposition—between ego libido and object libido. As a result, we can no longer be quite sure what a narcissistic object choice is, nor why Freud proposed to discuss it. If we set aside the allusion to homosexuality (which is the *only* explicit example we are given of narcissistic object choice), we are obliged to note that Freud is intent upon describing *pure* types that stem either from narcissism or from object-oriented sexuality, even though the "speculative" insight of the first section ought to have led him to emphasize the mixed or "impure" character of all libidinal cathexes.

All this is all too obvious: Freud is backing away from his own insight, is maneuvering to divorce himself, as it were, from himself. And all his visible confusion, his awkward hesitations, would certainly not be worth dwelling on, except for the question of just *what* Freud is backing away from. Is it only from the need to reformulate his entire theory of sexuality, once narcissism has been introduced? This is one possible explanation. The clearest benefit of the movement of retreat outlined here is unquestionably the maintenance of the attachment theory, intact: type II is not contaminated, as it were, by narcissism. But the opposite is just as true: type I is not contaminated by type II, and that advantage is undoubtedly just as significant, if not more so. For this way the fiction of narcissism can be maintained, the fiction of a *pure* and *purely non-object-oriented* narcissism. The term "fiction" is not to be taken in the sense of a "theoretical fiction," a "speculative hypothesis" that sketches the phantom of something that, rigorously speaking, *is* not and never *presents* itself in person. Let us take the term in the sense in which Freud has just denounced the illusion of a nonspeculative—that is, nonmediate—approach to narcissism. Woman (womanly woman, child-woman, cat-woman), in this context, is such a fiction. She is the example, the exemplary figure of a narcissism that in principle ought to have remained without example, since it is inaccessible to direct observation. Speculation, by this very token, reverts to dogmatism.

Freud believes in this fiction; he believes in woman's narcissism. He believes in it because he believes in the possibility of a *purely object-oriented* love. Indeed, narcissism is all the purer for being opposed to an object love that is itself purified of any narcissism. We must bear in mind from now on that the affirmation of the inherently object-oriented character of object love, far from contradicting the hypothesis of a primary narcissism, is in fact its strongest guarantee. If narcissism were visible in object love, and *only* in object love, it would mean, on the contrary, that narcissism "loses" itself in object love at the outset. It would also mean that the ego is never itself, never present to itself in the love of itself, whereas it is present everywhere and, by that token, fundamental: the foundation is abyssal, because it is always already superficial. Confronted with that possibility, which is a disconcerting one for any conceptualization of the subject (of the substructure, the *subjectum*), Freud finally retreats. (And thus the theory of narcissism once more demonstrates its narcissistic character.)

Do we stop here? To do that would entail a failure to read. We have just traced one particular development within Freud's text—the most obvious and the most substantial one, and also the one that most often attracts commentators. We had to do this, if only to situate its stakes—the mirage, let us say, that orients it. This mirage is inscribed in the text and thus has to be taken into account. But the mirage does not account for everything. Freud approaches the issue only by piling up the most openly contradictory statements, and the sort of reckless haste he manifests is all the more telling. It is impossible to pin down his argument in a *thesis* (in *a* thesis) that is not immediately nullified, swept away in a contrary movement. We may regret this; we may find all the turmoil irritating. We may also see its possibilities, and think in terms of a "successful failure." The mirage of narcissism, and its power, are such that one can only denounce it, perhaps, by putting its disappearance to the test, albeit unwittingly. (A procedural matter: it is possible to progress by taking steps backward.)

A very significant factor, in this regard, is Freud's inability to distinguish between the two libidinal regimes *at the very moment* when he is trying to oppose them as two distinct types of libidinal cathexis. This lack of differentiation necessarily affects sexual difference, given that man and woman represent "complete object-love of the attachment type" (p. 88) and narcissistic self-love, respectively.

Man

To begin with, man. As we have seen, he loves the woman who substitutes for his mother, who has already substituted for herself as object of need. But Freud goes further, and we deliberately broke off the quotation at this point:

It displays the marked sexual overvaluation which is doubtless derived from the child's original narcissism and thus corresponds to a transference of that narcissism to the sexual object. This sexual overvaluation is the origin of the peculiar state of being in love, a state suggestive of a neurotic compulsion, which is thus traceable to an impoverishment of the ego as regards libido in favour of the love-object. ["On Narcissism," p. 88]

Were things not already complicated enough? "Complete object-love" now turns out to be narcissistic love, and Freud here superimposes the schema of libidinal "yielding" on that of attachment. The overvaluation (*Überschätzung*: an economic notion, once again—*Schatz* means treasure) consists in a transference of narcissism (a transfer of assets) to the benefit of the object. The third section of "On Narcissism" develops this point: by exalting the object, by praising it to the skies, the lover has "forfeited part of his narcissism," and that loss can be compensated for only on the condition that love (that is, overvaluation) is paid back in return (p. 98). When this does not happen (which is the most frequent case, if the lack of "congruence" of the masculine and feminine types is taken into account), the lover's self-esteem is diminished proportionately—hence the erotic vassalage, the blind submission to the Lady, to the Mistress (*domina*) who keeps the ego in her castle, and so on.

Unrequited love? Yes and no. Yes, if "the aim and the satisfaction in a narcissistic object-choice is to be loved" (p. 98), as Freud writes, and if the transference of narcissism is negotiated in view of a counter-transference. And no, because the ego, in the last analysis, is by no means lost in erotic ecstasy. On the contrary, one might even say that woman is all the more apt to represent the ego (and thus to satisfy her narcissism), in that she is more inaccessible to object love—that is to say, *more narcissistic*. That is why Freud also remarks that those men "who have renounced part of their own narcissism" (p. 89), far from choosing women who will love them (as men), are attracted to those women who reflect back to them the image of an intact narcissism.

In Freud's view there is no "incongruity" here, Girard notwithstanding,[40] but a logical incongruence. For if it is true that the nonnarcissistic woman "gives back" to man a quantity of libido equivalent to the amount he has "yielded" to her, "the fact remains that man will not find in her the narcissistic self-sufficiency that he has had to give up and that he is seeking by every means to "recover."[41] The choice of the femme fatale is thus a fatal one. Only in a haughty and sovereign beauty can Narcissus find himself again *as he was* (choice I.b.). As Denis de Rougemont would say, erotic love is a necessarily unrequited love (a quest for the "obstacle") because each lover loves "from the standpoint of self."[42] Narcissism triumphs, in other words, in the defeat of love. And it finds satisfaction in submission, in that peculiar "voluntary servitude" that submits it to *itself* in the figure of the Lady.

(But is that Lady, that *domina*, still a woman? Are we not faced with *domination* pure and simple, prior to any sexual characterization? And is it still so astonishing that this battle of the sexes closely resembles the struggle of consciousness described by Hegel in the chapter of *Phenomenology of Spirit* entitled "Independence and Dependence of Self-consciousness; Lordship and Bondage"?)

Here we have a decidedly paradoxical definition of love, one that does not point precisely in the direction of a consummated sexual relationship. And we might note in passing that it illuminates the phenomenon of "transference" at least as much as the latter illuminates the phenomenon of love: in this regard, we should recall Freud's discussions of transference-love; *Übertragungsliebe*, in which he even goes so far as to say that nothing distinguishes this transference-love from "'genuine' love" ("Observations on Transference-Love," *SE* 12: 168). It may be pointed out that this definition comes into play just when erotic love is in question, erotic love being a manifestation which is, after all, rather rare in object love and whose quasi-pathological, "compulsive" nature Freud emphasizes. This may well be; however, as it happens, "pathological" love routinely provides Freud with a paradigm for "normal" love. We have already had occasion to see this in the Schreber case, where *Verliebtheit* represented object love in its opposition to the "gloomy tyranny" of the narcissistic ego;[43] elsewhere, in "A Special Type of Choice of Object," Freud judges that *Verliebtheit* "betrays," in the manner of an informer, the "maternal prototype of the object-choice."[44]

What is true of *Verliebtheit* is thus also true of object love in general. This implication is all the more decisive in that the interpretation of erotic overvaluation by way of the narcissistic "transference" takes over quite manifestly, here, *from the interpretation* by way of attachment, that is, *from the Oedipal interpretation*. Indeed, the "object-choice of the attachment type" is never anything but another name for Oedipal love (choice II.a.), and this is how "A Special Type of Choice of Object" earlier explained erotic overvaluation—through the irreplaceability of the unique and inimitable Mother:

The trait of overvaluing the loved one, and regarding her as unique and irreplaceable, can be seen to fall just as naturally into the context of the child's experience, for no one possesses more than one mother, and the relation to her is based on an event that is not open to any doubt and cannot be repeated. [*SE* 11: 169]

What happens, then, when overvaluation proves to be inherently narcissistic? When the irreplaceability of the loved object replaces not the mother's irreplaceability, but the ego's? Does this not mean that the mother was, after all, never Irreplaceable, never Unique? Does it not mean that even though she was the first love object she was not loved for herself but *for the ego*, in the unsubstitutable place of narcissism? Let us leave these questions unanswered. They already lead us to suspect that narcissistic love does not enter into the framework of the Oedipus complex, but grounds the complex in an even earlier phase.

The questions are in any event inevitable, given that overvaluation, the principal feature of narcissistic erotic love, characterizes *all* the examples of "complete object-love" proposed by Freud. This holds true, as we have just demonstrated, for men of the masculine type. But it also holds true for women who love as men do. As Freud readily acknowledged, women often "love according to the masculine type"; they then develop, not coincidentally, "the sexual overvaluation proper to that type" ("On Narcissism," p. 89). As for those who do not love (as) men, the "road that leads to complete object-love" is not entirely closed to them: "in the child which they bear, a part of their own body confronts them like an extraneous object, to which, starting out from their narcissism, they can then give complete object-love" (pp. 89–90).

But this road (choice I.d.) "starts" from narcissism, and the following passage explains how. Maternal love is never anything but a case of parental love; now,

if we look at the attitude of affectionate parents towards their children, we have to recognize that it is a revival and reproduction of their own narcissism, which they have long since abandoned. The trustworthy pointer constituted by overvaluation, which we have already recognized as a narcissistic stigma in the case of object-choice, dominates, as we all know, their emotional attitude. Thus they are under a compulsion to ascribe every perfection to the child . . . "His Majesty the Baby," as we once fancied ourselves. The child shall fulfil those wishful dreams of the parents which they never carried out—the boy shall become a great man and a hero in his father's place [*an Stelle des Vaters*], and the girl shall marry a prince as a tardy compensation for her mother. . . . Parental love, which is so moving and at bottom so childish, is nothing but the parents' narcissism born again, which, transformed into object-love, unmistakably reveals its former nature. [pp. 90–91]

For now, let us sidestep the abyss over which this whole tyrannico-familial novel is constructed (we shall fall into it soon enough). Let us simply note that this passage confirms once again that no object love escapes the "narcissistic stigma." We need only tally up the various forms: whether we are talking about man's love for woman or woman's love for man, the child's love for the mother or the mother's (parents') love for the child, all the object choices Freud enumerates turn out to be more or less explicitly classified in I.b., I.c., or I.d.—in other words, in the categories labeled "narcissistic object-choice."

Woman

And woman, the typically feminine woman? Her position in type I.a. may appear unassailable, and the attitude Freud adopts toward her strangely resembles that of parents toward children: "at the most touchy point in the narcissistic system, the immortality of the ego, which is so hard pressed by reality, security is achieved by taking refuge in the child" ("On Narcissism," p. 91)—or, by implication, in the eternal feminine. But the breach is inscribed within the text. A portion of a sentence that we have not yet cited opens up a crack in the type, imperceptibly but implacably:

Strictly speaking, it is only themselves that such women love with an intensity comparable to that of the man's love for them. Nor does their need [*Bedürfnis*] lie in the direction of loving, but of being loved; and *the man who fulfils this condition is the one who finds favour with them* [*sie lassen sich den Mann gefallen, welcher diese Bedingung erfüllt*]. [p. 89; emphasis added][45]

Woman, whom we thought incapable of loving, loves the man who loves her. Or at least (and it amounts to the same thing) she needs to be loved—needs the man who loves her. Her cruel indifference was only a ploy, a trap laid for man's credulity. She chooses the one whom she can lead to believe that she is not choosing, in order to be able to dominate him from a libidinal position which he, in his stupidity, will not notice he has yielded to her. This "bluff," we must suppose, is carried out very quickly—in the time it takes to fall in love at first sight—and the rapidity with which Freud skims over it supports our supposition: he, too, is struck down by the woman's master blow. The fact remains, nevertheless, that woman makes an object choice (needs an object), if only to renounce it, and that this tarnishes the purity of her narcissism—that is, of her femininity: she loves as man does. More precisely, she loves like the man who loves a woman who loves as a man does—in order to be loved.

Plainly, sexual difference is no longer relevant, and the stereotypes rapidly merge or intersect. It is not surprising, then, that the positions of "man" and "woman" are perfectly symmetrical, precisely by virtue of their narcissism: since each loves him/herself in the other, and since each is speculating on a mirrored love, the other is in each case an other self, a likeness. Love does not adapt itself to the two sexes; on the contrary, it neutralizes the sexual opposition on the basis of a fundamental homosexuality. "Men" and "women"—men *as* women—love themselves as homosexuals. And was homosexuality not the only explicit example of narcissistic object choice? The man/woman difference turns out to be incapable of organizing the analysis of love, and this limitation has inevitable implications for the distinction between object orientation and narcissism that the difference was supposed to illustrate. If the libidinal positions of men and women are ultimately identical, this means that ego libido and object libido are once again indistinguishable, inseparable, *ununterscheidbar*.

Thus there is no narcissism but object-oriented narcissism, and vice versa. This statement can and must also be understood as follows: there is no narcissism but the narcissism of the other. It takes two (at least) to make a Narcissus, and we have here a sort of transcendental illusion that demands the active collaboration of both parties. Since each begins by crediting the other with a narcissism that the other lacks, the overvaluation is at first reciprocal, even if this initial congruence leads inevitably, according to the law that we were spelling out earlier, to the incongruity that Freud identifies.

Of course, neither partner can be satisfied with a shared—that is, imperfect—narcissism, and that is why the narcissistic couple is immediately thrown off balance. Since there is room for only one Narcissus, it must be "he (she) or I"; the whole question then boils down to discovering which one of us will succeed, by trickery or by chance, in monopolizing the overvaluation of the other to his/her own profit. This dissymmetry depends nevertheless on an initial symmetry that relates the subjects to each other—or, more precisely, subjects them to each other and divides them into each other—according to a

chiasmus that eludes the structure of opposition, eludes the oppositional form in general (lover / loved one, object orientation / narcissism, overvaluation/self-sufficiency, servility/mastery, and so on).
And when Freud persists in placing woman in the role of Narcissus,
we may be sure that he himself, in this "dialectics" of mistress and
slave, occupies the servile position. This entire theory of love is written from the clouded vantage point of the slave who believes in the
narcissism of the other, does not want to see that he has yielded her
"his own," and thus avoids acknowledging that there is no narcissism
that has not always already been "yielded," no subjective property
that is not borrowed, no mastery that does not depend on servitude.

The Turning Point

> The Child is father of the Man.
>   Wordsworth, "My Heart Leaps Up When I Behold"

Our reading is further corroborated by the example of the parent-
child couple that closes the second section of "On Narcissism." Thus
far we have been looking at the issue strictly from the viewpoint of
parental love. We need to add, now, that this is a slave's viewpoint.
Indeed, it coincides precisely with the lover's blind spot: parents see
themselves in their child as they would like to be; they see themselves
outside themselves as they "are" in their fantasies, in their "egoistic
dreams"—as great men, heroes, princesses, and so on. Thus we are
not surprised to find the child occupying the same place as the
woman in the love relationship: the place of the tyrant, His Majesty
the Baby. The couple in love and the parent-child couple are of the
same type, and they produce the same effect.

Let us note, however, that in the second case Freud *describes the
couple* and exhibits it *as such*, something he did not do in the first
case. The reason is simple; it is no longer possible to be misled as to
the presumed narcissistic autonomy of the child (whereas this was
still possible with the typically female woman). For the child-king,
the family hero, is an infant who is bathed, put to bed, and tucked
in, the child with his gaze anxiously raised toward his parents, the
child as he is being *brought up*. Can a more destitute tyrant be imagined, or a more fragile kingdom? If there is any case in which the

overvaluation of the other is overwhelming, heedless, and unmistakable, it is that of the infant delivered up mercilessly to its parents' omnipotence. It is impossible, then, to maintain a belief in the omnipotence of infants. Quite obviously, only a derived, secondary narcissism is possible, one that would not "stand up" for a moment without parental care, so that its "reality" resides nowhere except in their idolatry. Freud ends up acknowledging this, obliged as he is, now, to emphasize the fact that narcissism is by nature wholly relational and mediate, and thus also "speculative": "The primary narcissism of children which we have assumed and which forms one of the postulates of our theories of the libido, is less easy to grasp by direct observation than to confirm *by inference from elsewhere*. If we look at the attitude of affectionate parents toward their children . . ." ("On Narcissism, p. 90; emphasis added).

These remarks may appear to be extremely banal, and they are: what is more banal, after all, than man's inherent finitude? However, they make a crucial difference to Freud's argument. The passage in question deals with infantile narcissism, that is, with *primary* narcissism, which woman's narcissism merely reproduces or perpetuates. The whole theory of narcissism thus depends on this paragraph, especially since this is the only passage in the essay in which Freud answers (so to speak) the question he had left open in the first section, namely, the question of the *origin* of primary narcissism. That question was inevitable once Freud had acknowledged that "a unity comparable to the ego cannot exist in the individual from the start" and that "there must be something added to auto-erotism—a new psychical action—in order to bring about narcissism [*um den Narzissmus zu gestalten*]" (p. 77).

Now the supremely naive (and there is a connection here with nativity, birth, *naissance*) and at the same time quite vertiginous character of Freud's answer to the question is perfectly plain. The answer consists (and this is why it is not, strictly speaking, an "answer") in exacerbating the question and in acknowledging the abyss that the question had encompassed from the start. For if narcissism has a point of departure, a beginning or an origin, this means, quite simply, that narcissism is not primary. The naïveté resurfaces here with the acknowledgment that the ego *is born*, in other words, that narcissism is not always already its own foundation as a subject (*sub-jectum*, *hupokeimenon*). "Something"—"something" that narcissism is not, itself, and that Freud calls "parents" here—has to bring it into the world, has to enable it to be born to itself, has to present it to itself by giving it a "form," a "figure," a *Gestalt*. Thus we may just as well say that there is no such thing as self-generation or self-conception, and that the orphan subject within which philosophy has been dreaming itself since Descartes is a *fiction*, in several senses.[46]

The idea that primary narcissism is a fiction can be understood, first of all, and as trivially as possible, in the sense that it is not the real beginning. The real beginning, as we have said, is much more modest—and in saying this we are only repeating what Freud had already written in "Formulations on the Two Principles of Mental Functioning" with reference to the initial self-sufficiency of the newborn:

It will rightly be objected that an organization which was a slave to the pleasure principle and neglected the reality of the external world could not maintain itself alive for the shortest time, so that it could not have come into existence at all. The employment of a fiction like this is, however, justified when one considers that the infant—provided one includes with it the care it receives from its mother—does almost realize a psychical system of this kind. [*SE* 12: 219n]

The same is true of narcissistic omnipotence, then: it presupposes parental overvaluation, exactly as the "pleasure-ego" of the newborn infant depends on the maternal supplement. The analogy breaks down, however, in the face of the fact that maternal care is real (it keeps the newborn alive), whereas parental overvaluation is wholly "unreal." Indeed, the "lost" narcissism in the image of which the parents form their child was obviously no less fictitious, in the beginning, than the one they "rediscover" in the little family tyrant. Freud hints at this when he writes, for example, "'His Majesty the Baby,' *as we once fancied ourselves*" ("On Narcissism," p. 91). "Once"—"once upon a time"—thus already had the shape of a myth or family romance. No matter how far back we go in the generational chain, we shall always rediscover the parent-child *couple* and the parental "fictionalizing" of the child[47]—unless of course we presuppose, back at the beginning of history, an absolute Father (or an absolute Child, which would be the same thing)—that is, a Subject.

This figure of the primitive tyrant is the one that blocked, as we know, the "regression" of "Totem and Taboo." But "Totem and Taboo," as Freud said himself, is a "scientific myth" (a "childish theory"?), and this is hardly a coincidence. If man is always a child of man, subject to the law of procreation, it is impossible for him to be a subject except by fiction. This is so not only because the child's narcissism (being-through-and-for-oneself) is a sort of *proton pseudos* that presupposes *in reality* a prior parental intervention, but, much more fundamentally, because there is no real beginning to that illusion and because everything begins, for that child as for those children his parents once were, with fiction.

It begins, that is, with a process of "fashioning," of "formation." That the subject emerges in and through a primordial fiction is what Freud has been saying from the outset, from the moment he declared (naively, to be sure, but finally more decisively than in the entire discourse on the transcendental ego) that "something" has to form the ego. This has to mean that the ego *is nothing*—not even amorphous matter, not even a "fragmented body"—*prior* to such a formation, prior to such a "creation." Thus we have no business speculating about the nature of the ego, the subject, the Narcissus complex, any more than we may presuppose any sort of property or subjective identity. Such identity will always be apocryphal and fictitious (but its falseness can no longer be truthfully expressed), inasmuch as there can be no subject except one that is initially *modeled on* or *modeled by* (here we have no way to distinguish activity from passivity, spontaneity from receptivity) something that "precedes" it.[48] This is why Freud's regressive "inference from elsewhere" can only go on and on, recurring indefinitely until it finally aborts in its confrontation with the constant priority of modeling. For it is the recurrence itself that is primary: the congenital infantilism of the subject—the insuperable infantile obstacle—is such that the subject is no sooner itself than it is "behind" with respect to its own origin. And the origin has to be expressed through myth, not because it is inaccessible to "direct observation," but because everything begins with myth—for example, with the wish-dream that already pervades the parents themselves: "I am a great man," "I am a princess." (Was it not on just such a familial myth that Freud's own self-analysis ran aground in *The Interpretation of Dreams?*)

Freud stops far short of spelling out all these implications clearly. Not only does he fail to pursue his "inference" to the end, he even takes it as a "confirmation" of the concept of primary narcissism. The paragraph in question can thus be read as a concluding paragraph that recapitulates the hypothesis and corroborates it one more time—at least on the surface. In reality, however, a sort of suppressed anxiety has come to light, as attested by the fact that Freud starts the whole analysis of narcissism over again, this time taking it in the opposite direction. In fact, Freud's earlier arguments consistently *presupposed* the ego. Whether the ego "kept" its libidinal cathexis or, on the contrary, "yielded" it to objects, the ego itself nevertheless constituted the point of departure for the entire process. By the same token, the narcissistic relation to objects could only be specular, and that is why the analysis of love ultimately led back—by extremely twisted paths, to be sure—to a dialectics of recognition. And even though this dialectics was blocked by an initial aporia (given that each of the partners *began* by *re*cognizing him/herself in the object—did so, in other words, prior to any knowledge of self), the fact remains that the narcissistic object continued to be defined as a secondary reduplication of the ego: "what he himself was" (I.b.) or "someone who was once part of himself" (I.d.). Finally, we must bear in mind that homosexuality, the paradigm for the narcissistic relation to the object, was described as a relation of model (*Vorbild*) to copy—in short, as a mirror imitation.

Now this language can no longer be used, or at least not *in the same sense*, once the question of the "formation" of the ego itself has arisen, however indirectly. The difficulty raised by this question is easy enough to formulate. It is the one we identified a moment ago: if the ego is not "present from the outset," if it is nothing prior to accepting in (and as) "itself" a form that comes "from without," it follows not only that the relation to the object (to the other, to the "non-ego") is primary, but also and especially that this first relation cannot have been a *specular* relation, nor even, ultimately, a *relation* at all.

This consequence may be obvious, but it is obvious as well that the reasoning gives rise at once to a major and perhaps insurmountable linguistic confusion. It is an understatement to say that it muddles Freud's language: it renders this language wholly obsolete, and with it, the entire language of representation, of re-cognition, of reflection, redoubling, and so on. For one can no longer say that the ego rediscovers *itself* or represents *itself* in another that resembles it like a brother. The easy way out—which consists in positing the ego *in advance*, that is, as the infinite pre-sence of the subject to all that is presented *to it*—has been disallowed. As a result, it is impossible to speak of the ego as a "model" reflecting itself in objects and narcissistically enjoying itself in that self-reflection. But it is likewise impossible to adopt the opposite "easy" answer, which would consist in postulating that the ego "models itself" on objects or "forms itself in the image" of the other. However relevant and even necessary this reversal may be (it is Lacan's—a Lacan more faithful to Freud than ever, as we shall confirm in a moment), it only turns the problem around *within the same language*.

It would be useless indeed to insist on the inaugurating and formative character of the mirror (phase), to inflect the specular image as an *imago* and the imago as a *Gestalt* or a "type,"[49] to develop, under the heading of the Imaginary, a theory that reverses the model/imitation relationship, which is here the very language of the difficulty.[50] For "in the beginnning" there is no one to *see* anything at all; there is no "one" to see *oneself* in front of oneself in a model-image (or, as it is so aptly put in German, in a *Vor-bild*, a "picture-in-front"). Here, in short, we are brought back to the spot—the other's spot, the "point of otherness"—where we have been led once before by the analysis of fantasies and dreams. Where the ego forms itself in the image of the other, where it mimes the other, one can no longer speak either of "form" or "image," either of "self" or "other." Where the id was (neither *himself* nor *myself*), the "I" arrives. And the id can no longer be expressed in the language of the visible, of perception, of phenomenality, nor, by the same token, in any sort of theory of models and images. The other stage becomes a beyond-stage, a fore-stage of the primary mimesis.

Nor must we be astonished if the difficulty that this "fore-stage" designates is left unspecified in Freud's text and even remains, quite literally, imperceptible. Freud does not "see" it, which is hardly surprising, since he continues to speak the language of theoretical evidence. That there is nevertheless a difficulty and that it affects Freud's thought—even, so to speak, in the obscurity of the evidence—is corroborated by the movement of the third section of "On Narcissism," where Freud once again confronts the same difficulty in the same language, but this time *in reverse*, or perhaps *from another point of view*. The main part of this section is devoted to an elaboration of the concept of the narcissistic ego ideal. The text thus appears to pursue the analysis in a completely new direction, inasmuch as it focuses on identifying incidences of narcissism in the "psychology of repression" rather than in the "psychology of erotic life":

We have learnt that libidinal instinctual impulses undergo the vicissitude of pathogenic repression if they come into conflict with the subject's cultural and ethical ideas. By this we never mean that the individual in question has a merely intellectual knowledge of the existence of such ideas; we always mean that he recognizes them as a standard for himself and submits to the claims they make on him. Repression, we have said, proceeds from the ego; we might say with greater precision that it proceeds from the self-respect of the ego. . . . We can say that [the subject] has set up an *ideal* in himself by which he measures his actual ego. . . . For the ego the formation of an ideal [*Idealbildung*] would be the conditioning factor of repression. [pp. 93–94]

But the distinction between love and repression is not as clear-cut as it appears, and we shall see it fade away in a moment. More remarkable is the reversal that occurs here with the introduction of the ego ideal. The object of narcissistic love was "what one has been oneself"; but the ego ideal, if we follow the definition given in advance by the table of object choices, is "what one would like to be" (type I.c., p. 102). The inversion is flagrant. "What one *would like* to be" is what one is not and also what one has never been. Thus no "yielding" of a preexisting subjective identity or property occurs, since we find *identification* with the other, instead. As for "*what* one would like to be," this can only refer to a model that one desires to resemble, that one imitates, copies, and so on—a crucial nuance, since it is no longer the ego that is in the position of *Vorbild*, but the other (the parents, first and foremost, and thus *their* ego ideal—what they would like to be through their child, and so on).

Freud's text is actually not quite this clear. Beyond the fact that he completely avoids using the words "model" and "identification"—so that these terms stand out by their absence—he describes the emergence of the ego ideal in terms that associate it, once again, with an economic process ("loss,"/"recovery," dispossession/reappropriation). The ego ideal (*Ichideal*) would thus be an ideal ego (*Idealich*), a displaced ego, transferred, objectivized, projected outside itself in front of itself:

This ideal ego [*Idealich*] is now the target of the self-love which was enjoyed in childhood by the actual ego. The subject's narcissism makes its appearance displaced on to this new ideal ego [*ideale ich*], which, like the infantile ego, finds itself possessed of every perfection that is of value. As always where the libido is concerned, man has here again shown himself incapable of giving up a satisfaction he had once enjoyed. He is not willing to forgo the narcissistic perfection of his childhood; and when, as he grows up, he is disturbed by the admonitions of others and by the awakening of his own critical judgement, so that he can no longer retain that perfection, he seeks to recover it in the new form of an ego ideal. What he projects before him as his ideal is the substitute for the lost narcissism of his childhood in which he was his own ideal. [p. 94][51]

The reversal of perspective is thus not so simple as it may have appeared, and Freud does not shift without a struggle from the language of narcissistic "yielding" to the language of identification. On the contrary, the paragraph we have just cited begins by making short shrift of the schema that presided over the analysis of narcissistic love. The ego "projects itself" in the ideal ego, and consequently it is always already there "at the beginning," before the "formation of an ideal." But this should not surprise us. If he had conflated the phase of "ideal formation" with that of ego formation, Freud would have found himself obliged to confront the difficulty head on—the difficulty that is announced here with the enigmatic statement "he was his own ideal" and that will later be called "primary identification." But what Freud specifically fails to do is acknowledge the difficulty, at least as the *primary* difficulty. This is why he resituates it at another level as a merely secondary problem, since the entire maneuver (but it is a maneuver that is blind to itself) consists, finally, in *splitting* the difficulty: instead of considering the *Idealbildung* and the *Ichgestaltung* as two sides of a single question, Freud begins by positing an already-constituted ego, then goes on to speculate about its formation. It is only *then*—Freud's rear guard having been protected, as it were—that the question can arise anew, in terms of a problematics of modeling, identification, imitation, and so on.

This is why Freud seems less concerned, in what follows, with the problem of the emergence of the ideal through a projection of narcissism than with the exactly inverse problem of the formation of an ideal agency *within* the ego. It is a problem of introjection, so to speak: the ideal is no longer what one was, it is what one wishes to be (and must be), and it is therefore the object of *assimilation*. It is a problem of education as well, and the expression *Idealbildung* does not appear here by chance: it signifies not only the ideal agency constituted within the ego (the ideal formation, as one would speak of a "cloud formation"), but also the way in which this instance is constituted (the formation of the ideal, the *Bildung des Ideals*, as Freud puts it at least once). The *Bildung* is, then, formation as education, as education by example: the ideal ego-agency is formed in the image (*Abbild*) of a model (*Vorbild*)—that is, in the image of an ideal: the *Idealbildung* involves the constitution of an internal ideal through a mimetic internalization of an external ideal. This accounts for Freud's seeming carelessness when he situates the ego ideal sometimes outside the ego and sometimes inside. Indeed, the ideal sometimes seems to arise *in front of* the ego (the "real ego"). It is then a question of a model to be imitated, an ideal to be attained, as prescribed by the discourse of others:

What prompted the subject to form an ego ideal [*die Anregung zur Bildung des Ideals*], on whose behalf his conscience acts as watchman, arose from the critical influence of his parents (conveyed to him by the medium of the voice), to whom were added, as time went on, those who trained and taught him and the innumerable and indefinable host of all the other people in his environment—his fellow-men—and public opinion. [p. 96]

However, Freud sometimes states that the ego establishes an ideal "in itself" or (and this amounts to the same thing) that a "psychical agency . . . constantly watches the actual ego and measures it by that ideal" (p. 95). Here we have the internalized ideal, the "voice of the conscience." The ego speaks to itself as others speak to it; it mimics their discourse, and out of this mimicry "moral conscience" is born. Such a conscience is consequently neither a submission to constraint nor an "intellectual knowledge" of the law, but rather the mimetic self-prescription of a model of behavior. Without this identification, there would be no moral subject, no law, no authority. The ego might bend under the yoke of a prohibition imposed by force, but it would not espouse the prohibition as its own, whereas here the ego spontaneously imposes prohibitions on itself: in repression and censorship (which are never anything but the negative side of the ideal prescription: "Be like this," "Imitate me"), the ego is not dealing with an other, but with itself.

This, at least, is what we should be able to say if the ideal were not in principle heterogeneous with the ego. Freud insists strongly on this point: the genealogy of morals is external, and irreducibly so. Paranoic delusions bear witness to this, for in them the ideal moves back outside:

Patients of this sort complain that all their thoughts are known and their actions watched and supervised; they are informed of the functioning of this agency by voices which characteristically speak to them in the third person. . . . The institution of conscience was at bottom an embodiment, first of parental criticism, and subsequently of that of society—a process which is repeated in what takes place when a tendency towards repression develops out of a prohibition or obstacle that came in the first instance from without. The voices, as well as the undefined multitude, are brought into the foreground again by the disease, and so the evolution of conscience is reproduced regressively. . . . [The patient's] conscience then confronts him in a regressive form as a hostile influence from without. [p. 96]

Though the external ideal may be transformed into an internal conscience, and the Word incarnated in the ego, nothing is really changed by this: the ego remains subject to the ideal as to an *other*. The ego splits in two, internally, by interiorizing the distance that separates it from the model that it wants (that it *has* to want) to imitate and against which it "measures" or compares itself. The mystery of the undecidable incarnation of the Father in the Son[52] gives way, therefore, to a *topographical* distribution of psychic spaces and agencies—that is, to a problematics of the subject divided into several different "people," each one provided with an identity and a proper name (ego/conscience and/or ego ideal).

This topographical division of the subject corresponds exactly to the gesture with which we have seen Freud divide up the problem of the formation of the ego "itself." In short, where the consideration of the *Idealbildung* as modeling-through-the-ideal ought to have led him to return to this problem (for what is modeled if not the "ego," if not that "X" which as yet has no form, no name, no identity?), Freud is only concerned with the formation of *one part of the ego*. And it must be admitted that this hardly solves the problem, or that it only "solves" it by removing it to another level, displacing it onto another agency. The ego, like the fabled porcupine, is always there, and it stays the same, from the beginning to the end of the process, always in relation to an external model (outside-external or inside-external, it makes little difference) with which it has to conform but with which, as well, it never identifies *itself*.

Under these conditions, it is understandable that the relations between the ego and the ego ideal which "requires" sublimation or, at the very least, repression) might sometimes be very tense: since the ethico-mimetic injunction ("You must imitate me") comes from without, the ego experiences it as a constraint, and the supposed auto-nomy of the moral subject ("self-criticism," "self-observation," and so on) thus harbors an inner conflict. What is less easily understood, however, is why the parental ideal is "incarnated" in the conscience. For while conscience doubtless represents only a part of the ego, this "part" is totally identified with the ideal, and without any *distance* whatever between them. And this part, like it or not, has to be part *of the ego*, so that the problem only springs up at another stage, a little further on.

How are we to explain that an ego (fragment) assimilates (itself) (to) the other and *thereby forms itself*? That it begins by incarnating (itself) (as) voice, law, ideal? That it emerges by incorporating (itself) (as) the other, the object? These are inevitable, and inevitably hopeless, questions, as long as we continue to posit a preformed, ready-made ego. For it is not clear why such an ego would need to identify itself, even "partially," with an ideal imposed from without, or why it would desire to submit to the law that imposed imitation. If the subject is "at the beginning," why would it subject itself?

This will be the main problem of Freud's second topographical distribution, in the 1920's. When this second topography has to confront the question of the formation of the superego (alias the ego ideal, alias conscience) through identification with the Oedipal father, it only becomes more deeply enmeshed in the difficulty inherited from the 1914 text. The problematics of identification comes back up openly, where all the other questions intersect: the question of the Oedipus complex (how does one "enter" into it? how does one "get out" of it? and who is "one," anyway?); the question of topographical differentiation (how does the id constitute itself as an ego, a superego?); the question of the relation to law (in other words, of peaceful relations with others: how does "one" pass from identification with the Oedipal *rival*, who is a likeness, to identification with the Oedipal *Father*, who is an Other?); and that of desire (desire to be or desire to have? mimetic desire or object desire?). This is more than mere coincidence. The entire second topographical distribution can and must be read as the relentless, stratified, ever more complex and ever more inextricable reworking of a question perpetually deferred, and at the same time reproduced, in its successive "solutions": the pre-topological, utopian question of primary identification (mimesis or modeling) of the ego itself, *prior* to any subjective identity—prior, then, to any Model, any Ideal, any Law, any Other (and any "alienation" in the Imaginary and any "refissuring" by the Symbolic).

But we are getting ahead of ourselves. It must suffice for the moment to note that the "turning point" of the second topological distribution is introduced here and that it is no different, in principle, from the "turning point" that moves "On Narcissism" from a specular problematics of narcissistic "yielding" to a problematics of identification, or formation-through-the-ideal. This reversal, as we have tried to show, does not overcome the difficulty which, in a way, it "resolves." The fact remains that the two problematics cohabit in a single text, and this unstable, impossible cohabitation does not keep us from glimpsing something that transcends *both* of them.

To become aware of this, we have only to grapple with the third section of "On Narcissism" as a whole, "literally and in all senses": it is unreadable. For how can the statement that the ego is rediscovered in the ideal as it *was* be reconciled with the assertion that the ego conforms to the ideal that it *would like to be*? How can we conceive of that strange figure of an ego that forms its ideal in its own image and forms itself in the image of its ideal, that projects itself in the ideal and introjects the ideal, that identifies the ideal with itself and itself with the ideal? Is this not the unfigurable, the unimaginable *itself*? And to try to think that, must one not leave behind the "topology of the imaginary," abandon the *theory* of imitation, the ideology of the mirror and the idealogy of the model?

Freud never even hints at such a development. But by dint of circulating within this theory of the subject, by dint of turning around and around in it, he manages to knot it around itself to the point of rendering it inconceivable, enigmatic, incomprehensible. Incomprehensible for us, of course, as readers who do no more than read his text in order to decompose it (on the one hand . . . , on the other hand . . .), in order to be able to follow it quite simply in its strange theoretical *contortions*. But incomprehensible for Freud as well, since it leads him to tie up the theory of narcissism around a sort of internal impossibility, around a "solution" that is untenable in terms of psychoanalytic dualism—but that will henceforth "hold together" the entire system of the second topographical distribution. Here, then, is that enigma, that Sphinx (Oedipus is not far off): the ego ideal, regulatory model and agency of law, is an object of narcissistic love—or vice versa. Freud asserts this at least three times in "On Narcissism":

1. First, when he classifies the ego ideal among the objects of narcissistic love (type I.c.: "what he himself would like to be").

2. Second, when he hints that the love object can substitute for the ego ideal, for example, in transference-love:

The sexual ideal may enter into an interesting auxiliary relation to the ego ideal. It may be used for substitutive satisfaction where narcissistic satisfaction encounters real hindrances. In that case a person will love in conformity with the narcissistic type of object-choice, will love what he once was and no longer is, or else what possesses the excellences which he never had at all . . . [cf. type I.c., above]. The formula parallel to the one there stated runs thus: what possesses the excellence which the ego lacks for making it an ideal, is loved. . . . [The neurotic] seeks a way back to narcissism from his prodigal expenditure of libido upon objects, by choosing a sexual ideal after the narcissistic type which possesses the excellences to which he cannot attain. This is the cure by love, which he generally prefers to cure by analysis. Indeed, he cannot believe in any other mechanism of cure; he usually brings expectations of this sort with him to the treatment and directs them towards the person of the physician. [p. 101]

3. Third and last, when he defines overvaluation in love as an idealization, or the inverse:

Sublimation is a process that concerns object-libido and consists in the instinct's directing itself towards an aim other than, and remote from, that of sexual satisfaction; in this process the accent falls upon deflection from sexuality. Idealization is a process that concerns the object; by it that object, without any alteration in its nature, is aggrandized and exalted in the subject's mind. Idealization is possible in the sphere of ego-libido as well as in that of object-libido. For example, the sexual overvaluation of an object is an idealization of it. [p. 94]

This, then, is what remains to be conceptualized: love of the ideal, love of the law, love of authority.

The Primal Band

Thus we still face the task of conceptualizing Freudian politics. The closing paragraph of "On Narcissism" begins as follows: "The ego ideal opens up an important avenue for the understanding of group psychology [*Massenpsychologie*]. In addition to its individual side, this ideal has a social side; it is also the common ideal of a family, a class or a nation" (p. 101). This laconic program is carried out in a text published eight years later: "Group Psychology and the Analysis of the Ego." The central thesis—the *political* thesis—of that essay is very familiar: what underwrites the cohesion of the *Masse* (the group, i.e., society) is the love of all its members for the *Führer*—in other words, for the "object" that takes the place of their (paternal) ego ideal; thus sociality is necessarily structured according to the political model (there is no society without a leader) or, more precisely, according to a politico-familial model (the leader is a *Vaterersatz*, a father substitute).

Tirelessly repeated in countless works of "applied psychoanalysis," a thesis as straightforward as this one was bound to be transformed into a slogan, and by the same token was bound to *appear authoritative*, since it focused full attention on itself and immediately mobilized, in the customary interweaving of fascination and rejection, either parricidal rebellion or filial submission on the part of its readers. It almost goes without saying that "Group Psychology" has rarely been read, and that a certain political precipitation in the direction of Freud's "master thesis" has almost always masked the ex-traordinary theoretical imbroglio that this thesis supposedly sums up or commands, and whose very fragile cohesion is underwritten by this thesis, and this thesis alone.

Even a merely attentive reading soon discloses that politics by no means constitutes the primary object of *Massenpsychologie*. In fact, the "master thesis" comes into play (bluntly, as we shall soon see) only to answer a question that has to do first and foremost with the social bond. It would thus be quite imprudent to reduce the social bond in advance to the political bond properly speaking, even though Freud does everything possible to encourage such an amalgamation. To proceed with this sort of reduction would be to leave the crucial question behind, by supposing it to be settled from the start. There is something like an effect of intimidation here—a very powerful one, if we can judge by the ease with which appeals are made, in our own day, to "Freud's politics"—that needs to be forestalled at the outset. That is why, instead of hastily drawing up a platform of psy-choanalytical politics to be elaborately supported by quotations taken out of context, we shall begin by asking just *what* question Freud's politics answers, and why Freud answers as he does.

An-archy

> . . . as if it were a question of a discourse without conclusion; as if the logos that, in itself, is beginning, origin, ἀρχή—correla-tive of the pastless void of freedom—were, here, constantly sub-merged by pre-original substance; as if subjectivity were not freedom to adhere to a term that offers itself, but a passivity more passive than that of receptivity.
>
> Emmanuel Lévinas, "Humanisme et An-archie"

We shall begin, then, at the beginning—with the title, "Group Psychology and the Analysis of the Ego,"[1] and the introductory para-graphs that make its meaning clear:

The contrast [*der Gegensatz*] between individual psychology and social or group psychology, which at a first glance may seem to be full of significance, loses a great deal of its sharpness when it is examined more closely. It is true that individual psychology is concerned with the individual man and explores the paths by which he seeks to find satisfaction for his instinctual impulses; but only rarely and under certain exceptional conditions is individual psychology in a position to disregard the relations of this individual to others. In the individual's mental life someone else [*der Andere*: the other] is invariably involved, as a model, as an object, as a helper, as an opponent; and so from the very first individual psychology, in this extended but entirely justifiable sense of the words, is at the same time social psychology as well.

The relations of an individual to his parents and to his brothers and sisters, to the object of his love, and to his physician—in fact all the relations which have hitherto been the chief subject of psycho-analytic research—may claim to be considered as social phenomena; and in this respect they may be contrasted [*in Gegensatz*] with certain other processes, described by us as "narcissistic," in which the satisfaction of the instincts is partially or totally withdrawn from the influence of other people. The contrast between social and narcissistic—Bleuler [1912] would perhaps call them "autistic"—mental acts therefore falls wholly within the domain of individual psychology, and is not well calculated to differentiate it from a social or group psychology. ["Group Psychology," p. 69][2]

This passage does not aim at extending or "applying" "individual psychology" to the study of "social phenomena," but rather at *reducing* the latter to the former: psychoanalysis (since that is obviously what is at issue) is already a "social psychology," the analysis of the ego is already a mass psychology. The crucial step here is to understand what is at stake in that reduction, and how it operates.

What is at stake, first of all, is transparently clear. Freud is seeking to do away with the specificity of the discipline called "social psychology" by unveiling it as a false, derived specificity. Tarde, Le Bon, McDougall, Trotter, and others had made numerous attempts to account for sociality in terms of "instincts" or "tendencies," in contrast with the purely sociological studies of the social phenomenon (we need only recall the polemics between Tarde and Durkheim). Let there be no misunderstanding: Freud has no quarrel with the principle of this *psycho*social approach (even, for some, *biologico*social); on the contrary, he subscribes to it fully. But he intends to radicalize it. If one is going to ground the social in the psychological, why not turn toward the *psyche*, that is, toward the individual? Indeed, how could a psychological investigation of sociality proceed without exploring the social development of the individual or (as Castoriadis puts it) the "socialization of the psyche"?

There is no point in describing the psychology of individuals gathered into a crowd, as Le Bon had done, for example, if the problem of the passage from individual psychology to "crowd psychology" has not already been solved. Nor is Freud satisfied with the solution of invoking a specifically social impulse, a "gregarious instinct" (Trotter) or a "group spirit" (McDougall). Under the guise of minimizing the opposition between the individual and society, one would only be strengthening it, by rediscovering it at the level of instincts (individual instincts / social instincts). Now the problem, according to Freud, is precisely that of the continuity or bond between the two areas. Taken at its most radical extreme, the very project of a social *psychology* falls somewhat short of the distinction between an "individual psychology" and a "social psychology":

> Group psychology is therefore concerned with the individual man as a member of a race, of a nation, of a caste, of a profession, of an institution, or as a component part of a crowd of people who have been organized into a group at some particular time for some definite purpose. When once natural continuity has been severed in this way, if a breach is thus made between things which are by nature interconnected it is easy to regard the phenomena that appear under these special conditions as being expressions of a special instinct that is not further reducible—the social instinct ("herd instinct," "group mind"), which does not come to light in any other situations. But we may perhaps venture to object that it seems difficult to attribute to the factor of number a significance so great as to make it capable by itself of arousing in our mental life a new instinct that is otherwise not brought into play. [p. 70]

And we still need to locate the mainspring of Freud's demonstration, which consists in a substitution. In the place of the secondary opposition (*Gegensatz*) between "individual psychology" and "social psychology," Freud puts the fundamental opposition (also *Gegensatz*) between "narcissistic psychic acts" and "social psychic acts." This substitution has at least two consequences.

First, the question of the social bond is transformed into the question of the *relation to others*. According to Freud's argument, it is clear that if individual psychology can absorb social psychology, so to speak, this is because individual psychology already involves social psychic acts, which are not defined here except as relations to the other, the *Andere*: any relation to another person is a social relation, whoever the other may be (model, love object, adversary, and so on). Thus Freud is not emulating the sociologists by describing definite, established social relations; rather, he is seeking to work back toward the very possibility of social relations, a possibility that such relations necessarily presuppose. No sociality can be instituted before the opening toward others comes about, and whoever holds the key to that "before" also holds the key to everything that comes "after."

It would thus be quite mistaken to suppose that Freud is proposing to launch some sort of "sociology inspired by psychoanalysis." *Sociology* continues to be unable to account for the relation to others, since it fetishizes the pseudo-specificity of social relations. By returning toward the issue of the other, Freud intends, on the contrary, to establish a (psycho)sociology based on an archisociology that is ultimately no more and no less than *psychoanalysis*. There is no need to expand psychoanalysis or to "apply" it to the field of sociology; it is itself more sociological than any sociology, since relations with others—the *earliest* relations with others: parents, brothers and sisters, and so on—constitute the sole object of its studies.

This proposition is not new in Freud's writings: after all, the same statement provided the basis for the ontogenesis of social relations as Freud outlined it in the Schreber case, in the margins of his development of the concept of narcissism. Furthermore, there is no doubt that Freud is relying on his earlier analyses here, since the opposition he sets up between narcissistic psychic acts and social psychic acts presupposes, implicitly but straightforwardly, the identification of the latter with libidinal object cathexes. This, as we know, was Freud's major theoretical advance in his discussion of the Schreber case: narcissism is opposed to object love in the same way that a-sociality is opposed to sociality—or again, to go back to the terms used in "Thoughts for the Times on War and Death," in the same way that egoism is opposed to altruism. A great deal of knowledge about the social (archisocial) relation to others is thus enveloped in these few preliminary considerations. And it ought to suffice—such is the plan—to expose this knowledge so as to establish "social psychology" on a new basis: by replacing it with psychoanalysis.

Second, this substitution signifies that the opposition between "individual psychology" and "social psychology" comes back into play, more bluntly than ever, within psychoanalysis itself. For psycho-analysis clearly appropriates for itself both the field of "individual psychology" and that of "social psychology," once it unlocks the se-cret of the social psychic acts that constitute their common object. But then it is the domain (*Bereich*) of psychoanalysis itself that turns out to be split down the middle, following the line that separates narcissistic psychic acts from social psychic acts. Indeed, it soon be-comes apparent that this opposition only reproduces, in a more rad-ical form, the opposition between individual psychology and social psychology, especially because Freud first presents it in a simplified, rigid form; he seems to have forgotten everything that blurred, com-plicated, or even eliminated the distinction between narcissism and object orientation in "On Narcissism." For the psychology of nar-cissistic psychic acts is nothing if it is not the psychology of an in-dividual (an ego) that has for once managed to elude all sociality, all "influence," and all relation to others.

Thus the problem of the social bond is dismissed, only to reassert itself as an *intra-psychoanalytic* problem. It is one thing to method-ically reduce the question of the social bond to the question of the individual relation to others; it is something else again to solve the issue raised by that relation itself. This question (which is also the question raised by the "and" and the title "Group Psychology and the Analysis of the Ego") becomes inevitable as soon as the relation thus posited is charged with linking a narcissistic subject with an "object"—that is, an "ego" with an "alter." Since archisociology is in tandem with an egology, it cannot fail to collide with the powerful solipsism inherent in every egology: if the ego relates only to itself (and this is the case with the Freudian Narcissus), how can it ever be thought to enter into a relation with another in the strict sense, with an other, an *Andere*? How can "I" be thought to apprehend the other *as other*—that is, as (an)other "I," and so on? The Freudian definition of sociality only exacerbates the difficulty of the transition from "individual psychology" to "social psychology": far from dis-missing the opposition between the ego and the *socius*, it stresses their alterity instead. What intervenes here to block or inhibit the "reduction" begun by Freud is the narcissistic evidence, the (self-)

evidence of the subject. It is because Freud continues to operate in full view of that evidence, without confronting it, that the problem of the social bond remains a problem, and a problem of the "other."

Indeed, the "question of the other," with its classic inextricable complexity, only arises from the presupposition (the prior position) of the subject, and it is therefore a trick question, a trap. On the one hand, its very formulation precludes ever finding a solution for it;[3] on the other hand, it is constructed so as to preserve the subject itself from any questioning. As we shall see, it is precisely here that the ultimate issues of "Group Psychology and the Analysis of the Ego" are shaped. Perhaps we can now formulate these questions as follows: Does primary sociality begin in the stage of transition toward the object, of the face-to-face encounter with others? Or does it precede the *positioning* of others, which means the positioning of the ego as well? And in the second case, must we not imagine *that*, such a strange and unnameable thing for a problematics of the subject— a mass-ego, a primordial crowd—by means of which the analysis of the ego (psychoanalysis) would go well beyond itself, by *identifying* itself with (and as) mass psychology?

It is not yet time to raise these questions, however; and in any event, these are not the questions Freud addresses first. On the contrary, it is as if he were satisfied to have reduced the psychosociological problem to the problem of the individual's relation to the *Andere*, and as if the solution to the latter problem had already been provided by "psychoanalysis." That is why "Group Psychology" first appears to be a discussion—which is an attempt at destruction—of the theses of social psychology, rather than an intra-psychoanalytic exploration of the concepts of ego, narcissism, object, and so on. These concepts are taken for granted, presupposed as nonproblematic; they form the base on which Freud undertakes to give social psychology a new foundation. The principle behind the enterprise, expressed in the title of Chapter 4, "Suggestion and Libido," is a simple one. In brief, Freud's strategy is to summarize the various concepts used by social psychology under the heading of "suggestion"; he then replaces or translates that word by the terms "libido" or "love": "What we are offered as an explanation by authorities on sociology and group psychology is always the same, even though it is given various names, and that is—the magic word [*Zauberwort*] 'suggestion'" (p. 88).

This magic word, in the last analysis, is only a screen or shield designed to conceal love relations (p. 91). The translation of "suggestion" by "libido" plainly functions as an unveiling, and as such, it serves to unveil the reasons for "veiling" (resistance, repression). In short, it is a sort of psychoanalysis. Archisociology has no need to construct a new theory of the social bond; it needs only to reestablish the hidden truth of those that already exist, by translating them word for word into psychoanalytic terminology. This also means that psychoanalysis is saying the same thing as social psychology here, even though its terminology may differ.

We should point out in advance that Freud is not disputing the facts set forth by the "social psychologists"; he is merely proposing a new explanation for them, and in so doing he shows signs of a certain rivalrous *identification* with social psychology. At stake in this identification is nothing other (and nothing less) than the *identity* of psychoanalysis—that is, its capacity to differentiate itself from social psychology and to have the last word, to make the definitive statement. What would happen if the word "libido" proved incapable of translating the word "suggestion"? Or, worse still, if "suggestion" translated "libido"? Would psychoanalysis not be threatened with loss of its own identity? And could it still control the borders of its realm, the boundaries of its property?

But we are getting ahead of ourselves. First, we need to know precisely with whom Freud is competing. With quite a number of people, it would seem: with Gustave Le Bon and William Mc-Dougall first of all (he devotes his second and third chapters, respectively, to their work), and also, though less directly, with Tarde. (Trotter is only mentioned at a later stage of the analysis, since he makes no use of the concept of suggestion and, for the time being, Freud intends to debate only the "magicians.") Is it a coincidence that Le Bon appears first? Among all these psychosociologists who are already very close to psychoanalysis, Le Bon is closest of all: "We have made use of Le Bon's description by way of introduction, because it fits in so well with our own psychology in the emphasis which it lays upon unconscious mental life" (p. 82).

Upon what does this proximity depend? First of all, on the way the problem of sociality is addressed. Le Bon's approach was intended to be psychological, and his *The Crowd* (*Psychologie des foules*, 1895) has often been considered the inaugural work of social psychology.[4] In particular, Le Bon's psychology is a psychology of regression, which makes his work especially close to Freud's. Like Freud, Le Bon uses "pathological" states as the key to decoding "normalcy." The two share a common conviction (along with the vast majority of late-nineteenth-century psychologists) that the pathological return to a previous state bears witness to the existence of a stage of ontogenetic and phylogenetic development that has been surpassed (that is, integrated and by the same token recovered). "Pathological," in this sense, does not mean abnormal; on the contrary, it is archinormality itself, primary normality. And the origin (the essence) can thus be read in the symptom.

Le Bon's social psychology thus logically took the form of a psychology of crowds and not of institutions. For Le Bon, the crowd is to the social and political realm what pathological states are to the realm of normalcy—in other words, its buried truth. Beneath the civilized individual there lies the "barbarian" or "primitive"; behind "people" there lurks the crowd and "primitive communism";[5] behind the statesman, finally, we find the "leader." The idea, then, is that the crowd—seemingly a marginal phenomenon or even a transgressive one with respect to normal sociality—manifests the deepest essence of normal sociality better than social institutions do. This is Freud's hypothesis as well, and his approach is exactly the same: virtually all the examples invoked in "Group Psychology" (girls in boarding schools, instances of collective "idolatry," the primal horde, and so on) are examples of "psychological crowds" in Le Bon's sense.

Indeed, when Freud appears to be countering Le Bon, in Chapter 5, with examples of "artificial," "highly organized" crowds with a leader, as opposed to the elementary, unorganized, and "leaderless" crowds to which Le Bon limits himself, there is a good deal of bad faith involved, as we shall see. On the one hand, Le Bon does not believe in the possibility of a leaderless crowd any more than Freud does (a whole chapter of Le Bon's book is devoted to this problem); and on the other hand, among the "artificial crowds" that Freud himself analyzes (the Church and the Army), he retains only what he needs to define them as "elementary crowds" (a unanimous group plus a leader). Moreover, the fact that he speaks of "crowds" with regard to the Church and the Army is significant in itself: even when he turns toward differentiated, structured, hierarchical, and stable collective formations, Freud is only interested in what constitutes their common basis; and on this point he ends up in complete agreement with Le Bon: this common basis—sociality reduced to the zero degree, as it were—is the crowd, the *Masse*. Archisociology will thus necessarily take the form of a crowd psychology or (to revert to Jankélevitch's misreading, which is ultimately a useful one) a mass psychoanalysis.

But Freud's proximity to Le Bon does not end here. According to Le Bon, crowd psychology is not only a regressive psychology, it is also a psychology of the unconscious. To regress is to go back toward the archaic unconscious: the crowd lays bare the "unconscious substratum" that all its members have in common and through which they belong to a single "race." This accounts for the abolition of individual distinctive features (but these are also *social* distinctive features: class, profession, and so on) in favor of what Le Bon calls the "mental unity" or the "soul" of the crowd. The crowd acts as a single individual, because its members are driven by the same ancestral unconscious:

Our conscious acts are the outcome of an unconscious substratum created in the mind in the main by hereditary influences. This substratum consists of the innumerable common characteristics handed down from generation to generation, which constitute the genius of a race. . . . It is more especially with respect to those unconscious elements which constitute the genius of a race that all the individuals belonging to it resemble each other, while it is principally in respect to the conscious elements of their character—the fruit of education, and yet more of exceptional hereditary conditions—that they differ from each other. . . . It is precisely these general qualities of character, governed by forces of which we are unconscious, and possessed by the majority of the normal individuals of a race in much the same degree—it is precisely these qualities, I say, that in crowds become common property. In the collective mind the intellectual aptitudes of the individuals, and in consequence their individuality, are weakened. The heterogeneous is swamped by the homogeneous, and the unconscious qualities obtain the upper hand.[6]

Thus Le Bon and Freud use the very same term. The same term need not mean the same concept, however. As Freud hastens to point out in a note, Le Bon's unconscious covers the realm of the unrepressed unconscious—"the 'archaic heritage' of the human mind" ("Group Psychology," p. 75)—but he still lacks the idea of a repressed unconscious. Apart from that detail (an essential one, to be sure), the two views of the unconscious are very much alike, and Freud does nothing, at least at first, to attenuate their similarity. Not only does he subscribe unreservedly to Le Bon's description of crowd phenomena, but he also concedes that Le Bon's terms "harmonize well with the fundamental postulates of our own depth psychology" (p. 73).

Thus Freud sets about conscientiously translating (that is, appropriating) Le Bon's crowd psychology into psychoanalytic terminology. The translation is astonishingly easy: the crowd is impervious to contradiction, to logical argumentation; credulous, it knows neither doubt nor degrees of conviction; it cannot be restrained, for it tolerates no lapse between desire and its realization, to the point of being careless about its own preservation; the only reality it recognizes is psychic reality (image, illusion, the "magic word"). But surely psychology had recognized all these features long ago in the unconscious primary processes? It seems, then, that at the end of this enumeration the matter is settled: crowd psychology is nothing but the psychology of the unconscious, as Freud had described it on the basis of individual neuroses and dreams. The unconscious, in other words, is the archaic group, sociality or collectivity. (And the only question left is *in what sense* the unconscious is [the] collective. Is the unconscious collective because it is common to all individuals—in which case collective psychology would indeed fall "within the limits of individual psychology," as Freud clearly intends to prove? Or because it is *in itself* "communitarian" or, to borrow Bataille's term, "communial"—in which case collective psychology would go beyond the internal boundaries of individual psychology? We shall see.)

What, then, is the basis for Freud's disagreement with Le Bon, since there does appear to be some disagreement? As we have just seen, it does not involve Le Bon's psychological description, nor does it bear upon the word "unconscious." Instead, it concerns the *concept* of the unconscious as Le Bon uses it. And we still need to make clear that Freud is not objecting to the "hereditary" unconscious. Le Bon's unconscious, except for the biological racism, is Freud's as well. This is obvious from the remainder of "Group Psychology," in which the hypothesis of an unconscious patrimony transmitted phylogenetically plays a large part. Freud's opposition has much more to do with the basis—or rather the lack of basis—of Le Bon's theory of the unconscious, namely, the theory of hypnotic suggestion.

The theoretical "regression" set forth in *The Crowd* did not end with the "unconscious substratum," the "racial soul." For Le Bon, the "racial soul" already marks a first degree of crowd *organization*. It may well be older, more archaic, than the individual subjects it melds into a whole, but it is still a "soul"—that is, a *subjectivity*, albeit a supra-individual one. Since it is the same for all individuals, it is what gives them the unity and identity of a "people," with its own characteristics, its own traditions, and especially its own "ideal" (the term is again the same as Freud's): "At times no doubt [the race] will still be a crowd, but henceforth, beneath the mobile and changing characteristics of crowds, is found a solid substratum, the genius of the race which confines within narrow limits the transformations of a nation and overrules the play of chance."[7]

But underneath the race, as its hybrid and monstrous base, there is the crowd, the horde of barbarians whose "only common bond . . . is the half-recognized law of a chief"[8] and whose menacing return Le Bon prophesies. And that crowd, unlike the race and the people, has no identity of its own. It is profoundly "anonymous,"[9] even unnameable. The racial unconscious was still a *substratum*, a *subjectum*—"solid," stable, permanent, identifiable. The crowd's unconscious is entirely different, first of all because it has no content of its own. The paradox of the crowd is such that its homogenization is based not on a common ground but on the absence of any "subjectal" ground. Le Bon insists strongly on this, at the very point where he is attempting to shore up the thesis of the crowd's supra-individual "soul": "If the individuals of a crowd confined them-selves to putting in common the ordinary qualities of which each of them has his share, there would merely result the striking of an av-erage, and not, as we have said is actually the case, the creation of new characteristics. . . . Different causes determine the appearance of these characteristics peculiar to crowds."[10]

Now how are these "new characteristics" defined, as distinct from inherited-unconscious qualities? Precisely by their total lack of spec-ificity. Le Bon lists three features—"a sentiment of invincible power," mental "contagion," and "suggestibility"; the second and third (the most decisive, in his argument) are manifestly non-characteristics, or nonspecific characteristics. In fact, to say that "opinions" and "sentiments" are spread through the crowd by con-tagion is to say both that no members of the crowd draw these opin-ions and sentiments from their own reserves, and that the crowd as a whole receives them from without, like a virus. And to say that the crowd is suggestible is to say the same thing all over again: as Freud points out in his summary of *The Crowd*, "suggestibility" designates nothing but contamination by suggestions that come from "another source" ("Group Psychology," p. 76).

Thus there will be as many crowds as there are suggested opinions and feelings, and this means that a crowd has no identity of its own (it has no "soul"). It is impossible to define crowds except through their "impulsiveness," their "mobility" and their "irritability," and of course their "femininity" (hysteria and bacchanalia are waiting in the wings).[11] It is just as impossible to speak of an unconscious *of* the crowd. The crowd does not *have* an unconscious (an inherited, archaic unconscious), simply because it is not a subject or an aggre-gate of subjects. At the very most, the crowd may be said to *be* the unconscious "itself," the crowd-unconscious or the mass-unconscious: neither substratum nor substructure, but rather a soft, malleable, plastic, infinitely receptive material without will or desire or any specific instinct of its own. A matrical mass: the group as womb.

It is clearer now in what sense Le Bon's psychology of the un-conscious is a "social" psychology, and in what sense, too, it differs profoundly from Freud's. The Freudian unconscious characterizes desires, representations, fantasies of an essentially monadic subject (Freud speaks, for example, of the "narcissistic asocial productions of dreams" ["An Autobiographical Study," *SE* 20: 65]). Le Bon's unconscious, however, is indissolubly nonsubjectal and "social," to the extent that he never designates anything but immediate communion with others (their representations, desires, affects) prior to any consciousness of self, and thus also prior to any consciousness of others. Taken to the extreme, it is thought transmission, telepathy.[12] The transfusion or merging of subjects is such, here, that one can no longer speak of communication (feelings, opinions, but also "communication between unconsciousnesses") because there are simply no more subjects communicating among themselves: the members of the crowd are merely *mediums* controlled (entranced, possessed) by suggestion.

The model underlying Le Bon's description is significant: it is the hypnotic trance, the sleepwalker given over, body and soul, to the hypnotist's suggestions (motor, perceptual, sensory, and so on). Can a more perfect, more complete osmosis be imagined between "self" and "other"? (We need the quotation marks here: under hypnosis, *I* no longer distinguish myself from the other—I *am* the other.) In particular, can a more striking illustration of the unconscious be imagined? The sleepwalker instantly carries out the hypnotist's suggestions, without being present "himself" to "his" own representations. The other's discourse might be said to function in him without him (and yet it is "he"), and irresistibly.

It remains an understatement to say that hypnosis *illustrates* the fact of the unconscious. For Le Bon, it constitutes, rather, the paradigm of the unconscious. We must not forget that Le Bon's era (and that of the "young Freud," 1895) is the era of the great equation between hypnosis and the unconscious. The works of Charcot, Liébeault, and Bernheim had just rehabilitated Mesmer's old "animal magnetism" and had aroused extraordinary enthusiasm from which Freud, as we know (or rather, as many do not know) was not exempt.[13] In these writings readers discovered with amazement the possibility of a *psychological* unconscious (or, to use Janet's terms, an "automatism"). For hypnosis seemed to take subjects back toward an unmistakably psychic activity that nevertheless lacked the quality of consciousness: it was automatic, reflexive, involuntary, passive.[14] Hypnosis, as Bernheim explained, bears witness to the initial psychology of the individual, which is a psychology of the unconscious. Before it is consciousness (consciousness of self, reflexivity), the brain is a pliable material, a sort of wax that accommodates "ideas" ("suggestions") from elsewhere. As for hypnosis itself, it can never be anything but a regression (a particularly spectacular one that can be reproduced experimentally) to that state of native receptivity called "suggestibility."[15]

Le Bon draws on this whole set of hypotheses, and from this point of view his construction is hardly original, except that he "applies" suggestion theory to sociology and in the process makes plain its most important (though also its most problematic) implication. For what is the psychology of the hypnotized patient (unconscious-archaic psychology) if it is not, in fact, a "social psychology"? The relation to others is inscribed in it from the outset, in the form of the strange relation (without relation) of hypnotic suggestion: the hypnotized person is a non-individual, a quasi-individual, since he is literally penetrated by (the discourse of) the other; and if there is an unconscious, in this instance, it must be said, strictly speaking, to belong to no subject (it comes from the other, through the other).

In short, hypnosis provided the highly paradoxical model of a pre-individual, pre-subjective psychology. Consequently, it sufficed to go beyond the framework of two-party hypnosis (a two-member *crowd*, as Freud later says, not at all coincidentally) in order to end up with the collective hypnosis that, according to Le Bon, defines archaic sociality and psychology: that is to say—and now we understand why—archaic sociality *as* archaic psychology:

We know to-day that by various processes an individual may be brought into such a condition that, having entirely lost his conscious personality, he obeys all the suggestions of the operator who has deprived him of it, and commits acts in utter contradiction with his character and habits. The most careful observations seem to prove that an individual immerged for some length of time in a crowd in action soon finds himself—either in consequence of the magnetic influence given out by the crowd, or from some other cause of which we are ignorant—in a special state, which much resembles the state of fascination in which the hypnotised individual finds himself in the hand of the hypnotiser. . . . He is no longer conscious of his acts. In his case, as in the case of the hypnotised subject, at the same time that certain faculties are destroyed, others may be brought to a high degree of exaltation. Under the influence of a suggestion, he will undertake the accomplishment of certain acts with irresistible impetuosity. This impetuosity is the more irresistible in the case of crowds than in that of the hypnotised subject, from the fact that, the suggestion being the same for all the individuals of the crowd, it gains in strength by reciprocity.[16]

This, then, would be the origin both of society and of the individual—the *primordial crowd*, of which every crowd would constitute the reappearance or the repetition: something like a hypnotic, somnambulic, undifferentiated magma, spurred into action (or rather agitation) by suggestions. In other words, everything would start with suggestion. But it is immediately obvious that this "origin" gets carried away beyond itself, and that in the last analysis it is incapable of originating anything whatsoever. On the one hand, the crowd gives rise to no individual, no subject, since it brings us back to a psychology that antedates all individual psychology (we can scarcely speak yet, here, of "psychology," for example, of a "crowd psychology"); on the other hand, it is impossible for the crowd to give rise to a society—at least if we mean by that a totality or a political body with the characteristics of a supra-individuality (autonomy, sovereignty, and so on). For there is no doubt that the members of the crowd form a homogeneous whole, to the extent that they are moved to action by the same suggestions; however, their unity comes from elsewhere, from an "other source." Since members of a crowd are, by definition, incapable of acting and thinking by themselves, suggestions always come to them from "without," from an "other," and this means that none of them can ever be *at the origin* of the *initial* suggestion (the suggestion that is propagated by contagion, unifying the mass).

Whether applied to the "individual" or the "collective" order (but it undermines this very opposition), suggestion theory finally refers back to an unassignable, impossible origin. No more than the "I" can be at the beginning of itself can the crowd (the "we") institute itself on its own (and still less can it manage itself) as a social body or political entity. The instituting suggestion, if there is one, has to come to it from the outside (thus preventing the crowd from closing in on itself at the very moment when the suggestion imparts to it a unity and an identity), and from an "outside" which is itself already transcended by a prior suggestion (since according to the hypothesis, whoever makes the suggestion must first have received it from another source, and so on: it is impossible to *fix* the limit or the external boundary of the crowd or group, of the whole).

Exempt from any beginning or *principium*, the crowd thus eludes any principality or leadership. This is another way of saying that no subject will ever emerge from the initial magma and that no leader who might come forth from the heart of the crowd could ever dominate or subject it. Since subjection (a-subjectivity, suggestibility) is the rule, where would the leader get the authority, mastery, independence, or will (personal, individual will) to dominate? Nothing, in the hypothesis of primal suggestion, ultimately authorizes the institution of any sort of political power—that is, the self-institution or self-performance of a subject (a Narcissus) advancing to say "I want," "I order," "Obey!" and so on.

The crowd, in short, is defined by unpower. Which does not mean by the *absence* of power. Unpower is precisely not untrammeled freedom, as might too readily be assumed. If the members of the crowd are barred from all authority, it is *to the very extent (and this is the paradox) that they lack any freedom to give up*. Alienation comes first; it is no longer even a question of wondering about the origin of submission (interest? desire? voluntary servitude?), nor about how power, Politics, the State are instituted (by contract? by force? and so on). All these classic questions of political philosophy are discouraged here in advance, undermined in their very principle. For if subjection is the origin, there is no origin for subjection, nor, by the same token, is there primordial power. Because the command (the suggestive injunction) is always already older than the subjects it directs, it belongs to no one. No one can appropriate it—that is, *begin* to command. Thus there is no starting point to commandment, and there is no commandment: the "primordial" crowd—this ought to be the strict consequence of suggestion theory—is archaic an-archy, primal (a)politics.

Such ought to be, such ought to have been the consequence. However, Le Bon retreats, quite significantly, at the very point where he might have drawn this conclusion (which is in fact an untenable one:

it makes neither an end nor a beginning). Everything is blocked, in *The Crowd*, at the point where a leader, a *Führer*, is peremptorily assigned. Crowds, according to the *leadership thesis*, want a master. More precisely, crowds want nothing, therefore they have a master. "Men gathered in a crowd lose all force of will, and turn instinctively to the person who possesses the quality they lack";[17] that person's will then becomes the general will, "the nucleus around which the opinions of the crowd are grouped and attain to identity."[18] In other words, the mere fact of having a will confers on the leader a power that is all the more absolute (Le Bon says "despotic") in that it meets no opposition—and here we have *hypnotic* power, "suggestive capacity," or "prestige," a mysterious quality that provokes "sentiments . . . of the same kind as the fascination to which a magnetised person is subjected."[19]

Le Bon thus by no means neglects the role of leader, as Freud claims with persistent bad faith, any more than he leaves the hypnotist out of the picture.[20] Rather, the contrary is true: the thesis of the hypnotist-leader is all the more explicit, in Le Bon, in that it comes up in the manner of a *Diktat* and is exhausted, finally, in dogmatic and definitively mysterious assertions: "there is leadership," "there is magnetic prestige." For where does the "first" leader get his will? By what miracle has this strong individuality emerged from the primordial crowd? We remain in the dark about this.[21] The thesis is set forth, it is not proved; and it is set forth *because* it is not proved.

Now this gesture, in its very brutality, should interest us considerably, if only because it is also found in Freud: the figure of the hypnotist-leader also constitutes the final example of "Group Psychology," and it arises just as abruptly, artificially, dictatorially. Since the motivations behind the gesture are the same in both cases, as we shall see, it is worth lingering over briefly, even if we get ahead of ourselves in the process.

First of all, the gesture is a profoundly political one, a sort of coup de force or coup d'état that comes down violently in favor of power, against unpower. Despite the obvious fascination that they hold for him, Le Bon is afraid of crowds (they are barbarian, fanatic, blind, and so on). And his fear is not only, as some have said, that of a reactionary thinker confronting revolutionary masses (the Commune is not long past, and before it the French revolution). Much more fundamentally, it is fear of an-archy as such, and of the vertigo that it threatens to provoke. Hence the reaction, the abrupt about-face. A leader is *required* in order to dominate and control the otherwise unmasterable unleashing of the crowd.[22] "There is leadership" translates this "requirement": better an absolute and total power than an absence of power. This is a classic argument (used by all tyrannies), but it brings us back, here, to the extreme limit of the Political, to the point where the Political, in all senses, is decided. In fact, it is at the threshold of the formless (undecidable) threat of chaos that, in Le Bon's text, the figure of the Leader arises as a last resort and ultimate guarantee of the cohesion of the social body. Only the *figure* of the leader is capable of giving form to chaos—and it is the political form.

Or the Subject-form, for the Leader, as we have just seen, is a subject. Strictly speaking, he is even *the* subject. First of all because there is a *single* "strong will," a single hypnotist. (What would happen if there were two, or several?) Then because the crowd is identified entirely with this leader; it constitutes a body or unanimous mass, acts as *a single man*, and so on. Political unity is equivalent here, strictly speaking, to the unity of a subject. The crowd has a "soul" (that is the "law of the mental unity of crowds"), and that "soul" is the Leader. Thus it is apparent that *Le Bon brings forth the Political and the Subject in one and the same gesture.* There would be no body politic if there were no individual at the outset; and if this is so, it is because the body politic is defined as a supra-individual. This complicity between the political form and the Subject-form, found in Freud's writing as well as in Le Bon's (and not there alone: this complicity underlies the modern concept of the Political), has to be examined at this point. It allows us to foresee that everything that threatens the schema of the Subject in one way or another will also threaten the Political. And vice versa.

We shall have ample evidence in what follows of the extent to which "Group Psychology," in its deepest logic and even in its literality, reintroduces the theses of *The Crowd* concerning the hypnotist-leader. Why is it, then, that Freud's criticisms bear precisely on this part of Le Bon's argument? In fact, it is in a recollection of the leadership theory that he concludes his summary of *The Crowd* and then declares his dissatisfaction:

What Le Bon says on the subject of leaders of groups is less exhaustive, and does not enable us to make out an underlying principle so clearly. . . . Le Bon does not give the impression of having succeeded in bringing the function of the leader and the importance of prestige completely into harmony with his brilliantly executed picture of the group mind. ["Group Psychology," pp. 80–81]

Why this reticence? Is it because Freud sees the forced and arbitrary character of the leadership theory too clearly? Is it so he can invoke a theory of leaderless groups, a theory of the social bond that is finally *acephalous*? Not at all. Freud disagrees so little with Le Bon as to the need for recognizing a Leader at the origin and head of the social body that he never ceases to reproach him, quite oddly, for not having insisted enough on this point. It is not to the organico-political structure of the crowd (of society) that he objects; quite the contrary. He does not disagree with Le Bon about this, but only about the theory Le Bon proposes to account for it, in other words, the theory of suggestion.

The Suggest

> sug · gest, tr. v. [Latin *suggerere* (past participle *suggestus*), to carry or put underneath, furnish, suggest: *sub-*, underneath + *gerere*, to carry]
>
> sub · ject, adj., n., tr. v. [Middle English *su(b)get*, *subject*, from Old French *su(b)get*, from Latin *subicere* (past participle *subjectus*), to bring under: *sub-*, under + *jacere*, to throw]
>
> American Heritage Dictionary

In Chapter 4 of "Group Psychology," Freud's argument begins to crystallize around suggestion theory. Power (and, by extension, society) cannot be explained by the suggestive "prestige" of the leader or, conversely, by the "suggestibility" of those who are led. Such explanations explain nothing, in Freud's view. Le Bon is the immediate object of his criticism, of course, but Tarde and McDougall (to whom Chapter 3 was devoted) are also included: Tarde's "imitation" and McDougall's "sympathetic induction of emotion" are nothing but synonyms for "suggestion." We shall not take the time to confirm the validity of this last statement: it could be demonstrated in detail, but the process would be tedious and pointless. With these writers, as with Le Bon, everything converges toward the magic word, the *Zauberwort*, "suggestion"[23]—that is, toward the word and theory proposed by Bernheim. Freud's objections, from this point on, are ready at hand: after all, psychoanalysis had refuted the theory and practice of suggestion from the beginning. Indeed, was it not by rejecting suggestion that psychoanalysis had constituted itself *as* psychoanalysis? Does not this very rejection embody the Freudian break with the past? Everything seems to boil down to a familiar quarrel: psychoanalysis contesting its own prehistory. Now that the testimony is in and the principal culprit identified, the trial of magic can begin. The charges against it are twofold; they involve both the use of hypnosis for therapeutic purposes and the concept of suggestion.

First, hypnotic suggestion as practiced by Bernheim is tyrannical, violent, and unjust, because it subjugates or "subjects." Freud's forceful accusation is deontological—that is, ethico-political—in nature, and he grounds it in the rights of free subjectivity: Bernheim's patients "certainly had a right to counter-suggestions if people were trying to subdue [them] with suggestions" ("Group Psychology," p. 89). The declaration of patients' rights of course recalls the whole series of "technical" motifs Freud cites elsewhere to justify the abandonment of hypnotic therapy (the incapacity of hypnosis to overcome resistances or to prevent the return of symptoms, and so on). But there is more, in the liberal or libertarian tone that surfaces here—a tone that illuminates Freud's technical innovations at least as much as it is justified by them. Let us recall that the fundamental rules of psychoanalytic technique all stem from what has to be called an anti-authoritarian politics. Thus the decision to abandon hypnosis in order to focus treatment on "free associations" and the analysis of resistances is always ultimately justified by the need to free the subject's (unconscious) discourse from all outside influence. Hypnotic suggestion, on the contrary, does violence to the unconscious, imprinting something on it from without (*per via di porre*) rather than patiently removing (*per via de levare*) the internal obstacles that prevent the subject from reappropriating it as its *own* unconscious.[24]

The same is true of the prescription directing the analyst to refrain from intervening in the patient's daily life and to abstain from direct instruction: this rule, too, is aimed at preserving the patient's freedom, by preventing analysis from deteriorating once again into suggestion.[25] In this sense, psychoanalytic treatment is always opposed to suggestive therapy as an enterprise of liberation is opposed to an enterprise of subjection (whether or not this is actually true is a question we shall not attempt to answer here). The stakes are clearly political, and it is no accident that Freud speaks of the "tyranny of suggestion" (p. 89): at the origin of psychoanalysis we find something like a revolt or an uprising against the hypnotist's unjustifiable power. We must keep this in mind when Freud invites us to view society in its essence as a horde subjected to a tyrannical and hypnotizing Father. Do we then find a contradiction, a radical break with the de-alienating thrust of psychoanalysis? No; we find, rather, an underlying continuity within a single "politics of the subject," to borrow a term from Lacoue-Labarthe and Nancy.

Second, suggestion, a totalitarian and omni-explanatory concept, does not explain itself. Presented by Bernheim as a "fundamental fact in the mental life of man" (p. 89), it is actually baseless, rather like the box from which the magician draws the rabbit. Suggestion works in a void, it does not hold up: "Christopher bore Christ; Christ bore the whole world; Say, where did Christopher then put his foot?" (p. 89, n. 3).

Freud's irony here is fierce and bitter; it is kindled, as we can see, by the fear of a kind of bottomless pit. Freud prefers to have his feet on the ground, and this means that there must *be* a ground, a base, a foundation, a *subjectum*. Like Descartes in the second *Meditation*, Freud requires an Archimedean point, "a fixed and sure point" on the basis of which the "terrestrial Globe" can be "pulled from its place." And like Descartes, he looks for it in what is, properly speaking, for Decartes' descendents, *the* solid ground, *the* foundation: the subject. Not, of course, in the subject of the *Cogito*, but in the subject of the *libido*: in desire.

The rest of Chapter 4 tells us that *underneath* hypnosis, *under-*

neath suggestion, there is libido, love. For if the subject allows himself to be hypnotized, if he agrees to let himself be possessed this way by the hypnotist, it must be because, somewhere deep down inside, he desires this and derives pleasure from it. His servitude somehow has to be voluntary. It must be. What would be inexplicable, unacceptable (the theoretical requirement of the foundation cannot be dissociated from the ethical prescription of freedom) would be the absence of anyone to want or desire anything at all—except the strange and disquieting *suggect* of hypnosis, always already in submission, subjected to the will of another. "Even then," in 1889, that had awakened in Freud a silent opposition, a "suppressed hostility," a sort of resistance or counter-suggestion arising from the depths of his being.

We must linger a moment over the tone of these objections, for, very strangely, in this passage Freud's remarks never go beyond the bounds of mere indignation. This is all the more peculiar given that Freud's passionate quarrel with Bernheim quite obviously reproduces the founding scene of psychoanalysis: the abandonment of suggestive psychotherapy and the cathartic method in favor of free associations, the repudiation of the "hypnoid" unconscious in favor of a dynamic and repressed unconscious, a waning of interest in "artificial sleep" in favor of analysis of "spontaneous dreams," and so on. Freud might have been expected to formulate arguments, to justify his reticences, to advance facts that would contradict Bernheim's theory. He does not do so. Why not? One answer, of course, is that he does not need to do so, since he is implicitly relying on a critique that has already been developed elsewhere; in short, Freud would be alluding to what is already "well known" in psychoanalysis. And yet, can we be sure of this? Do we really know what psychoanalysis defined itself *against*, and why? Hypnotic suggestion had undoubtedly been relegated to the obscurity that bordered and preceded psychoanalysis. But precisely *as obscurity*: it had been rejected with no one the wiser as to exactly *what* had been rejected. Freud acknowledges this in a strangely inconclusive passage that directly follows the attack on Bernheim: "Now that I once more approach the riddle of suggestion after having kept away from it for some thirty years, I find there is no change in the situation. . . . But there has been no explanation of the nature of suggestion, that is, of the conditions under which influence without adequate logical foundation takes place" (pp. 89–90).

Freud is speaking here of "the literature of the last thirty years," but what he is saying applies to psychoanalytical literature as well. Nothing seems to justify taking this passage as a simple rhetorical transition in which Freud might be feigning ignorance, the better to dissipate it later on. Hypnotic suggestion is indeed the name of a riddle (in Chap. 10 it is called a *Rätselwort*), something mystical and mysterious (*mystisch*: Chap. 9), uncanny (*unheimlich*: Chap. 10). Freud claims to have kept his distance from this riddle. Thus the initial irony turns back against its source; the *Zauberwort* returns as *Rätselwort*. The magic has not been dispelled, it has only been avoided, rather as one avoids a haunted site inhabited by phantoms and ghosts. Hypnosis was abandoned, in other words, not because suggestion theory had been incorporated within a more powerful theory; rather, it was abandoned by virtue of a denial, a rejection, a suppressed hostility that was obscure, so to speak, to itself. Freud simply wished to hear nothing further on the subject of hypnosis. Now the refusal to confront a riddle obviously does not constitute an epistemological break. At most, it constitutes a repudiation, a *Verwerfung*, we might say, if the concept of *Verwerfung* were not perhaps ill-suited to account for the effects of return, *revenance*, or haunting that here threaten psychoanalysis at its very core.

For it must be understood that hypnotic suggestion had returned *into* psychoanalysis, *as* psychoanalysis. The dependence of the hypnotized subject on the hypnotist; the establishment of an elective, exclusive, somnambulic bond; suggestibility; even thought transmission[26]—all this had come back up, at the very core of analytic treatment, in the form of transference. Freud says so himself, in a relevant passage of the *Introductory Lectures* that deserves to be cited here. The passage is fully as ambivalent, as inconclusive, as aporia-laden as the one just cited:

A capacity for directing libidinal object-cathexes on to people must of course be attributed to every normal person. The tendency to transference of . . . neurotics . . . is only an extraordinary increase of this universal characteristic. . . . Bernheim, with an unerring eye, based his theory of hypnotic phenomena on the thesis that everyone is in some way "suggestible." His suggestibility was nothing other than the tendency to transference, somewhat too narrowly conceived, so that it did not include negative transference. But Bernheim was never able to say what suggestion actually was and how it came about. For him it was a fundamental fact on whose origin he could throw no light. He did not know that his *suggestibilité* depended on sexuality, on the activity of the libido. *And it must dawn on us that in our technique we have abandoned hypnosis only to rediscover suggestion in the shape of transference.* [*Introductory Lectures, SE* 16: 446; emphasis added]

That last sentence is disconcerting, and it brings the argument to a halt—for a long time, it would seem.[27] For just where does the last instance originate? In transference (libido)? Or in suggestion? What translates or transfers what? If transference translates suggestion and if suggestion translates transference, what are we to make of this reciprocal translatability, this conceptual *mimesis*? Does it not threaten to undermine our confidence in a unidirectional translation, and at the same time our confidence in this science of translation (of transference, displacement, deformation, and so on) that is called psychoanalysis? In particular, does it not threaten to make psychoanalysis definitively opaque to itself? For if transference and suggestion are one and the same thing under two different names, the "riddle" of suggestion inevitably contaminates transference and all that this word (this *Rätselwort*? this *Zauberwort*?) governs in psychoanalysis—namely, everything, in a sense: psychoanalysis as a whole.

It is clear that the stakes of Freud's argument with Bernheim and social psychology are nontrivial. In brief, the very originality of psychoanalysis is at stake: its capacity to resolve the issue of the origin and basis of suggestion once and for all, and hence to resolve the issue of the origin and basis of psychoanalysis itself. This issue has *not* been resolved, contrary to what Freud's irony and nonchalance might lead us to think: thirty years later, suggestion still remains a riddle for psychoanalysis. It might be expected, then, that having reached this point, Freud would confront the riddle, would linger near the Sphinx. But he does no such thing. No sooner has the riddle been recognized than it is sidestepped, exorcized. The paragraph that follows abandons hypnotic suggestion to its oblivion in order to move on to the familiar concept of libido, "a concept which has done us such good service in the study of psychoneuroses" ("Group Psychology," p. 90).

In objection, it will no doubt be argued that the opposite is true and that Freud, far from seeking to avoid the difficulty, calls upon libido to solve the riddle. Of course; we have no intention of denying this. For Freud, it is a matter of dissipating the mystery of hypnotic suggestion by returning it to its libidinal base, and this is consistent with everything he said on this topic. As early as 1890, in "Psychical (or Mental) Treatment," he had sketched out a parallel between hypnosis and love.[28] This parallel was transformed into an explanatory theory when the episode of Anna O.'s nervous pregnancy and other manifestations of "transference-love" allowed him to grasp the erotic nature of the "mysterious element that was at work behind hypnosis," as he explains in "An Autobiographical Study" (*SE* 20: 27). Scattered remarks in his discussion of the Dora case,[29] in "Three Essays on the Theory of Sexuality,"[30] in "Five Lectures on Psycho-Analysis" (*SE* 11: 51), and so on, had expanded on that idea, which Ferenczi systematized, in 1909, in "Transference and Introjection":[31] hypnosis, in this view, is a transference—that is, a reproduction or "re-edition"—operating by means of a displacement onto the doctor's person of an older attachment or libidinal bond. All these issues had been settled long ago. But in that case, why the term "riddle"? Once again, Freud's perplexity is not feigned, as what follows will show, for it reintroduces not a riddle that has been solved, but one that remains intact.

This is another way of saying that it remains a riddle *for libido theory*. In this sense, we are not claiming that Freud does not attempt to solve the problem; rather, we are emphasizing the strangeness of the procedure that leads him to put forward a solution—the libidinal solution—whose failure he has just implicitly acknowledged. For the problem, here, is manifestly the solution. Would it not have been better, then, to change the solution, in order to avoid a situation in which the riddle would come up later on, even more implacable, even more incontrovertible? Most enigmatic of all is Freud's insistence on invoking a solution that is condemned in advance to failure. Must one not suspect that behind his inconsistency we may find the very tenacious consistency of a resistance? A resistance of the ego, as always?

Political Love

> He who thus domineers over you has only two eyes, only two hands, only one body, no more than is possessed by the least man among the infinite numbers dwelling in your cities; he has indeed nothing more than the power that you confer upon him to destroy you. Where has he acquired enough eyes to spy upon you, if you do not provide them yourselves? How can he have so many arms to beat you with, if he does not borrow them from you? The feet that trample down your cities, where does he get them if they are not your own? How does he have any power over you except through you?
>
> Etienne de la Boétie, *Discourse on Voluntary Servitude*

> L'Etat, c'est moi.
>
> Louis XIV

These questions must be left unresolved for a time. They will come up again soon enough. For the moment, let us look at the "solution" Freud has to offer. And let us not forget that he undertakes all his analyses in an effort to solve what he calls once again, in Chapter 8, "the riddle . . . of the constitution of groups" ("Group Psychology," p. 193). The same riddle is posed in both contexts: the riddle of suggestive "influence." Since the concept of libido has made it possible, according to Freud's hypothesis, to solve the problem at the level of individual psychology, it ought to suffice—here is the supplementary hypothesis—to apply this same concept to group psychology. The reasoning is simple: Freud's explanation now focuses not on the hypnotist's power, but rather—prior to any notion of suggestibility, prior to any influence of the other on the ego—on the desire that presides over submission, that is, over the collective desire of the individual. The key to collective psychology is to be sought, following the essay's preliminary definitions, in individual psychology. Here we have Freud's new hypothesis: "We will try our fortune, then, with the supposition that love relationships (or, to use a more neutral expression, emotional ties) also constitute the essence of the group mind" (p. 91).

But what is a love relationship?

In particular, what is a bond of affection, an emotional tie? Is it the same thing as an erotic, libidinal bond, as Freud's parenthesis suggests? We cannot yet say. All that can be said for the time being is that the second expression is "more neutral"—as Strachey's interpretive translation puts it—than the first. The reference to sexuality in the second expression is vaguer and looser, we might say. Freud has just emphasized this a few lines earlier, as if he were already anticipating an objection: the concept of libido is borrowed from the theory of affectivity (*Affektivitätslehre*, a term he uses rather seldom), and it has to be understood here in an encompassing, "broadened" sense. It designates the energy of the various instincts grouped together in the name of love. And love may well always refer ultimately back to its core, as it were: to sexual love proper, that is, to sexual *union*. But it also encompasses all the forms that are derivations or deviations from that fundamental tendency toward conjunction, or even fusion, and sacrifice of self: friendship, family ties, love of humanity, and even self-love (as narcissistic unity). Thus broadened, the concept of love is consistent with the ideas Freud had developed a year earlier in "Beyond the Pleasure Principle," and is equivalent to Plato's *eros*, understood at once as platonic love and as re(as)sembling or (re)unifying power (with an implicit reference to the myth of the Androgyne in the *Symposium*).

The indetermination or neutrality of the notion of emotional tie (*Gefühlsbindungen*) is therefore not coincidental. It corresponds to the indetermination or neutrality of the concept of libido. Thus we are alerted in advance that the love relationships that make up the essence of sociality will not necessarily belong to the category "sexual love with direct aims." What is certain, in any event, is that they constitute a bond, a social bond: the *Gefühlsbindungen* bind or link together the members of a crowd, lash them together so that they form a unit, a group, a *Masse*.

But what is a bond?

We must pay close attention to the term *Bindung*, which does not appear here by chance. It has to do, as we know, with one of the most crucial notions of the Freudian apparatus (one of the most problematic, as well). Indeed, it provides the most general concept of union, understood as formations of coherent, homogeneous, *mas-*

sive units. As early as the "Project for a Scientific Psychology," Freud found in the tying up of free or unconquered (*ungebändigt*) energy the condition for the establishment of stable units, with a fixed cathexis: there the ego, for example (but this example is telling), is defined as "a mass like this of neurones which hold fast to their cathexis—are, that is, in a bound state, and this, surely, can only happen as a result of the effect they have on one another" (*SE* 1: 368).

This is the hypothesis that the speculation on something "beyond the pleasure principle" had just amplified, by investing the *Bindung* with a critical role to play midway between the economic and the biological registers. What is in question is in fact the most "precocious" and most "important" function of the psychic apparatus, which consists in binding—so as to master them—the large quantities of destructive stimuli that come from without; this occurs even before the intervention of the *Lustprinzip* as a tendency toward the unleashing of pleasure, toward *Lustenbindung*. More generally speaking, the *Bindung* is the means used for the life instincts (through Eros) to maintain the cohesion and consistency of living matter and form new units.[32] Thus it is in binding these together within a "cellular State," or by binding the stimuli that come from outside, that single-celled organisms defer their own death (instinct). The same is true for all organic units of higher rank: it is always in binding (oneself) (with) the *other* or the *outside*—by uniting oneself to him/it, and vice versa, in a higher unification (*Vereinigung*) or a binding (*Verbindung*)—that the various organisms neutralize the lethal unbinding tendency that pushes them to constitute a separate band, that is, to live and die alone—as Freud says, rather like "narcissistic" cancer cells.[33]

Freud now extends all this economico-biological speculation (and we must not forget that it constitutes the ever-present theoretical background of "Group Psychology") to crowds, with a crowd conceived as a social organism or perhaps as a cellular super-State. For if a crowd, as Le Bon proposed (and as Freud acknowledged), is "a provisional being formed of heterogeneous elements, which for a moment are combined, exactly as the cells which constitute a living body form by their reunion a new being,"[34] this must owe something to the erotic *Bindung* as principle of organicism, of beings-bound-together, of systematic assemblage. The crowd must *hold together* by means of Eros: "a group is clearly held together by a power of some kind: and to what power could this feat be better ascribed than to Eros, which holds together everything in the world?" ("Group Psychology," p. 92).

Freud's hypothesis, then, posits Eros as primitive social bond, as *primal band*.[35] According to this hypothesis, the tendency to form a band or crowd represents a biological extension of "the multicellular character of all the higher organisms" (p. 87). The individual would sacrifice his own individuality to that of the "supra-individual," that is, the group,[36] exactly as the single-cell organism sacrifices itself to the cellular State by "copulating" with other cells, or as the narcissistic ego sacrifices its libido to the object—given that we are dealing with an analogy of proportionality within which each individual (the narcissistic ego, for example) is bonding (life-sustaining) with respect to the individual of immediately lower rank and unbonding (life-destroying) with respect to the individual of immediately higher rank, each individual representing a determinate union or blend of death instinct and life instinct. Sociality, on this basis, would always be only one of the "degrees" of Eros, as a binding, agglutinating, and in this sense archisocial life force: instead of coupling in pairs (*una cum uno*) to form a little lovers' cell or family cluster, individuals would couple together severally to form a group, a society, a State.

But what this hypothesis—this *organicist* hypothesis—implies is immediately obvious: a fully political, and—why avoid the term?—*totalitarian* concept of the social bond, since society is posited from the outset as single, unified, unanimous, undivided. The term "mass" or "masses" says the same thing in another way: as Hannah Arendt's work has shown, these are the catchwords par excellence of modern totalitarianisms.[37] But the social organicism that subtends these analyses makes the point even clearer, and it ought to allow us (while avoiding the naive trap of constructing the absurd image of a Stalinian or Fascist Freud) to reconstitute the underlying logic that accounts for the coexistence within a single text, as we indicated earlier, of a libertarian protest against the hypnotist's power and an authoritarian theory of the social bond. This logic is, in a word, the logic of the Subject. For when Freud rises up against the tyranny of suggestion, he is of course militating in favor of the autonomy of the individual subject. But when, like Le Bon and many others, he conceives of society as an organism, he is likewise militating in favor of a collective subject or Subject-State. Declaring the organic unity of the social body is tantamount, as Philippe Lacoue-Labarthe and Jean-Luc Nancy have clearly shown,[38] to declaring a unity of the Subject (we need only think of the frontispiece of Hobbes's *Leviathan*, where a great body crowned with a head is formed of small bodies looking up toward that head). The opposition between the individual and the collectivity remains quite secondary, from this viewpoint, and it is produced within a fundamental identity: the "we" is still "I" (the cellular superstate is still a supercell).

As for the omnipresent and all-powerful figure of the Leader, which appears throughout Freud's text, it in no way contradicts this logic of the Subject; quite the contrary. That body which is society requires a head; the organism requires a center of organization. And the group cannot set itself up as a Subject except by setting up, and setting *itself* up *as*, the figure of an independent, autonomous subject taking its authority from itself alone—hence of an authoritarian leader. Hence of a Narcissus, as we shall see. Only a narcissistic Leader can endow society with the unity of a body proper. And conversely, by subjecting themselves to the organic and narcissistic figure of the subject, subjects are only subjecting themselves, in the final analysis, to themselves. The politics outlined here is a narcissistic politics.

This may appear to contradict Freud's declarations on the erotic, and especially the *object-oriented*, character of the social bond, the social *Bindung*. After all, from the very first chapter of "Group Psychology," he has posited an opposition, a *Gegensatz*, between "narcissistic" (non-object-oriented) "psychic acts" and "social" (object-oriented) "psychic acts." It may be argued that he is in the process of amplifying that hypothesis when he proposes considering social bonds as erotic, libidinal bonds, and that an individual's narcissism is consequently incompatible with the erotico-social bond that links him with others. The issue is all the more important given that, from here on, Freud unfailingly treats the opposition between narcissism and object orientation (egoism vs. altruism, asociality vs. sociality, individual vs. collectivity, and so on) as if it were an opposition between an unbinding and a bond (*Entbindung* vs. *Bindung*). Thus it is important to establish the secondary or relative nature of this opposition.

Let us recall, first of all, that within the framework of Freud's third theory of the instincts, narcissistic libido stems just as much from Eros as object libido does. Freud made this clear in the sixth chapter of "Beyond the Pleasure Principle": the ego's narcissistic libido belongs to the life instincts, since it derives from "the stores of libido by means of which the cells of the soma are attached to one another" (p. 52). The ego's unity, in other words, is already the work of an erotic *Bindung*. This unity, of course, is not prevented from functioning as an *Entbindung* with respect to the higher-level erotic unit (as when the ego refuses to form a couple or when the individual refuses to become integrated with the group). But then we are dealing with a secondary contradiction, so to speak, in which narcissism comes to *represent* unbinding (= the death instinct) to the higher unit, without ceasing to be an erotically bound unit itself. Narcissistic autarchy is still a *union*, of self to self, self with self.

But this also implies, conversely, that the erotic union is profoundly narcissistic in nature. For if the erotic *Bindung* has the function of opening up the narcissistic monad to the other (the object, the *Andere*), the result is a union, the formation of a new narcissistic unit. From this point of view, the *Bindung* never encounters the monad as its *other*. When the cell, for example, is bound to or within the cellular state, it only repeats the process by which it was narcissistically bound to itself, was already tied up so as to form a compact whole. And the same is true for individuals when they are bound to or within the group.

The *Bindung*, in this sense, does not serve to tie up the subject (or, as it may be called, the cell, the ego, the individual, and so on) from the outside. It *starts from within*, like a "biological extension" of the subject itself. The best model of this process no doubt remains the one Freud used in "On Narcissism"—the pseudopods sent forth by "narcissistic" protoplasm toward "objects": an emission of this type is an emission of self, a sort of expansion of the living substance, and the subject never goes beyond its own bounds, even when it appears to exceed itself or to pour itself out toward the other. On the contrary, by mixing its own substance with the foreign substance (amphimixis, binding of exogeneous stimuli, copulation, crowd), it encompasses the foreign substance within its *own* limits so as to form a new subject, a new bound set, a new *Bund*. The subject remains the same, as compact and ab-solute as ever, since it is related and bound only to itself. There is thus no opposition between the *Bindung* and what it binds: the subject is not bound, it binds *itself*. And because it binds itself in this manner, binding the other within itself, it remains master and subject of its own liaison; it determines itself. The movement of *Bindung*, like the self-binding movement of living substance, is precisely a movement of reducing opposition in general: a conquering movement on the part of the *autos*, a self-movement on the part of Narcissus, opposing or objecting the other *to itself*, the better to absorb it into itself (Eros is then the pseudopod of Narcissus).

The fact remains that the opposition must first be deployed *as opposition* in order to be reduced: in this instance, as opposition between subject and object, between ego and other. Such an opposition is necessary, in a way, to the narcissistic process. If everything begins with the subject and if everything returns to the subject, this is because the opposition not only is produced from the vantage point of the subject's initial and preliminary position but also confirms that position. The other must first be an other-than-I so that I may bind *myself* to it and thus bind it, overpower it, master it. But if the "other" were from the outset the "same" as myself, in some sort of blend or union that would precede any liaison, any binding-together, then all assurances of "myself" would be subtly threatened, undermined.

Now did Freud's hypothesis not attest to this very possibility? What else is hypnotic suggestion, if not a "bond" that inextricably mingles the "self" with the "other"—a bond that transcends all (op)position of identity or identities and that must therefore be characterized as a non-bond? Hypothesis: Is it not this undifferentiated, indeterminate (undialectizable) sameness that Freud rejects when he repudiates hypnosis? Is That (the id, neither "I" nor "thou") not what most profoundly motivates his resistance to the theories of Bernheim and Le Bon? Is it not that fusion which he *determines* here as union, as unifying *Bindung*?

Such is the conclusion of Chapter 4 of "Group Psychology." If sociality consists in fusing with others in a group or mass, the process must depend on a bond that emanates from the subjects themselves; and if suggestibility is involved in the case in point (Freud does not deny that it may be), it must be because subjects allow themselves to be open to suggestion, out of love: "When the individual gives up his distinctiveness in a group and lets its other members influence him by suggestion, it gives one the impression that he does it because he feels the need of being in harmony with them rather than in opposition to them—so that perhaps after all he does it *ihnen zu Liebe* ("Group Psychology," p. 92).

Once these metapsychologico-speculative preliminaries have been put in place the stage is set for group psychology—for the psychology of groups *with leaders*. Chapter 5 in fact begins by distinguishing between several types of groups, following the lines of classification laid out by Le Bon and McDougall. Thus there are homogeneous crowds, consisting of individuals who already have features in common, and nonhomogeneous crowds ("heterogeneous" ones, in Le Bon's sense); there are artificial, differentiated, organized crowds whose permanence is ensured by some external constraint, and natural, primitive, undifferentiated, unorganized crowds (McDougall's classification); finally—and this is a distinction to which the psychosociologists have not paid enough attention—there are crowds with a leader (*Führer*) and leaderless crowds. Freud then proposes, "in complete opposition to the usual practice," to limit his investigation to organized groups, to the "Church" or "Army" type. Why this choice, which may seem arbitrary at first glance? Because "certain facts, which are far more concealed in other cases, can be observed very clearly in those highly organized groups which are protected from dissolution" (p. 93).

In other words, these examples are exemplary examples, paradigms according to which the essence of all crowds can be read. This means two things at once. In the first place, *there are no unorganized groups*, not even those that are "unorganized" in McDougall's sense:

every group includes an embryonic organization, and from this point of view there is no difference between passing crowds and stable groups such as the Church or the Army; once this is understood, we may as well turn our attention to groups of the latter sort, since that embryonic organization is more developed, more observable in them.

In the second place, and conversely, the organization of artificial groups (of established societies), however complex it may be, is finally of the same type as that of the crudest, most primitive groups. That is why Freud, very significantly, takes virtually no interest in the differentiated structure of the Church and the Army, in the distribution of social roles, in the division of labor, and so on—that is, in precisely what McDougall called "organization." He is only interested in the feature of minimal organization that is observable in any group, namely, in the relation between the leader and the led (Christ and the Church, the commander-in-chief and the Army). That relationship—the *political* relationship—is the one that constitutes the group embryo, the primitive band. As we shall soon see, without that elementary organization (that minimal element of difference *and* of articulation), the group would disintegrate at once, would no longer constitute a body. "There are no unorganized groups": this statement has to be understood, then, as follows: "there is no group without a *Führer*"; "there is no such thing as a leaderless band."

Indeed, the love that establishes the group would first be directed toward the leader rather than toward the other members of the group. This is not surprising: Eros is a unifying force channeling love toward the principle of political unity from the outset. Love, here, is immediately a political economy. And vice versa: it is from the subjects' love that the leader (temporal or spiritual, real or ideal) draws his power. He extorts submission by extorting love—in particular, by dispensing the "illusion" that he loves all members of the group equally. The lack of individual freedom, "the principal phenomenon of group psychology" (p. 95) thus results neither from a constraint imposed by force nor from a social contract of the juridical type, nor from a natural suggestibility, but from a sort of seduction destined to extort from each Narcissus the free gift of his freedom. Love for the leader is thus the first social bond or *Bindung*, the first binding-of-self-to-other.

As for the second *Bindung*, the one that links group members among themselves, it follows automatically from the first, inasmuch as the lack of freedom of the individuals bound to the leader produces among them a relation of *equality* and, by the same token, of *fraternity*. The organization of the group thus reproduces that of the family. The members of the group are like brothers vis-à-vis the Father, and the libidinal-political economy is analogous to the libidinal-domestic economy (patriarchal, as always):

It is not without a deep reason that the similarity between the Christian community and a family is invoked, and that believers call themselves brothers in Christ, that is, brothers through the love which Christ has for them. There is no doubt that the tie which unites each individual with Christ is also the cause of the tie which unites them with one another. The like holds good of an army. The Commander-in-Chief is a father who loves all soldiers equally, and for that reason they are comrades among themselves. [p. 94]

Freud does not have much more to say, for the time being, about the second bond. Is it libidinal, like the first? Are the brothers also love objects? What is certain is that there are two bonds and that the second derives from the first. Without the bond with the Commander-in-Chief/Father, individuals would not be bound to one another (and thus it must be recognized that the second bond is much less spontaneous than the first). According to Freud, to prove this it would suffice to show that the suppression of the bond with the leader would immediately bring about the dissolution of the crowd, an *Entbindung*, a complete rout. This proof is provided in the two examples of the Army and the Church.

What happens when an army loses its head? *Panic* strikes. As long as the leader is present, the soldiers are capable of confronting the greatest dangers, even of sacrificing their lives—a supplementary proof, in Freud's eyes, that it is not the interest of the ego (self-preservation) that leads crowds, but libido. But as soon as the leader disappears, fear (or anxiety—*Angst*) takes over and it is every man for himself, the anarchic scattering of narcissistic egos: "Each individual is only solicitous on his own account, and without any consideration for the rest" (p. 96). Thus it is not fear or anxiety that provokes the narcissistic rout, but the loss of the libidinal bond that constitutes the group: "The loss of the leader in some sense or other, the birth of misgivings about him, brings on the outbreak of panic, though the danger remains the same; the mutual ties between the members of the group disappear, as a rule, at the same time as the tie with their leader" (p. 96).

And when the Church loses its leader? This eventuality is not so easy to observe, Freud says, since here we are dealing with an ideal, "invisible" leader, all the better protected against disappearance. Thus we have to resort to a sort of theoretical fiction—for example, an English novel in which it is imagined that conspirators spread the word about a false archaeological discovery tending to destroy the dogma of the resurrection of Christ. Because the leader appears to be dead, in this fiction that Freud judges plausible, the result would be a dissolution of the religious group. This dissolution, however, would not be manifested by a narcissistic every-man-for-himself rout, as in panic, but by the violence of each against all. The leader's disappearance would in this case liberate, unleash hostile impulses devoid of any respect for others, impulses that the community of love had bottled up, had confined by directing them beyond the bounds of the group (intolerance toward infidels, cruelty toward enemies of Christ, and so on). And since Freud hypothesizes that such channeling of aggressivity is not peculiar to the Church but characterizes every group bond (*Massenbindung*) that can be put in the Church's place (the "socialist" bond, for example), we must conclude that whenever any leader—political, religious, or ideological—disappears, the same unleashing of violence is bound to follow.

What is the outcome of this dual demonstration? Love for the leader is doubly necessary to the constitution of a group, first because it binds narcissism (attaches individuals to each other), second because it binds destruction (bottles up and channels the aggressivity of all members). The group, like a fine-tuned, organic, harmonious whole, would not survive an instant without that founding bond, without that political Love or that Politics of Love. This is what had to be demonstrated.

Dangerous Liaisons

But just why did this *have* to be demonstrated? What is this strange prescription (a leader is required, or else)? Why knot, bind, subordinate all bonds to the libidinal-political bond? Why make that one *the* bond, without which no bond would be possible? Are there no other bonds—pre-political, perhaps, but nonetheless bonding, binding? And then where does the leader, the deus ex machina, come from? What has made him a leader? Why is he loved? Must that be taken for granted?

These questions lead into the most problematic phase of the text, for Freud does not conclude "Group Psychology" here. He might have: he has already said everything he intended to say; in a way, he will say nothing else right to the end. Yet he continues, starting the whole analysis all over again. The chapter that follows is entitled "Further Problems and Lines of Work," and we are not even halfway through the essay. Freud took five chapters to establish the main thesis (the leadership thesis); he takes seven more to work it over, to shore it up, to bolster it with all the conceptual resources of psychoanalysis.

If Freud finds it necessary to go on, it is obviously because the preceding explanations have left a residue, an unassimilated remainder involving the bonds linking crowd members to one another. Indeed, the exact nature of these bonds has not yet been established. All that we know for the moment is that love for the leader has come into play to keep crowd members from reverting to the narcissism and violence that seems to be their natural bent. In this regard, Chapter 6 only repeats in a positive vein what Chapter 5 has already established negatively: since the group brings to light a "limitation of narcissism" and a lack of reciprocal aggression, we have to see this as "cogent evidence" of the unifying and pacifying action of love. Such action would thus be necessary. But even so, is it sufficient? In other words, are bonds of the second type libidinal *in themselves*, prior to, or apart from, the intervention of love? We might suppose so, since Freud has thus far seemed to recognize no liaison but the libidinal one. If we turn to the very last lines of Chapter 6, however, this appears not to be the case. In this passage Freud acknowledges, quite disconcertingly, that libidinal bonds ("object-cathexis, as we know it in sexual life") are not "the only manner of emotional tie with other people [*die einzige Weise der Gefühlsbindung an eine andere Person*]" ("Group Psychology," p. 103). Libidinal ties or bonds do not exhaust the field of the *Gefühlsbindung*; this realm also encompasses the *bonds of identification*. And as we will learn in the following chapters, these are the bonds that unite crowd members among themselves.

What is the nature of these identifications? (The word appears in the plural.) And how are they compatible with love? How are they libidinalized? Let us set these questions aside for now, and ask rather what impels Freud to produce this new speculative output. Why does he feel the need to complicate his initial schema by introducing the concept of a nonlibidinal, nonerotic bond? Strangest of all is the fact that Freud says nothing about what he is up to: identifications are brought up *ex abrupto*, without any indication as to the need they must be meeting. We are thus reduced to hypotheses. One sign, however, should alert us: the identifications in question, *nonlibidinal bonds*, are situated precisely at the intersection of two series that Freud has set in opposition to each other up to this point: *Bindung*, object libido (Love, Eros), altruism, sociality versus *Entbindung*, narcissism, violent egoism, asociality.

Is it not therefore plausible that, owing to the inadequacy of these oppositions (or even of opposition as such), identification should intervene in compensation? Must we not suppose that the initial grid was still too coarse, that it allowed narcissistic bonds, for example, or altruistic non-bonds, or a nonlibidinal sociality, to slip through? When we look closely enough, we find that these kinds of ill-assimilated residues do seem to be left over from the preceding analyses. Thus we shall do well to take a closer look at them, in an effort to better understand what motivates Freud's introduction of identifications.

Let us go back to the example of panic, a Freudian paradigm of the narcissistic rout, and let us admit, with Freud, that it is the disappearance of the libidinal tie to the leader, and not fear, that produces panic. But what, then, is panic? Can it really be described as the brutal breaking of all bonds with others? McDougall saw it as a typical manifestation of one of the principal social tendencies, the sympathetic induction of emotions.[39] Freud had summarized Mc-Dougall's theory in Chapter 3:

> The fact is that the perception of the signs of an affective state is calculated automatically to arouse the same affect in the person who perceives them. The greater the number of people in whom the same affect can be simultaneously observed, the stronger does this automatic compulsion grow. The individual loses his power of criticism, and lets himself slip into the same affect. But in so doing he increases the excitement of the other people, who had produced this result in him, and thus the affective charge of the individuals becomes intensified by mutual interaction. Something is unmistakably at work in the nature of a compulsion to do the same as the others, to remain in harmony with the many. [p. 84]

"Sympathetic" communication from ego to ego (the term "sympathetic" approximates the German *Einfühlung*, and Freud recognizes "sympathy" as the "affective contagion" with which psychoanalysts were so familiar) would explain the at once epidemic and disproportionate nature of panic. Freud immediately pinpoints the paradox: by making panic the exemplary example of the group mind, a paradoxical result is achieved—namely, that "this group mind does away with itself in one of its most striking manifestations" (p. 97), since panic is equivalent, as well, to the group's dissolution. But at the same time the paradox simply reasserts itself in Freud's own text, for Freud, oddly enough, never denies that panic is a "sympathetic" phenomenon. His disagreement with McDougall has to do with the cause that sets off panic (fear vs. disappearance of the leader), not with the process itself: "The contention that fear in a group is increased to enormous proportions through induction (contagion) is not in the least contradicted by these remarks" (p. 96).

At this point the paradox, which brings us to the heart of the difficulty Freud is confronting, is the following: the disappearance of the libidinal-political bond that ensured the cohesion of the group does not liberate narcissistic egos in a pure and simple unbonding. In a way, it liberates nothing at all, and especially not autonomous subjects (individuals), since panic consists precisely in an unmasterable overflowing of ego by way of (affects of) others; or, to put it differently, panic consists in a mimetic, contagious epidemic narcissism. The example of panic is thus not the counter-example of the group, and Freud's argument can easily be turned around: by making panic the exemplary example of individual psychology, a paradoxical result is achieved—namely, that narcissism does away with itself in one of its most striking manifestations, since panic is tantamount to a gaping, more or less bewildered opening toward others. Narcissistic egos are in fact *bound* by the sympathy of panic just as tightly as they were earlier bound by military love.

What are we to make of this bond? We can see at once that it brings Freud up against a double (and identical) difficulty. The first level of this difficulty concerns the theoretical rivalry that binds him to the psychosociologists, for by conceding to McDougall that panic is propagated by "sympathetic induction of emotions," Freud concedes virtually everything to suggestion theory. "Sympathy," as he had just confirmed in Chapter 4, is nothing but the phenomenon of suggestion, considered from the angle of affect: it makes me experience the *same* affect as another person, just as verbal suggestion makes me think *like* the person making the suggestion, just as imitation makes me *reproduce* the conduct of the model. We must not forget that this entire set of mimetic or mimic relations to others is what Freud had claimed to explain by libido. But he has now rediscovered the same set of relations in panic—*in other words, in a phenomenon that, according to his hypothesis, no longer stems from libido*. Far from being a manifestation of libido that would disappear with it, the sympathetic (suggestive, imitative) bond is precisely what *remains* when the libidinal element has been removed from the crowd. What are we to make, then, of this remainder, this suggestive, affective, nonlibidinal bond? In particular, what are we to make of this *narcissistic bond*?

For panic bonds, binds each Narcissus to the others: this is the second and by far the more formidable difficulty. The pinnacle of the sympathetic relation to others is simultaneously the pinnacle of non-relation to others. Affective assimilation to others is rigorously equivalent to a deassimilating dissimilation. Thus it does not suffice to say that the panic bond is nonlibidinal; it is necessary to add that it binds in the mode of a non-bond. The panic bond transcends the alternative between *Bindung* and *Entbindung*, as do all the related oppositions Freud deploys: an unbinding bond or band, a stampeding horde (une bande débandante), it must be labeled both narcissistic and non-narcissistic, object-oriented and non-object-oriented, egoistic and altruistic, social and asocial. Narcissism is constituted in this bond, so to speak, *in the manner of* the relation to the other, *like* the other—thus in an *identification* with the other.

Thus we have the paradox of a non-relation to the other, of a relation without relation (let us note in passing that this intractable double band undoubtedly maintains the closest possible relationship with what is called elsewhere a double bind, a pragmatic paradox, undecidability, and so forth). From this point on, if panic designates the limit or breaking point of the group, as Freud would have it, it can no longer be conceived as the group's outside or external limit. This limit is, rather, an ultimate internal impossibility ensconced at the very heart of the group: a cancerous growth, we might say, that proliferates from within and uses the paths of unity to propagate disunity, narcissism, death.

The panic bond must necessarily stand in some relation to the internal violence of each against all, which is the second type of unbonding observed upon the disappearance of the libidinal bond with the leader. What sort of relation? In Chapter 5, Freud merely juxtaposes the narcissism of panic and fratricidal violence without examining the relation between these two phenomena. In Chapter 6, however, he specifies that narcissism and hatred constitute one and the same lack of "altruistic" relation to others: hatred is therefore fundamentally narcissistic.

There are two modalities of narcissistic hatred, then, depending on whether this hatred is mixed or not, linked to object love or not. The first possibility is that of affective ambivalence, which affects all relationships between individuals or social groups (with the exception, as a disconcerting note points out, of the mother-son relationship, which is said to be "based on narcissism"). In this case, the hateful-narcissistic element is bound to and by love: in other words, either it is tempered or else it is displaced onto outsiders, as Freud had shown in Chapter 5. The second possibility is that of pure hatred—unbound, unleashed, narcissistic; this corresponds quite precisely to what emerges when the libidinal bond linking group members with one another is broken:

In the undisguised antipathies and aversions which people feel towards strangers with whom they have to do [*nahestehende Fremde*] we may recognize the expression of self-love—of narcissism. This self-love works for the preservation of the individual, and behaves as though the occurrence of any divergence from his own particular lines of development involved a criticism of them and a demand for their alteration. . . . In this whole connection men give evidence of a readiness for hatred, an aggressiveness, the source of which is unknown, and to which one is tempted to ascribe an elementary character.*

*In a recently published study, *Beyond the Pleasure Principle* (1920 . . .), I have attempted to connect the polarity of love and hatred with a hypothetical opposition between instincts of life and death, and to establish the sexual instincts as the purest examples of the former, the instincts of life. [p. 102]

Now this narcissistic hatred raises many more problems than it solves, within Freud's argument. No doubt we better understand now how narcissism and violence constitute one and the same unbonding, one and the same hatred of the other. But that is just the problem: how can we continue to speak of *unbonding*? Hatred, even the most cold-blooded, even the least ambivalent, still implies a relationship to the other, and it is no accident that Freud speaks here of *nahestehende Fremde*, of strangers in the vicinity with whom one enters into contact: as the text "Inhibitions, Symptoms and Anxiety" later declares, contact is "the immediate aim of the aggressive as well as the loving object-cathexis."[40] Hatred seeks to strike out at others, seeks to touch others even when it is attempting to destroy them. The "narcissism" of hatred thus has to be put in the same quotation marks as the "narcissism" of panic: this absence of bond is still a bond. And vice versa, since the bond of hatred is equivalent to the dissolution of all relationship: alterity is immediately suppressed, annihilated, absorbed by the assimilating violence of the Same. Thus we find ourselves confronted with the same "paradox" as before, that of an unbinding bond that can be classified neither on the side of bonding nor on the side of unbonding—or else on both sides at once. Once again ambivalence rules, and it resurfaces in the very spot where, according to Freud, a pure, unmixed, elementary hatred should have appeared, that is, the absolute other of the bond, the without-relation of the death instinct as such.

It will be said, perhaps, that all this must be read against the background of Freud's speculation about what lies "beyond the pleasure principle," as his footnote indicates, and that there is no reason to be too surprised if narcissistic hatred is not yet pure unbonding, not yet the death instinct *itself*. It is only the "delegate" of this instinct, sent to appear before the life instincts (or their "delegates"), but still without constituting unbonding as such. If Freud sets up an opposition between narcissistic hatred and object love as if between an unbonding and a bonding, it is only by analogy with the ultimate—and irreducible—opposition between the *Entbindung* of Thanatos and the *Bindung* of Eros. And what may seem to be a contradiction when we encounter it in this passage of "Group Psychology" is no longer a contradiction at the level of the theory of the instincts that supplies its framework.

So be it. But this only enhances and increases the difficulty, by raising it to the level of Freud's more general speculation on *Bindung* and *Entbindung*. For even if narcissistic hatred only "represents" unbonding vis-à-vis love, the fact remains that it does so not by refusing to bond itself with another organic unit, *but by establishing the bond* in the mode of ambivalence. And we must then suppose that what is *thus* represented was already a mixture of bonding and unbonding: if hatred is to love what Thanatos is to Eros, this must mean that Thanatos itself is united, mixed, monstrously coupled with Eros. Thus, finally, one would never find an unbonding in the pure state—nor, by the same token, a pure bonding.

This is confirmed in exemplary fashion by the passage in "Beyond the Pleasure Principle" to which Freud's note alludes. The analysis of the "polarity of love and hatred" comes into play in "Beyond the Pleasure Principle" at the point when, having categorized narcissism and the instincts of self-preservation on the side of Eros, Freud suddenly remarks that according to his hypothesis there might be "no other instincts whatever but the libidinal ones. At all events there are none other visible" ("Beyond Pleasure," p. 52). No matter how far we may look, we see only the erotic *Bindung*, and we are then in danger, according to Freud's objection, of falling back into Jung's libidinal monism, by undermining the hypothesis of a death instinct opposed to Eros. Thus it is imperative to find an example (*Beispiel*) of the death instinct—that is, an example of what is without example, of something that works in silence and never comes to light. And this is the example of hatred, more precisely of the polarity between love and hatred. The passage should be read in its entirety:

In the obscurity that reigns at present in the theory of the instincts, it would be unwise to reject any idea that promises to throw light on it. We started out from the great opposition between the life and death instincts. Now object-love itself presents us with a second example of a similar polarity— that between love (or affection) and hate (or aggressiveness). If only we could succeed in relating these two polarities to each other and in deriving one from the other! From the very first we recognized the presence of a sadistic component in the sexual instinct. . . . But how can the sadistic instinct, whose aim it is to injure the object, be derived from Eros, the preserver of life? Is it not plausible to suppose that this sadism is in fact a death instinct [*eigentlich ein Todestrieb ist*] which, under the influence of the narcissistic libido, has been forced away from the ego and has consequently only emerged in relation to the object? It now enters the service of the sexual function. During the oral stage of organization of the libido, the act of obtaining erotic mastery over an object coincides with that object's destruction; later, the sadistic instinct separates off, and finally, at the stage of genital primacy, it takes on, for the purposes of reproduction, the function of overpowering the sexual object to the extent necessary for carrying out the sexual act. It might indeed be said that the sadism which has been forced out of the ego has pointed the way for the libidinal components of the sexual instinct, and that these follow after it to the object. Wherever the original sadism has undergone no mitigation or intermixture, we find the familiar ambivalence of love and hate in erotic life.

If such an assumption as this is permissible, then we have met the demand that we should produce an example of a death instinct—though, it is true, a displaced one. [pp. 53–54]

Thus it would be necessary to acknowledge that hatred proves the death instinct, proves the absolutely improbable. And we know, moreover, that hatred and aggressiveness maintain this status henceforth in Freudian theory, to such an extent that the term *Destruktionstrieb* tends more and more to alternate with that of *Todestrieb*, as if the illustrating (enlightening, illuminating) example were perfectly equivalent to the dark obscurity of what is not seen. But this example, as we have just *seen*, is not an example of the death instinct itself, any more than it is a counter-example of the life instincts—first of all because we are dealing with an example of the death instinct displaced, turned away from its own path, expelled from within the ego, which is also a way of saying that it is allied, bound to the life instincts. This example—the only one, or at least the purest, most characteristic one—proves nothing, except perhaps that there is no example of the death instinct, or (the same thing) that there is no death instinct except exemplified, impure, improperly stated—*bound* (*bandée*). Freud acknowledges this a little later on, by laying to rest, as it were, a bit of speculative contraband:

> A very extensive fusion and amalgamation, in varying proportions, of the two classes of instinct takes place, so that we never have to deal with pure life instincts or pure death instincts but only with mixtures of them in different amounts. Corresponding to a fusion of instincts of this kind, there may, as a result of certain influences, be a *de*fusion of them. How large the portions of the death instincts are which refuse to be tamed in this way by being bound [*solcher Bändigung durch die Bindung*] to admixtures of libido we cannot at present guess. ["The Economic Problem of Masochism," *SE* 19: 164]

But this is not all. Not only is hatred an example of the death instinct already (always already) bound to the life instincts; it also seems to provide the example par excellence of the erotic *Bindung*. Freud is not content to proclaim that sadism is added to or mixed with an *already* established love bond (through the addition of a shade of hatred, a nuance of aggressivity). He adds—in what is doubtless the most inextricable proposition in this discourse on intrication and disintrication—that sadism breaks the path to the libido, opens the narcissistic ego toward the object. The paragraph that follows specifies that what is involved may be a primary masochism (primary narcissism as suicidal narcissism) projected onto objects: auto-aggression would be transformed into hetero-aggression, the death instinct would turn into a life instinct. Thus we learn that Eros is *none other* than Thanatos (or Narcissus): aggression, a deferred narcissistic death instinct, *inaugurates* the object relation and thus libidinal liaison in general. Far from putting itself "at the service" of the sexual function, as Freud seems to be saying, aggression introduces that function as "ascendancy" or "mastery" over the object, and it does so in the mode of an ambivalence that is anterior to any composition or addition or mixture: at the absolutely initial, primary stage of oral incorporation, hatred *is* love, indissociably, just as the ego and the object, the ego and the other, are indissociable.

Everything begins, then—or rather is broached, and deferred, and repeated—in this consubstantiality of love and hatred, in this strange murderous intussusception which is the incorporation of (what is not yet) the object—maternal substance, foreign protoplasmic substance, and so on. Everything is begun and broached, in other words, in that primitive double band which is doubly primitive, since it is only in the erotic destruction of the "object," in the (non-)relation to the "other," that death *and* life come into the world.

Double Band or Triangle?
(The Holy Trinity of Identifications)

Appearances notwithstanding, we have not really strayed far from "Group Psychology," for we can no longer settle for the initial schema of a harmonious group or mass soldered together by exclusively libidinal bonds. Far from confirming this schema, the examples of panic and hatred have surreptitiously sapped, undermined, destroyed it. In the first place, this has happened because the phenomenon of panic has at the very least brought to light the nonlibidinal character of the "horizontal" bonds between crowd members: "sympathetic," "suggestive," mimetic, these bonds remain indefinitely refractory to the opposition between the libidinal bond and the narcissistic non-bond, so that they can neither be excluded from the group nor simply included within it. Between the group and the non-group, and articulating each with the other, there is this extremely problematic fringe of relations of non-relation to the other, of detaching attachments, of centrifugal attractions. And since this fringe defines a certain exterior that is *internal* to the group, it has to be taken into account. In the second place, and even more seriously, hatred has brought us back to the place where the possibility *and* the impossibility of the bond in general (thus also of the social bond) open up, *whether we are dealing with the "vertical" bond with the leader or with "horizontal" bonds*: non-relation to the other haunts every relation to the other from the outset (it *is* this "relation"), and once again, it has to be taken into account.

The problem, then, is no longer the overly simple, too quickly solved problem of the passage of any individual Narcissus into object love (and hence into sociality). It is the problem of the *transformation* of this whole set of double bands of panic and hatred into social bonds—that is (and Freud has no doubt about this), into peaceful bonds. This new problem is a much more difficult, more overwhelming one, inasmuch as the social-erotic bond can no longer be opposed to its other. In a way, this bond can only be established on the basis of what threatens it from within, and this allows us to see that it will never be *established*, will never establish itself as a stable relation.

Indeed, how can "sympathy," "suggestion," "imitation"—or identification, as Freud is about to call it—ever give rise to the homogeneity of a social body, if this body is truly pregnant with panic? Worse still, how can love for a leader, which institutes the social, ever be purified, expunged of hatred, which institutes love? Is not the founding bond of being-together itself (in itself) ambivalent? Are there not, as Freud wondered briefly at the beginning of Chapter 6, cases in which "the leader or the leading idea might . . . , so to speak, be negative; hatred against a particular person or institution might operate in just the same unifying way, and might call up the same kind of emotional ties as positive attachment" ("Group Psychology," p. 100)?

It is noteworthy that Freud does not consider this latter sort of question, at least not right away: only in Chapter 8 does the bond of loving submission to the leader begin to require a complementary investigation. At the point we have reached in Chapter 7, Freud begins by splitting up the difficulty, limiting his interest to the bonds that unite crowd members among themselves. Let us summarize and anticipate: we are dealing with identificatory bonds (more precisely, with a certain *type* of identificatory bond), and these are nonlibidinal, unlike the love bond linking member to leader. Freud is thus complicating his initial schema by making a place for nonlibidinal *Gefühlsbindungen*; and we can now identify (or at least begin to glimpse) the problem this revised schema aims to address. But we also see that the revision bears for the moment only upon bonds of the second type: the bond with the leader, for its part, remains exempt from scrutiny.

It would thus seem that the unanticipated intervention of identification does not pose a fundamental challenge to the general schema. On the contrary, it reconfirms the schema while partially modifying it. In fact, it is difficult to understand Chapter 7 properly without noting that it is wholly organized so as to bring about that confirmation. In this chapter, as we now need to show, Freud concedes the existence of *purely* nonlibidinal bonds only to the extent that he thinks he can make certain of these bonds depend on a *prior* libidinal bond, which is to say a bond that is *pure*, free of any contamination by the nonlibidinal. Thus love (pure political love) would preside over the origin of identification (pure social identification) and reign over it henceforth.

But which identification? For there are several, which Freud enumerates in a disorder that is completely disconcerting if we fail to notice that a perfectly clear classification is being proposed, one that is valid for all the identifications listed in Chapter 7, even though the principle of classification appears in the middle of the list (and not at the beginning or end, as a scholarly exposition would have it). Let us take this classification, therefore, as our guide. In it Freud distinguishes three types or kinds of identification:

First, identification is the original form of emotional tie with an object; secondly, in a regressive way it becomes a substitute for a libidinal object-tie, as it were by means of introjection of the object into the ego; and thirdly, it may arise with any new perception of a common quality shared with some other person who is not an object of the sexual instinct. [pp. 107–8]

How is it that these three types of identification belong to a single genre? Quite obviously, all three consist in a total or partial assimilation of an ego to some other. On this basis, they are all apt to account—and this of course is one of the objectives of the chapter—for the mimetic phenomena said to be based on "suggestion," "imitation," "sympathy" (or "empathy," *Einfühlung*). Let us note, however, that identification can be produced either before or after the establishment of a libidinal object bond, as the case may be. This point is clearly critical, and it leads us to suspect that not all identifications will be equally eligible for the role of social emotional bond (*Gefühlsbindung*), given that this latter is supposed to be explained by way of the libido. Preceding any libidinal bond (*mimesis* without *libido*), identification would in fact elude the reign of love.

Primary Identification

Such is apparently the case with the first identification, which, as we have seen, would constitute "the most primitive form" of emotional bond with others. The first sentence of Chapter 7 of "Group Psychology" says exactly this: "Identification is known to psychoanalysis as the earliest expression of an emotional tie with another person" (p. 105). And Freud repeats it a little further on: "Identification is the earliest and original form of emotional tie" (p. 107). As we read these unequivocal declarations, it may appear that the case is closed: the identificatory bond *precedes* the libidinal object bond. But the question is murkier than this, for Freud never stops swinging back and forth, in a quite disconcerting way, between diverse chronologies. In the very same pages, in fact, we learn that identification is *contemporary* with the libidinal object bond, or even *posterior* to it.

How can these contradictory statements be reconciled? The question is not incidental: these chronologies involve two different theories of identification, at least one of which is radically incompatible with the general problematics of "Group Psychology," that is, with psychoanalysis. Psychoanalysis is henceforth divided or doubled: for it, these few extraordinarily awkward (and embarrassing) pages are the locus of a fundamental ambiguity. They must therefore be read attentively, without pressure to find a coherence that may not exist.

The identification that concerns us at the moment is the one that Freud labels "primary," two years later, in Chapter 3 of "The Ego and the Id." Now the term "primary" (and here is the ambiguity) has to be understood in Freud's text both in the sense of chronological anteriority and in the sense of elementariness, or irreducibility. It is in this second sense that identification is said to be "possible before any sexual object-choice has been made" ("Group Psychology," p. 106). Identification and libidinal object cathexis would be, in fact, "psychologically different ties [*psychologisch verschiedene Bindungen*]" (p. 105), and hence mutually independent. It would thus be *possible* for identification, as the primary and elementary bond, to appear prior to object love—which does not mean that this possibility is always realized. The opposite may also be true, as we shall see.

What are we to make, then, of the "psychological difference" between the two types of tie or bond that conditions their reciprocal independence? The libidinal bond bears upon the "object" of the ego (*Objekt des Ichs*), which the ego wants to "have" so as to enjoy it. But the identificatory bond takes hold of the "subject" of the ego (*Subjekt . . . des Ichs*), in other words, of what the ego wants to "be" (p. 105). The ego is bound to another ego by constituting itself as (that) ego, by making itself or being (like) the other. This definition basically characterizes identification as a mimetic relation, and not an object relation, to others. Freud goes on to explain that it tends "to mould a person's own ego after the fashion of the one that has been taken as a model" (p. 106). That is why "a little boy will exhibit a special interest in his father; he would like to grow like him and be like him, and take his place everywhere. We may say simply that he takes his father as his ideal" (p. 105).

This formative, modeling identification (*vorbildliche Identifizierung*) precedes the Oedipus complex, belongs to its prehistory. But once again, this does not mean that it necessarily precedes the object bond. The object cathexis of the mother, according to the anaclitic (attachment) type, may take place simultaneously with the identification with the father, "or perhaps even earlier" (p. 105). Freud's casual approach to chronology is clarified once we have grasped that he is bent, above all, on establishing the mutual *independence* of identification and the object bond. There have to be *two* distinct bonds if he is to produce the Oedipal *triangle*, and this triangle provides the model, as we shall see, for triangular relations within the group. The prehistory of the Oedipus complex must be *pre*-Oedipal, that is, potentially triangulatable, and for this reason it must be double, the ego maintaining two types of relations (mimetic and object-oriented) with two different "others" (an ideal-model and an object): identification and object cathexis coexist "side by side for a time without any mutual influence or interference" (p. 105). They coexist without merging, then. It is only in a second phase that they interfere, by virtue of the Oedipal conflict for which they "help to prepare the way" (they already bear its seeds): identification with the father is reinforced and takes on a "hostile colouring" (p. 105) owing to the rivalry for possession of the mother. The child, in other words, wants to be the father in order to have the mother. And we know what comes next . . .

But our problem remains, and even becomes more difficult. For why does Freud simultaneously make identification a bond that is *necessarily* (and not *possibly*) anterior to the libidinal object bond? What compels him to make such an inconsistent move?

A first response comes readily to mind, although it never appears as such in Freud's text. It can be taken for granted that if identification designates a process that is formative of the ego (of the *Subjekt des Ichs*, in other words, of subjective identity), it is by the same token anterior in principle to any ego-object relation: the object relation, by definition, presupposes the constitution of the ego that is entering into relation with the object. Thus identification can no longer be viewed as just one relation among others, however "primary," nor even, taken to the extreme, as a relation at all. It is not something that might come upon or happen to the ego, since it is what has made the ego already come upon itself. And its anteriority (the anteriority of the very first identification, let us say) is absolute, not only because it precedes all relations but also, and more radically, because it exceeds all chronology: having taken place "before" the ego, it has never *presented* itself to the ego, it has never constituted a historical, datable, rememberable event. (That past, as Lévinas might say, has never been present.)

In addition, Freud's few and already quite enigmatic references to the merely chronological anteriority of a positive bond of identification are entirely inadequate with respect to the problem they raise. As a primordial relation, prehistoric identification will be from the outset exempt from relation, origin, and history; it will be a tie without tie (an umbilical cord?), origin without origin, an identification without model (*Vorbild*, *Ideal*, or *Gestalt*: all these are still present to view, and thus present to an already-constituted subject). The difficulty that arises here is, clearly, the one around which the conclusion of "On Narcissism" revolved (oscillated, wavered)[41]— namely, the difficulty involving the formation of the ego or the *birth of the subject*. This difficulty is at once absolutely binding and impossible to resolve within the conceptual framework of psychoanalysis. In a way, Freud cannot avoid it: in chronological order, the question of the genesis of the ego is the primary question, the one that governs everything else. But at the same time its rigor is such that it requires a regression beyond the ego-object or ego-model pairs, which belong to the history of an already-constituted ego. It is this regression that Freud visibly hesitates to undertake here—and ultimately avoids. Thus prehistoric identification is still, and in spite of everything, construed as a relationship or a relation that *happens* to the ego. At the very beginning—as early as the second sentence of Chapter 7—it is reduced to a formative identification (*vorbildliche Identifizierung*) with the paternal figure, that is, with the ideal of the Oedipal ego. And thus its anteriority with respect to the object bond becomes definitively mysterious, for if the primary identification is nothing other than a (pre-)Oedipal identification, it is no longer apparent why it would necessarily precede object love . . .

Unless the anteriority or non-anteriority of identification with respect to the object bond is itself a false problem. Let us note that Freud does offer us a path to follow, albeit a very tenuous one, and that this time it leads back beyond the identification/object-bond opposition, into a prehistory that has not confronted this contradiction. For no sooner has Freud spoken of the Oedipal ambivalence of identification with the paternal rival than he goes on as follows (thereby changing everything):

Identification, in fact, is ambivalent from the very first; it can turn into an expression of tenderness as easily as into a wish for someone's removal. It behaves like a derivative of the first, *oral* phase of the organization of the libido, in which the object that we long for and prize is assimilated by eating and is in that way annihilated as such. ["Group Psychology," p. 105]

This passage has to be compared with the third chapter of "The Ego and the Id," which deals with exactly the same motif:

At the very beginning, in the individual's primitive oral phase, object-cathexis and identification are no doubt indistinguishable from each other. [p. 29]

Henceforward his relation to his father is ambivalent; it seems as if the ambivalence inherent in the identification from the beginning had become manifest. [p. 32]

Thus we learn that the double pre-Oedipal prehistory of the Oedipus complex has its own prehistory—and, as Freud notes in both texts, this prehistory refers back to the collective prehistory of humanity, to primitive cannibalism, to the totemic meal, in short, to the whole great scene of the ingesting community or communion described in "Totem and Taboo."[42] Especially telling for our purposes is the fact that this prehistory inextricably blended together a devouring identification, as process of ego-formation, and the object bond, as tie or relation to the other. At the origin of the origin (but this origin is lost in the depths of time, it eludes memory by definition), hate-identification and object love must have been one and the same thing, one and the same *assimilation to* the other, *of* the other. To be and to have, these were the same: "I am the breast," as the famous London note will put it ("Findings, Ideas, Problems," *SE* 23: 299). The Narcissus, the ego (but we are now in the prehistory of the ego, in a sociality or a collectivity that precedes all individual history, and it is thus preferable to speak of "That," the id) had been formed *by way of* the other, *as* the other—by digesting it.

Thus it is finally pointless to try to find out whether identification precedes the object bond or vice versa: archi-incorporation does not allow for this alternative, quite simply because it knows, as yet, neither ego nor object nor model. And by the same token it is clear that the thesis of an original separation between identification and the object bond can no longer be maintained: identification is an "offspring" of the very first object relation, which is itself nothing but a devouring identification or an identificatory devouring. *It is no longer possible, in other words, to maintain the thesis of the Oedipus complex.* In fact, when Freud describes a prehistory of the Oedipus complex and brings into play three differentiated characters (the ego, the Father, and the Mother) and two types of bonds (identification and love), he is considering a situation that is already quite "historical," quite secondary. But prior to this little triangular society, making this society possible from the standpoint of a pre-individual (and nevertheless individuating) *socius*, one must now recognize a sort of group or *mass*, neither purely undifferentiated nor purely differentiated—the *Oedipal womb*: something, let us say, like a non-subject initiating itself as an ego in an unbinding bond of panic (and this is anxiety, and it is birth) to what is as yet neither object nor model, and what will be called "mother" only on the condition that it not be confused with the maternal character of the Oedipus complex.[43]

For this womb-mother (the nurturing breast, but also the womb from which I was born) is not *loved* in the Oedipal sense. This is so, first of all, because the womb-mother is not an object[44]—at least not an object exempt from the process of identification, as Freud suggests when he declares axiomatically that the primary identification involves the father. Since at the time of incorporation it is the very first "object" of the very first identification, the womb-mother is also the site of the very first erotic war. In fact, to say that identification is the original object relation is to say once again that this relation is equivalent to the immediate suppression of the object, to an absence of relation. To identify oneself with the object is to put oneself in its place or to place it within oneself, to kill it and live off its death. If I *am* the breast, then that breast *is nothing*—outside of myself, who have always already swallowed it up (and consequently *I* shall never come back to that place where *it* was I before I was). This first bond, this first *copula* that makes me what I am, is also the first unbonding, the first annihilation of alterity (a forgetting of the other, prior to any remembering): a matricidal Oedipus. Thus is confirmed, from a new angle, what we had already learned from "Beyond the Pleasure Principle": the *Bindung* is undertaken as love/hate ambivalence, as a double band or binding—and this is so, we must now add, because what is involved is an identification older than any relation of identity, a union more ancient than any individuation.

It follows—though this is a consequence that Freud does everything he can to evade—that the *Bindung*, if it is the condition of possibility of the relation to the other, and thus of the social bond, is also its condition of impossibility: for example, the condition of impossibility of Oedipal love and of all that that love is supposed to govern. For if devouring identification constitutes "the original form of emotional tie with an object" ("Group Psychology," p. 107), if everything begins (subject *and* sociality) in this indissoluble double band, can we still be satisfied with the official version of the Oedipus complex? Can we continue to separate the object bond and identification, love and hate? Can we slice through the double band, cut the Oedipus complex away from its womb, by imagining a *purely* libidinal relationship to the mother (free from any identification and from any violence) and a *purely* nonlibidinal identification with the father (which would only be colored by ambivalence in a second phase)? Is this not a reassuring construction, destined to preserve the myth of a peace that precedes violence, the myth of a primordially idyllic and harmonious sociality?

Secondary Identifications

These questions must be left wide open. Freud does not answer them; he does not even consider them, for they would completely destroy the argument he is seeking to develop. Thus the examination of identification comes to nothing, aborts: we pass abruptly on to other things, to *other* identifications, without being able to tell whether these latter "descend" from the primary identification or not. Among these other identifications we find those that "in a regressive way . . . [become] a substitute for a libidinal object-tie" ("Group Psychology," pp. 107–8). This is the second type in Freud's classification, and it encompasses the identifications that "The Ego and the Id" dubs "secondary." Unlike the primary identification, the secondary ones presuppose an object cathexis, inasmuch as they intervene secondarily in the loss of the loved object. As a result they should be more favorable to the Oedipal hypothesis of a pure love, free from any identificatory, mimetic element.

We shall see. If we keep to the definition of identification that has just been provided, we find three examples corresponding to it, among the numerous ones that Freud juxtaposes helter-skelter in this seventh chapter. The first appears via a list of the various forms of hysterical identification through symptoms: here we have the example of Dora, who imitates her father's cough and thus substitutes identification for object choice, the latter having been repressed.

Identification, in this case, "only borrows a single trait [*nur einen einzigen Zug*] from the person who is its object" (p. 107).[45] A second example, which Freud includes after his enumeration of the three types of identification but which clearly belongs in the category of "secondary identifications," is that of masculine homosexuality. Instead of replacing the Oedipal mother with a substitute object, the homosexual is transformed into that mother. Identification in this case is no longer partial, since the ego adopts the sexual nature of the object, which is therefore suppressed, abandoned. The last "instance of introjection of the object" into the ego is melancholia. As Freud has presented it in "Mourning and Melancholia," melancholic self-abasement would arise from the ego's identification with a loved/hated object and the simultaneous entrance of the ego into dissension with itself (more precisely, with its "critical agency," the ego ideal). In this case too, the identification is complete: "the shadow of the object has fallen upon the ego" (p. 109), the ego becomes the object.

The ego becomes, or rather *becomes again*—reverts to being—the object. For we must note that the secondary identifications are called "regressive." Freud insists on this with regard to identification of the "Dora" type: the object choice becomes identification again, and the movement of a so-called secondary identification thus consists in a reversion to "the earliest and original form of emotional tie" (p. 107)—that is, to *primary* identification. What reverts, in a so-called secondary identification, is quite simply primary identification, and the proof of this is that the reversion is accomplished by an "introjection"—in other words an incorporation—of the object into the ego.[46] It is clear at once that this hypothesis is hardly consistent with the Oedipal schema. Beyond the fact that Freud is now reaffirming the antecedence of devouring identification over the libidinal object cathexis, he is implying that the latter derives from the former. And to say that Dora's Oedipal love for her father (or the homosexual's for his mother) *regresses* into identification is to say, according to good Freudian doctrine, that identification subtended the object cathexis from the beginning, prior to the Oedipus complex and *right up to the Oedipus complex itself*. Otherwise, one could not hope to understand why regression adopts this form rather than some other:

we have to suppose that it is because the object relation is still haunted by identification (was therefore not yet Oedipal) that this relation gives up its place to identification so easily.

Freud had explained this in "Mourning and Melancholia," at the point where he was elaborating the idea of a regressive identification for the first time. It is worth taking a moment to look at this text, for it brings together virtually all the problems that are stirred up here. Why, Freud wonders, does the loss of the object provoke an identification with that object in melancholia, and not, as one might have expected, a displacement of the libido onto a substitute object? Because the lost object was a narcissistic object, as he begins by explaining:

> One or two things may be directly inferred with regard to the preconditions and effects of a process such as this. On the one hand, a strong fixation to the loved object must have been present; on the other hand, in contradiction to this, the object-cathexis must have had little power of resistance. As Otto Rank has aptly remarked, this contradiction seems to imply that the object-choice has been effected on a narcissistic basis, so that the object-cathexis, when obstacles come in its way, can regress to narcissism. The narcissistic identification with the object then becomes a substitute for the erotic cathexis. . . . It represents, of course, a *regression* from one type of object-choice to original narcissism. ["Mourning and Melancholia," *SE* 14: 249]

This passage rules out any understanding of secondary identification as a regression on the basis of a love object chosen according to the anaclitic or attachment type. If the ego turns itself regressively into the lost "object," it is because this latter *was* in some way the ego (let us recall that "On Narcissism" defined the narcissistic object as "what [a person] was," "what he himself would like to be," or as "someone who was once part of himself"). But conversely, if the loss of the narcissistic object is balanced by an identification, and not by a mere narcissistic retreat, it is because there was "a strong fixation to the loved object"—in short (the text cannot be understood in any other way), because the ego *was the object*. It follows that Freud is not satisfied, either, with the idea of a regression toward primary, "original" narcissism; and he continues:

> We have elsewhere shown that identification is a preliminary stage of object-choice, that it is the first way—and one that is expressed in an am-

bivalent fashion—in which the ego picks out an object. The ego wants to incorporate this object into itself, and, in accordance with the oral or cannibalistic phase of libidinal development in which it is, it wants to do so by devouring it. . . . If we could assume an agreement between the results of observation and what we have inferred, we should not hesitate to include this regression from object-cathexis to the still narcissistic oral phase of the libido in our characterization of melancholia. [pp. 249–50]

As we follow the rather strange logic of this argument, which leads us back once more to that mixture of narcissism and object bonding that is incorporation, we note that the identificatory outcome of melancholic regression is explained by the narcissistic nature of the object relation, which is characterized in turn as a relation of identification (and thus we learn in passing that the "narcissistic object choice," and *even narcissism itself*, is identification). To summarize: it is because the object relation itself was identificatory (i.e., "narcissistic") that the loss of the object provokes an identification, a devouring introjection. Consequently, regressive identification is defined not so much as the replacement of a pure object bond by a pure identificatory bond, but more as the exacerbation of the profoundly identificatory character of the relation to the object (to such an extent, moreover, that one may legitimately wonder whether the "loss of the object" is not the effect rather than the cause of this process). The same holds true for all the secondary identifications, which thus also escape the Oedipal framework. Within that framework, identification and object orientation are once again inseparable, at the beginning as at the end of the so-called regression, so that they bring us back to the double band or original incorporation, and not at all by chance: in the final analysis, they are only its reproduction or perpetuation *within the "Oedipus complex," like "Oedipus"* (Dora swallowing her father's cough, the homosexual incarnating the mother, and so on).

Triangular Identification

The last type of identification remains to be examined. According to Freud's definition, this third type comes about when the ego discovers it has "a common quality shared with some other person who is not an object of the sexual instinct" ("Group Psychology," p. 108).

As Freud declares in order to differentiate this third sort from identification of the "Dora" type, the ego does not copy a beloved person (*geliebte Person*) but a person who is not loved (*ungeliebte Person*). This point is a crucial one, for it implies that the identification does not involve the object, this time, but a third party. Hence it corresponds perfectly to the Oedipal schema: the third type of identification is triangular identification, triangulatable.

In other words, it is *hysterical* identification—at least as that identification has been described thus far. This last qualifier is needed because Freud proposes three examples of hysterical identification in Chapter 7 and because the second ("Dora"), as we have just seen, resists Oedipal triangulation. Here we have an innovation with respect to the "classic" Freudian theory of hysteria. Would it not have been appropriate, therefore, to re-elaborate the concept of hysterical identification? Might not the discovery of a "secondary" or "narcissistic" hysterical identification have provided a pathway toward quite a different understanding of hysteria in general? Had not Freud even outlined such a move in "Mourning and Melancholia," when he wrote that "narcissistic identification is the older of the two and it paves the way to an understanding of hysterical identification, which has been less thoroughly studied" (*SE* 14: 250)?

However, Freud does not embark upon this path. With a stubborn and striking persistence, he maintains his earlier problematics of hysteria as if no new element had appeared, as if all the examples of hysterical identification that he juxtaposes here coexisted peacefully within the same theory.

His first example of hysterical identification precedes the "Dora" example, of which it offers a sort of Oedipal version. For here is a girl who identifies with *her mother's* cough: the identification "may come from the Oedipus complex: in that case it signifies a hostile desire on the girl's part to take her mother's place, and the symptom expresses her object-love towards her father" ("Group Psychology," p. 106). Desiring to possess her father, the girl wants to be like her mother, in order to enjoy the object as her mother does, in her mother's place. The rivalrous triangle is in place, and it is obvious at once that this triangle is generated on the basis of the object-oriented pinnacle: it is on the basis of the desire for the object that the formative identification of the beginning is reinforced, becomes rivalrous, takes on a "hostile colouring," and so on. This means, too, that the rivalry (the hatred) *derives* from the girl's desire for the object, and that the identification has no other function but to *represent* or "express" this desire on the secondary scene of the fantasy or symptom. Such is, in fact, the "complete mechanism of the structure of a hysterical symptom":

1. The ego discovers that it has a quality or element in common (*Gemeinsamkeit*) with another person—having to do, it must be added, with a common desire for the same object. This "common sexual element," according to *The Interpretation of Dreams*,[47] or that "something in common, which may signify love"[48]—in short, this (same) desire—is what identification represents, in order to carry that desire out;

2. But because this identification is accomplished under the sign of Oedipal guilt and repression, it is limited to "a single trait,"[49] preferably chosen for the unpleasantness it entails (a painful cough, and so forth).

It does not take long to observe that this description of the "mechanism" of hysterical identification is simply a reworking of the one Freud had supplied in *The Interpretation of Dreams* concerning the "dream of the abandoned supper-party."[50] It involves the same relegation of hysterical mimesis to secondary status, the same accentuation of the object pole of desire, and so on—with one difference: the hysterical triangle is now associated, much more explicitly than before, with the Oedipal triangle proper. The same holds true for the third and final example of hysterical identification, which is similarly modeled on the notions of hysterical contagion that Freud annexed to the analysis of the dream of the abandoned supper-party. The only difference is that in *The Interpretation of Dreams* Freud cited a case of identification among patients in the same hospital, whereas here it is a question of identification among girls in the same boarding school. But we are obviously dealing with the same phenomenon and the same theory, and this is the sign that Freud does not distinguish between the "boarding school" mechanism of identification and that of hysterical-Oedipal identification, any more than he did earlier between the "hospital" identification and the triangular identification of the "abandoned supper-party." That is why we must not be misled by the fact that he presents the boarding-school identification as a *third* case of hysterical identification: "There is a third particularly frequent and important case of symptom formation, in which the identification leaves entirely out of account any object-relation to the person who is being copied" ("Group Psychology," p. 107).

This was already the case with the Oedipal identification with the "person who is not loved," and from this point of view there is no difference between the first hysterical identification and the third.[51] The latter may well be collective—and thus entail the problematics of group identification, as we shall see; all the same, it stems from the same "mechanism."

The mechanism is this. Freud imagines, exactly as he does in *The Interpretation of Dreams*, that one of the boarding-school girls "has had a letter from someone with whom she is secretly in love which arouses her jealousy, and that she reacts to it with a fit of hysterics" (p. 107). A first hysterical crisis, then, and one that is produced, it seems, on the basis of an Oedipal scenario (disappointed love, jealousy, identification with the rival). This symptom would then be propagated by psychic contagion and imitation, by virtue of the identificatory mechanism that we are acquainted with already: the other boarders would nurture a desire analogous to that of their classmate ("a common quality"), and they would identify, under the influence of guilt, with her symptom ("single trait"). Once again, as a result, identification comes about on the basis of a comparison of one desire to another—in other words, *on the basis of an object love*:[52]

The other girls would like to have a secret love affair too, and under the influence of a sense of guilt they also accept the suffering involved in it. . . . One ego has perceived a significant analogy with another upon one point—in our example upon openness to a similar emotion [*Gefühlsbereit-schaft*]; an identification is therefore constructed on this point, and, under the influence of the pathogenic situation, is displaced on to the symptom which the one ego has produced. The identification by means of the symptom has thus become the mark of a point of coincidence between the two egos which has to be kept repressed. [p. 107]

And, as in *The Interpretation of Dreams*, Freud points out that the boarding-school girls do not identify because of sympathy; instead, they sympathize because of identification:

It would be wrong to suppose that they take on [*sich aneignen*] the symptom out of sympathy [*Mitgefühl*]. On the contrary, the sympathy [*Mitgefühl*] only arises out of the identification, and this is proved by the fact that infection or imitation of this kind takes place in circumstances where even less pre-existing sympathy [*Sympathie*] is to be assumed than usually exists between friends in a girls' school. [p. 107]

But what does "sympathy" mean here? Several things, and we must be attentive to the particularly crafty and interested use Freud makes of this word.

We must keep in mind that Freud's "sympathy" is first of all McDougall's word and concept—that is, the induction of emotion by means of sym-pathy, *Mit-gefühl*, or affective mimesis. We must make no mistake about it: by declaring that sympathy proceeds from identification, Freud in no way means to make affect an effect of mimesis; quite the contrary. The concept of identification, as he uses it, has precisely the function of reversing the mimesis-affect relation implied in the concept of sympathy. It signifies that affect precedes mimesis instead of being produced or induced by it. The individual sentiment (*Gefühl*) is understood to be anterior to social sympathy (*Mitgefühl*)—even to empathy (*Einfühlung*);[53] the boarding-school girls already have the same *Gefühlsbereitschaft*, the same affective or emotional (pre)disposition *before* they identify with each other. Putting-oneself-in-the-other's-place or feeling-oneself-in-(or as)-the-other thus constantly presupposes the feeling of self and feeling itself. If, in hysterical identification, I feel (myself) to be like another, it is because I have previously recognized that he feels like me, because I have recognized myself in him (in his desire). Before he is a model with which I identify myself, the other is a likeness in whom I recognize myself, by comparison or analogy. In short (and this is the crucial point), affect (sentiment, feeling) does not come to me from or through the other. It is my own: I begin by having a feeling, *then* I identify with someone who has the same feeling, and not vice versa. There is no affective suggestion, and thus no sympathetic or empathetic contamination of the ego by the other—at least at the beginning. Social sympathy (psychology) begins here, to be sure, but its starting point is individual passion (psychology).

But this is not all, for sympathy is also, and more simply, a friendly and nonconflictual relation to others. To say that no sympathy precedes identification is thus to reaffirm that identification initially involves a libidinally indifferent person, "who is not an object of the sexual instinct": the imitated third party is not loved, not even in the mode of friendly sympathy, camaraderie, collaboration on the job, and so on. These social relations with others—which Freud always describes, we must remember, as sexual relations inhibited in their aim—are *generated* by identification, which itself has no sexual aspect at the outset.

This last statement is clearly decisive in Freud's reasoning, for it makes it possible to establish the link between the Oedipal schema and the group schema, via the boarding-school example: just as Oedipal identification comes about in the case of the *ungeliebte Person*, so social identification (contagion) occurs between persons whom no sympathy, no libidinal bond connects initially (since the group members are strangers to one another to an even greater degree than are the boarding-school friends). Hence we have reached the result in view of which this laborious treatment of identification was undertaken: the social *Gefühlsbindung* is hysterico-triangular identification, and therefore Oedipal identification. From the little family triangle to the social pyramid or cone, we do not escape the Oedipal structure: the boarding school is just a big family, structured along Oedipal lines, and the group in turn is a big boarding school, structured along the lines of collective hysteria. As for the axis around which all these triangles pivot (the "common element"), this is the members' love for the leader: "We already begin to divine that the mutual tie between members of a group is in the nature of an identification of this kind, based upon an important emotional common quality; and we may suspect that this common quality lies in the nature of the tie with the leader" (p. 108).

In summary, group members ("brothers") identify with one another by virtue of their common love for the *Führer* (for the father, who thus occupies, oddly enough, the place of the Oedipal *object*).

This is a robust and simple schema, which once again makes the social community a community of love, bound and tied together by Eros. And although the identificatory bonds are not in themselves libidinal, the fact remains that they *depend* on the libidinal object bond: just as the little Oedipus identifies with his father *because* he wants to possess the mother, so the members of the group identify among themselves *because* they love the leader. Or again, as Freud explains earlier with regard to the Church and Christ, "the tie which unites each individual" with the leader "is also the cause of the tie which unites them with each other" (p. 94).

The solution which is offered for the "riddle" of "the libidinal organization of groups" is thus easily reconciled, as we have seen, with Freud's initial hypotheses. *But not with the ones he had just been advancing with regard to "primary" and/or "secondary" identification.* These latter, as we now know, brought to light an original indissociation between the object bond and the identificatory bond that is incompatible with the Oedipal triangulation, and this means that the schema of the group could only be maintained in its first version if a series of theoretical decisions were taken—each one an application of arbitrary force. Here is what has been required, if our count is correct. (1) We had to bypass or repress the "womb" problem of primitive incorporation, in order to be able to construct the Oedipal triangle with its well-differentiated characters. (2) We had to lump hysterical identification together with Oedipal identification, by refusing to follow the path opened up by "narcissistic" or "regressive" identification. (3) We had to associate the phenomena of contagion and affective suggestion within crowds to hysterical identification thus understood, by refusing to recognize primary mimetic phenomena in them. All this adds up to a lot of choices taken at a lot of crossroads. We must then wonder why Freud chooses to embark upon one path rather than another. Why, among all the theoretical solutions available to him, the possibility of which he points to himself, does he systematically opt for "Oedipal" solutions? What are the reasons for this deepseated preference? What orients his choice? And what is it destined to preserve, to safeguard?

It preserves two things, which are one and the same: the Subject (and) Politics. As we suggested earlier, the peremptory installation of the Oedipus complex at the origin of the history of the individual subject is a way of short-circuiting the investigation of the subject's genesis in a pre-individual identification with the other. In this sense, it is no exaggeration to say that the Oedipal hypothesis intervenes to protect the autarchy of the subject—or, in what amounts to the same thing, the propriety of its desire (its "feelings," its affects, and so on)—in order to protect it against the possibility of *an alteration (which particularly does not mean an alienation) constitutive of its identity, its most proper "being."* As for Freud's obstinate refusal to grant primacy to "sympathetic" suggestion and contagion, this of course points in the same direction.

All these decisions ultimately add up to exempting the subject from the question—an infinitely disturbing one, to be sure, for it is infinitely abysmal, collapsing—of its being-(like)-the-other. This is (even though the term is, rigorously speaking, inadequate) the question of its *being-"social."* For this is no doubt the most impressive aspect of this chapter on identification: conceived by Freud as a sort of return toward the individual foundations of society, the text has, against all expectation, caused "social psychology" to resurface at the heart of "individual psychology," in the form of the identification of the ego itself. Far from supplying an origin or basis for the relation to others, the *sameness* of the ego it*self* has very paradoxically brought to light the necessity of thinking the other "before" the ego or, more precisely, "in" the ego, *as* ego. The group is thus at the origin (without origin) of the individual. Neither simply undivided nor simply divided, neither One nor Other (the One in diffe*r*ance from the Other, to borrow from Derrida), the ego is then inaugurated as (the) group.

Now by immediately concealing this possibility in the Oedipus complex, Freud is not simply closing off the subject within the security of its own limits (inside/outside, subject/object, ego/Other, and so on); he is also making a profoundly political gesture. For violence is involved here—in other words, the political evil par excellence. We have confirmed this repeatedly: the "social" womb or matrix of the ego is simultaneously the matrix of violence (hence the quotation marks that have to surround this "sociality"). Original identification with the other, if it is constitutive of the ego (but now we should be putting *all* the terms we have just used into quotation marks), is likewise radical violence with respect to the other—a devouring mouth clamped down on the alterity of others, an eye blind to what gave it light, an immediately destructive hand (grasping, grappling, appropriating) laid on the breast. The birth of the ego, we might say in a parody of one of Hegel's famous formulae, is the death of the other. It bears the death of the other in itself and it bears the other dead in itself.

In this sense, primitive identification constitutes at once the condition of possibility and the condition of impossibility of the ego *and* of sociality. An original alteration of the ego, primitive identification precludes, by definition, any purely pacific or "altruistic" relation to another, any ethical one-on-one between an "I" and a "thou," and any political dialogue—in short, any access to an other. (The other is from the outset inaccessible not, as is often claimed, because it would escape the egoism or solipsism of the ego, but because it is all the more other in that it is the same, the same as I who am the same as he.) It amounts to the same thing to say that the other paralyzes the ego from the starting-point of "itself" and that every relation to the other undecides itself, inaugurates itself as undecidable ambivalence of love and hate.

Thus the decision to decide the problem of the origin of the social tie in favor of the Oedipal hypothesis is not just one decision among others. In a way, it is *the* decision itself, the critical decree that cuts through what does not admit of dividing up. And here it is the political decision to decide between peace and war, by separating Oedipal object love from identification. This separation, which is flatly contradicted by everything Freud tells us elsewhere on incorporation, functions as an exclusion: violence is (violently) excluded from what becomes, by that very token, a decidable relation to the other, to the object. The violence (death-dealing disunion) that internally torments love (erotic union) is henceforth conceived as its *other*, as what assails it and threatens it *from without*. Thus the Greeks regularly purified the City of its internal miasmas by throwing a *pharmakos* outside the walls (and we know that Oedipus was such a *pharmakos*).[54]

By making everything begin—the ego and sociality—at the Oedipal stage, Freud thus makes everything begin with peace, and this is a way to preserve the possibility of a united society that would not be destroyed or sapped in advance by intestinal violence, violence internal to the social body. A myth of the origin of the subject, the Oedipus complex is consequently also a political myth, a myth with a political function. It is the myth of the Subject Politic, the Political (and the) Subject: the myth of an individual subject that would not be internally permeated with the stealthy violence of a relation without relation to the other, the myth of a political body lovingly closed in on itself that would not be continually disorganized by the relations of odious assimilation to and of the other.

Undecidable Oedipus

This myth was not constructed without considerable effort and some interpretive violence, as we have had ample opportunity to note. The extraordinary *internal* fragility of the construction still remains to be confirmed and demonstrated, if only as a finishing touch to our argument. At this point, we should note that the Oedipus complex offers no solution to the political problem of violence, either at the level of the "individual" complex or at the level of the group. For we have to remember that the Oedipus complex is a *crisis*—and a violent one at that. If the Oedipal mother is loved, the paternal model is hated. The Oedipal identification is straightforwardly defined as rivalrous, jealous, murderous. Even without referring to Freud's own remarks about the original ambivalence of "oral" identification, we cannot help noting that in the Oedipal context this identification is by no means "peaceful."

It makes no difference that Oedipal hatred may be attributed to a triangular rivalry rather than to an intrinsic ambivalence of identification, that it may be focused on the father instead of the mother, and that it may derive secondarily from love for the mother; from our point of view, all this changes nothing. If violence is eliminated on the side of what is called the object relation, it simply resurfaces, more virulent than ever, on the side of the identificatory relation. Hence the following problem in all its formidable simplicity: How can such a competitive and hate-filled identification with a rival ever lead to a peaceful relationship with that same rival? How can the violent, passionate desire to put oneself in the other's place ever give way, if not to love, at least to respect for the other? Here we have the problem known formally as the "dissolution of the Oedipus complex," from which one of Freud's later articles takes its title (*SE* 19). How and why is the Oedipal crisis resolved? How and why does the little Oedipus agree to give up the maternal object to the father? How and why does he internalize the paternal interdiction, that is, the law of the other, the Other as Law, and so on?

This problem, which is that of the norm in every sense (sexual, ethical, political) and of the origin (ontogenetic, phylogenetic) of this norm, is not contemplated by Freud here. At least not directly; we shall have to wait for the third chapter of "The Ego and the Id" to find the question raised on its own account, under the label of "ego ideal" or "superego." For the moment, let us postpone any analysis of the difficulties Freud will confront there. The mere statement of the problem suffices to show that Oedipal normalcy cannot be taken for granted. In and of itself, the Oedipus complex can only give rise to an endless state of war. It is one thing to enter into the Oedipus complex, quite another to emerge from it and to achieve a nonconflictual relation with the father, a relation governed by the law of private property ("this is mine, that is yours") and symbolic economy ("exchange your mother for another woman"). Yet nothing in the hypothesis of the Oedipus complex, as it is set forth here, ultimately authorizes such a "way out." It is not clear why the Oedipal rivalry should not go on forever, nor is it clear by what miracle identification with the father should be spontaneously transformed into tenderness or respect. *By the same token, it is not clear, either, why identifications within the group should be exempt from violence.* For why should they tend to generate peaceful social relationships, as Freud consistently implies? His own premises ought to have led him to declare just the opposite. If group identification is Oedipal in structure, it is necessarily rivalrous. Therefore pregnant with an at least latent violence. Therefore ill-suited to engender social ties that are positive, harmonious, stable, and so on.

This implication was not immediately obvious, it is true, in the case of "boarding-school" identification, for Freud used that example to show identification functioning on the basis of an *analogy* (*Analogie*) and not an *identity* of desire. Although the boarding-school girls shared an "openness to a similar emotion," they did not have a common love object. It followed that boarding-school iden-tification fell outside Oedipal rivalry proper. In short, the boarding-school Oedipus complex was the Oedipus complex minus hatred, a play Oedipus. The girls identified with each other without truly identifying; they behaved "as if," and thereby sympathized. But such sympathy becomes highly improbable when we move to the group Oedipus complex, which is an Oedipus complex in the strict sense, since group members are deemed to identify with one another by virtue of their common love for a common object (the leader)—in short, are considered to be in a position of mutual rivalry. And if this is the case, how can there be any sympathy at all among the rivals, Oedipal brothers?

There is a serious difficulty here of which Freud is fully aware, as we can see from the effort he makes to resolve it—or, rather, to get around it. Why, indeed, should he feel a need to declare that "sympathy . . . arises out of identification"? Why does he add, a lit-tle later, still speaking of hysterico-triangular identification, that "the more important this common quality [*Gemeinsamkeit*] is, the more successful may this partial identification become, and it may thus represent the beginning of a new tie [*dem Anfang einer neuen Bindung entsprechen*]" ("Group Psychology," p. 108)?

He adds a long note to the end of the chapter, explaining that

the manifestations of existing identifications . . . result among other things in a person limiting his aggressiveness towards those with whom he has identified himself, and in his sparing them and giving them help. The study of such identifications, like those, for instance, which lie at the root of clan feeling, led Robertson Smith (*Kinship and Marriage*, 1885) to the surprising discovery that they rest on the acknowledgment of the possession of a com-mon substance [by the members of the clan], and may even therefore be created by a meal eaten in common. This feature makes it possible to con-nect this kind of identification with the early history of the human family which I constructed in *Totem and Taboo*. [p. 110, n. 2]

Why does Freud do all this if not to gain recognition, more or less under the table, for a thesis that is astonishing in view of what preceded it—namely, that *identification creates sympathy, generates a positive bond with others?* This thesis must now appear as what it really is: a deus ex machina whose opportune descent from the rafters of psychoanalytic theory assures a "happy end" to the somber Oedipal drama, which otherwise would not have one. Without the intervention of such providential identificatory sympathy, the Oedipus complex would remain interminable, as would violence. This sympathy is thus absolutely indispensable to the argument Freud is making, from the moment he seeks to conceive of the Oedipal identification as the condition making a peaceful, controlled social tie possible. But it is at the same time absolutely unjustifiable, since he also gives us all the elements we need to think the opposite.

In a single gesture, Freud describes and eradicates the violence inherent in identification, affirms and denies Oedipal hatred. And does not the simultaneous, ambivalent affirmation of two contradictory propositions always mark—we have learned this lesson from Freud—the secret consistency of a desire? This is the case here, except that the desire in question is precisely the desire to abolish ambivalence, the desire to cut through the inextricable entanglement of love and hatred where every desire (proper, univocal, decidable, and so on) originates and is impeded. Describing and eradicating the violence of the Oedipal identification, Freud actually describes and eradicates its fundamental ambivalence—*describes it by eradicating it*. Undecidable Oedipus . . .

We shall perhaps be accused of attaching too much importance to a few fortuitous remarks that Freud scatters here and there in a single chapter without ever dwelling on them. However, such an objection would presuppose that the reader knows what is fortuitous in a text. And it might be demonstrated in any event that the enigmatic transmutation of rivalrous-Oedipal identification into "sympathetic" identification, here mentioned as if in passing, is regularly encountered elsewhere and always at critical moments. Already in "Totem and Taboo," it is the *erotic* identification implied in the *murderous* incorporation of the primal father that was supposed to generate "deferred obedience" to the father and thus to ensure the passage from war to law, from raw violence to Oedipal guilt, and so forth. Similarly in "The Ego and the Id," Freud again assigns to erotic identification with the "superegoistic" or "ideal" Father the role of pacifying the *rivalrous* identification of the Oedipus complex. Thus it is clear that this seventh chapter of "Group Psychology" is not the only place where Freud plays on the ambivalence of identification in order to eradicate it, where he relies on this ambivalence in order to escape it. This duplicity arises every time the Oedipus complex comes up, and each time it is the enabling factor behind the critical decision, the outcome of the Oedipal crisis.

But we need look no farther than "Group Psychology." In Chapter 9 we find the hypothesis of identificatory sympathy once again, here explicitly related to the problem of the transformation of hatred into a positive bond with others. The chapter is devoted to a discussion of the concept of the "herd instinct" (*Herdentrieb*) as proposed by W. Trotter. To this innate social instinct, which Freud immediately connects with the psychoanalytic Eros and which he praises Trotter for preferring to the mystery of "suggestibility," he nevertheless raises two objections:

1. As a social instinct, it is not sufficiently political; it leaves "no room at all for the leader" (p. 119). Man is not simply a herd animal (*Herdentier*) but rather a horde animal (*Hordentier*), "an individual creature in a horde led by a chief" (p. 121).

2. This instinct is not really an instinct, for Trotter was mistaken to consider that it cannot be split up, that it is "irreducible" and "primary" (p. 119).

Now this second objection, on which the entire chapter hinges, is of particular interest. If Freud refuses to concede any specificity to the herd instinct, it is not just to claim a more "primary" specificity for the sexual instinct instead. The objection goes much deeper, for it bears upon the instinctive or "drive-based" character of sociality, in other words, on its naturalness. Man is not *naturally* sociable, he is not a herd *animal*. Sociality cannot be deduced from *any* innate drive or instinct. Why not? Because the state of nature, which Freud infers here by analogy with the state of childhood, immediately implies war or, at the very least, the complete absence of relations with others. Any other, except perhaps the mother, provokes anxiety (*Angst*). The child's most primitive and spontaneous relation to a "stranger" is a non-relation, a vehement, uncontrollable, and panic-laden rejection of the other. Or else hostility, jealousy:

> For a long time nothing in the nature of herd instinct or group feeling [*Massengefühl*] is to be observed in children. Something like it first grows up, in a nursery containing many children, out of the children's relation to their parents, and it does so as a reaction to the initial envy with which the elder child receives the younger one. The elder child would certainly like to put his successor jealously aside, to keep it away from the parents, and to rob it of all its privileges. [pp. 119–20]

Harmony is thus not preestablished. Nature is not good; rather, it is likely to be naturally bad: *homo homini lupus*, man is a wolf among men, as Freud repeats after Hobbes in "Civilization and Its Discontents." This bleak remark, while it may justify the dismissal of Trotter's overly idyllic herd instinct, at the same time precludes imagining any natural sociality in general—for example, a libidinal or erotic sociality. Once again, loving one's neighbor cannot be taken for granted. It is the murderous ("egoistic," "narcissistic") wish that is primary—at least, if we follow Freud here, when it is not a question of the mother or the parents (the mother *and the father*). And consequently, *if* we *want* to conceive of a non-bellicose relation to others, we have to imagine hatred transformed into love of one's neighbor, we have to imagine an economy of violence.

Here is where identification comes in. Freud might have been expected to locate identification on the side of violence. After all, he has just finished describing the "fraternal complex," that is, the small child's jealousy toward his rivals for his mother's (or parents') affection—that is, the murderous identification of the Oedipus complex. However, he does nothing of the sort. Quite unexpectedly, identification now appears *after* the Oedipus complex or, more precisely, as the *end* of the Oedipus complex and conflict. Just after he has depicted the murderous desires of the older child toward a little brother or sister, Freud continues:

> But in the face of the fact that this younger child (like all that come later) is loved by the parents as much as he himself is, and in consequence of the impossibility of his maintaining his hostile attitude without damaging himself, he is forced into identifying himself with the other children. So there

grows up in the troop of children a communal or group feeling, which is then further developed at school. [p. 120]

Far from being confused with rivalry or maintaining it, identification thus brings rivalry to an end, by creating a sense of community (*Gemeinschaftsgefühl*) or sympathy (*Mitgefühl* and *Sympathie*). This may be so. But should it not be obvious by now that feeling like the other, in the place of the other, from the place of the other, is precisely the affect of jealousy par excellence? Was not that sympathy, that identificatory *Mitfühlen*, the very wellspring of Oedipal antipathy ("Get out of there so I can get in")? If this is the case, we have a right to be astonished by the sudden metamorphosis of identification that takes it from the realm of radical antipathy to the domain of friendly sympathy.

Here Freud makes a rhetorical concession: "This transformation—the replacing of jealousy by a group feeling . . . —might be considered improbable, if the same process could not later on be observed again in other circumstances" (p. 120). And then comes the example of the girls who have a crush on a pianist, a subtly modified version of the boarding-school example. Imagine them, Freud says, crowding around their idol after a concert. Since they all have the same love object (hence an Oedipal love object), each girl will want to possess that object for herself alone. *A priori*, therefore, we have rivalry, jealousy, and mutual hair-pulling. Consequently, we have the state of nature (woman is a wolf among women). And, finally, we have the state of law: recognizing the impossibility of winning the object of their love, the girls agree to give up their demands on the condition that all do likewise, so that no one is privileged. Since I cannot satisfy my desire, let it at least be *the same* for the others, let us at least all be in the same boat. This jealous contract, this egalitarianism rooted in envy, gives rise to fraternity, the sense of justice, social conscience, and the sense of duty—in short, as "Civilization and Its Discontents" says, to law in general:[55] "Instead of pulling out one another's hair, they act as a united group. . . . Originally rivals, they have succeeded in identifying themselves with one another by means of a similar love for the same object" ("Group Psychology," p. 120).

The "pianist argument" concludes as follows: "Thus social feeling is based upon the reversal of what was first a hostile feeling into a positively-toned tie in the nature of an identification. So far as we have hitherto been able to follow the course of events, this reversal seems to occur under the influence of a common affectionate tie with a person outside the group" (p. 121).

This is Freud's last word on the question, and it is worth noting that this position quickly hardens into a doctrinal thesis, a psychoanalytic dogma. Thus, when Freud wonders, in "Why War?" or in "Civilization and Its Discontents," how aggression and war are impeded, the answer is ready at hand: through identification, which channels libido toward others. Civilization, it is said in "Civilization and Its Discontents," aims at

binding the members of the community together in a libidinal way as well and employs every means to that end. It favours every path by which strong identifications can be established between the members of the community. [*SE* 21: 108–9]

Civilization has to use its utmost efforts in order to set limits to man's aggressive instincts and to hold the manifestations of them in check by psychical reaction-formations. Hence, therefore, the use of methods intended to incite people into identifications and aim-inhibited relationships of love. . . . [*SE* 21: 112]

Similarly, the 1922 article "Some Neurotic Mechanisms in Jealousy, Paranoia and Homosexuality" attributes the mutation of Oedipal hatred into homosexual love to an "exaggeration" of the identificatory process. This is to say, once again, that identification gives rise to love, libidinalizes the relation to the other (here we can read between the lines a reworking and a transformation of the theses of the Schreber case, Freud's treatment of social homosexuality and paranoia):

Observation has directed my attention to several cases in which during early childhood impulses of jealousy, derived from the mother-complex and of very great intensity, arose [in a boy] against rivals, usually older brothers. . . . Under the influences of upbringing—and certainly not uninfluenced also by their own continuing powerlessness—these impulses yielded to repression and underwent a transformation, so that the rivals of the earlier period became the first homosexual love-objects. Such an outcome of attachment to the mother . . . [is] first of all . . . a complete contrast to the development of persecutory paranoia, in which the person who has before been loved becomes the hated persecutor, whereas here the hated rivals are transformed into love-objects. It represents, too, an exaggeration of the process which, according to my view, leads to the birth of social instincts in the individual. In both processes there is first the presence of jealous and hostile impulses which cannot achieve satisfaction; and both the affectionate and the social feelings of identification arise as reactive formations against the repressed aggressive impulses. . . . The fact that homosexual object-choice not infrequently proceeds from an early overcoming of rivalry with men cannot be without a bearing on the connection between homosexuality and social feeling. [*SE* 18: 231–32]

And thus Freud can eventually write to Einstein that "the structure of human society is to a large extent based" on the *Gefühlsbindungen* generated by identification ("Why War?" *SE* 22: 212).

We can hardly fail to see, now, that these measures taken to ensure against the pacifying power of identification depend on a power play or perhaps a massive blinding. For the solution that is set forth here to the problem of sociality *is quite precisely that problem itself.* To say that identification overtakes rivalry like a reaction formation destined to limit, transcend, or surpass it is simply to say that rivalry reacts against itself, limits itself, transcends or surpasses itself—*since rivalry is already identification.* Identification is thus both the locus of the difficulty and the site of its resolution, or perhaps it is both the way one "enters into" the Oedipus complex and the way one "gets out" of it. In this connection, we need only reread the sentence that concluded the "pianist argument" to note that it can be understood in two different ways: "Originally rivals, they have succeeded in identifying themselves with one another by means of a similar love for the same object" ("Group Psychology," p. 120). To identify *by means of* a similar love, *because of* an identical desire—is this not the way Freud always describes the Oedipal rivalry? And presumably what he seeks to interpret here as a final pacification can just as well be interpreted, with him, according to him, as the beginning of the war. If the contract (the social contract) through which the belligerent parties give up their demands has the effect of compelling them to identification and social feeling, then it is an empty gesture, for identification came before the contract, just like the "social" feeling corresponding to it—which is hatred. The same causes bring about the same effects; it is difficult to see why the identificatory *Mitgefühl*, which was "negative" prior to the contract, would reverse itself and become a positive affect afterward.

The reality is that there is no social contract, quite simply because there are no parties to enter into one. A contract always presupposes the prior identity and individuality of the contracting parties. At least two are needed to establish a contract. This is not the case here, since identification precedes the supposed contract and implies an indistinction between "self" and "other" that precludes any agreement, any symbolic pact (such a pact would be possible only after the contract, after the impossible original contract). This does not in any way signify that it would prevent all sociality. Quite to the contrary, it is the original sociality—(a)sociality—except that this singular sociality can no longer be encompassed within the oppositions between individual and sociality, violence and peace, nature and civilization, law, and so on.

These oppositions are abolished without giving rise to any reconciling synthesis. Freud says this clearly when he invites us to conceive of identification *before* and *after* the "contract": in the first case it is marked by the negative sign of hatred, and in the second case by the positive sign of friendly sympathy or love—that is, identification is marked by both signs. But that is also what he does not say, when he persists in decomposing the ambivalence of identification into two contradictory values and into two successive phases, sometimes situating identification in pre-sociality, sometimes situating it within sociality, as sociality. He therefore says what he does not say, allows himself to say what he does not want to say: that the ego is the other, that peace is violence, that sociality is a-sociality. And vice versa.

"Be Me!" "Who's That?"

Freud has not yet mentioned the crucial bond, the bond with the leader. Chapters 7 and 9 of "Group Psychology" did not deal with this bond directly, because they consistently presupposed it, in keeping with the Oedipal concept of identification in general and social identifications in particular. *Without* a common libidinal bond, no identification would be established, either among Oedipal "brothers" or among members of the group. This has been a constant theme of our reading. Though it may have been temporarily set aside, the bond with the leader was nevertheless conceived as *the* founding bond of society. This political conception was implicit in the Oedipus complex. It has become quite clear that Oedipal politics entail some serious difficulties; indeed, we might be tempted to declare them insurmountable. Still, let us put them in parentheses for the time being and proceed as if we are unaware of them, in order to pursue the consequences of the Freudian argument as far as we can.

In Chapter 8, "Being in Love and Hypnosis," Freud spells out the nature of political love properly speaking. He has to take this step, for, as he explains in the opening paragraph, the word "love," as well as the concept (*Liebe*, and not the *Verliebtheit* of the chapter title), covers "a great many kinds of emotional relationships," and thus the particular kind under consideration has to be specified. Freud is therefore obliged to address certain questions. For example, is the love of group members for the *Führer* a love with a direct sexual aim or is it inhibited as to its aim? In the latter case, does it stem from sublimation or idealization? What becomes of libido? And is the love object chosen according to the anaclitic type or the narcissistic type?

One thing is certain: the answer cannot be sought in the direction of sexuality with a direct aim. Chapter 6 has already indicated as much, and in Appendixes C and D Freud dwells at length on this point: "In groups there can evidently be no question of [directly] sexual aims. . . . We are concerned here with love instincts which have been diverted from their original aims, though they do not operate with less energy on that account" ("Group Psychology," p. 103). This was already true for bonds of identification (moreover, that is why it was necessary to refer to them as *emotional* bonds), but it is just as true for the bond of political love: loving submission to the leader is quite clearly not equivalent to a directly sexual desire. Hence the need to resume and refine the analysis.

This was Freud's first stated reason. He adds another, however, which is no less crucial, even though he never acknowledges it as such. Not only is the leader not the object of direct sexual aims, but he can no longer be construed, strictly speaking, as an *object*. Speaking with full Oedipal rigor, he can no longer be an object, at least within the framework of a "positive" Oedipus complex. For if the Leader is a Father and group members are sons, it must become obvious that the sons' relations to the Father cannot be immediately assimilated to the object relation of the Oedipus complex, *since these son-to-father relations fall instead within the identificatory relation*. The Leader is not a Mother. On the contrary, in structural terms he occupies the place of the paternal rival. This implication cannot be avoided, since Freud consistently describes the group as a crowd (or horde) that is essentially masculine, led by a male chief. From this point of view, it is obvious that the examples on which Freud based his deciphering of the libidinal structure of the group were all selected or "arranged" so as to avoid this conclusion. By choosing examples of *female* crowds more or less systematically, Freud lent plausibility to the hypothesis of an Oedipal object love for a *masculine* leader—whereas this hypothesis is improbable, at least on the surface, in the case of a masculine crowd. And similarly, by deriving the social sentiment from a complex of fraternal jealousy aroused by love *for the parents*, Freud was surreptitiously lending credibility to the hypothesis of the brothers' love *for the father*—another improbable hypothesis, since according to conventional Oedipal doctrine the father is supposed to be the first rival (the first brother) for the mother!

There is doubtless no point in insisting further on this highly complex ruse. But it is important to understand this ruse as a sign of the confusion in which Freud finds himself as soon as he attempts to assert the libidinal and object-oriented nature of a relation which, within the framework of his own Oedipal theory, can be neither libidinal nor object-oriented. In short, love for the *Father* (the Leader) no more goes without saying than does love for a brother (one's neighbor). But conversely, without the *love* for the Leader-Father, the whole theory—the whole libidinal-political theory—would collapse. It would no longer be clear why (that is, in view of what, because of what) group members would identify with one another. Better still—or worse—it would no longer be clear how the bond with the leader would differ from identificatory bonds, how the "father" would differ from a "brother." Thus it is necessary at all costs—and here is the problem—to use the terms of a theory of love to describe a relation that, according to the evidence, is incompatible with a libidinal definition.

Is this possible? No, and we shall see spectacular proof of the point in a moment. But let us begin by following Chapter 8 as it progresses, for it reads like a kind of flight forward. Under the pretext of listing the various tenets of the psychoanalytic theory of love, Freud exhausts its possibilities as he confronts the problem to be resolved, somewhat as if he were reviewing all available "solutions," only to abandon them one by one. This chapter demonstrates, by way of the absurd, as it were, that the relation of authority (if it is a relation, and if it is authoritarian in the usual sense) does not fit within the framework of a theory of love.

We have seen that it does not fit, first of all, within the framework of a theory of sensitive, sensual, carnal love (*sinnliche Liebe*). This love inclines toward nothing other than direct sexual satisfaction, and it disappears as soon as it has achieved its aim. It gives rise to no fixed object cathexis, to no lasting bond, unlike the sexual tendencies that are inhibited as to their aims. Thus we must turn toward these latter tendencies if we are seeking the mainspring of political love.

For example—this is the second "solution," the second attempt at explanation—we must turn toward the inhibited sexual tendencies of the Oedipus complex. In fact, the repression that intervenes at the point of the destruction of that complex obliges the child to give up infantile sexual aims, and, according to Freud, a "modification" is then produced. The child is still tied to the previous sexual object, but by way of a tender feeling, although it is understood that the direct inclinations remain present in the unconscious. Thus we have two sorts of love: one is nonsensual, platonic, "celestial" (Uranian), while the other is sensual, "terrestrial" (Pandemian), and these may remain separated from puberty on, or they may be combined. In the first case, the result is a doubling of the love object—(the mother and the whore). In the second, which is the "normal" case, the result is a "synthesis" of the two loves in the same object—that is, a synthesis of *sinnliche Liebe* and *Verliebtheit*: "The depth to which anyone is in love, as contrasted with his purely sensual desire, may be measured by the size of the share taken by the aim-inhibited instincts of affection" (p. 112).

In spite of a certain textual ambiguity here, it is clear that *Verliebtheit* refers much more to the celestial or Platonic aspect of love—"as opposed" to its earthly aspect—than to their synthesis or combination. (Why, otherwise, would Freud measure it according to the contribution of aim-inhibited instincts?) *Verliebtheit* designates erotic passion insofar as it is capable of being purified, of detaching itself from any sexual aim—in short, of sublimating itself. That is what interests Freud, along with the overvaluation, the *Sexualüberschätzung*, that it implies: in erotic passion, he reminds us, the object is overvalued, exempt from criticism, idolized.

From this point on, we can see how easy it would have been to combine *Verliebtheit* and political love, to blend "celestial" overvaluation of the Lady with idolatry for the Leader. But that is precisely what Freud is unwilling to do—or at least he is not satisfied with that solution, for we see him shift surreptitiously toward a *different* theory of *Verliebtheit* and *Überschätzung*. The theory he has just summarized dates from 1912, when "On the Universal Tendency to Debasement in the Sphere of Love" was published. According to that earlier, Oedipal theory, the overvalued object represented the mother.[56] Freud's subsequent theory, expounded in 1914 in "On Narcissism," is incompatible with the first, for the object is now supposed to represent the *ego*, according to the hypothesis of a "yielding" or a "sacrifice" of narcissistic libido to the object:

We see that the object is being treated in the same way as our own ego, so that when we are in love a considerable amount of narcissistic libido overflows on to the object. . . . The ego becomes more and more unassuming and modest, and the object more and more sublime and precious, until at last it gets possession of the entire self-love of the ego, whose self-sacrifice thus follows as a natural consequence. The object has, so to speak, consumed the ego. ["Group Psychology," pp. 112–13]

Hence overvaluation (the "narcissistic stigmatum" par excellence, as "On Narcissism" indicated), hence abject blindness and servitude on the part of the ego—since the object is the ego, is oneself. This specular dialectics of Ego and Object has been a familiar one since our reading of "On Narcissism"; that it should reappear in connection with political love is hardly surprising, for it was already organized as a dialectics of Master and Slave, domination and servitude. This resurfacing of the problematics of narcissism nevertheless calls for a few brief comments:

1. It provides negative evidence of Freud's need to complicate the Oedipal schema. From here on, we know that the object of political love is not chosen according to the anaclitic mode (the object of political love is not, in the final analysis, an Oedipal mother).

2. On the positive side, it indicates that the leader is a narcissistic object: the group members love *themselves* in him, they recognize him as their master because they recognize *themselves* in him, and so forth. Here we have a well-known dialectics of "voluntary servitude" (dialectics in general) that attests once again to the profoundly narcissistic nature of Freudian politics.

3. Finally, and most important, the problematics of the narcissistic object brings back into view its own overwhelming *ambiguity*. Is narcissistic object orientation still object orientation? Is object narcissism still narcissism? This ambiguity cannot fail to have implications for the most general problematics of "Group Psychology." For example, if the bond with the leader, the founding bond of the social, is a narcissistic bond, can one still rely on the rigid opposition between "narcissistic mental acts" and (object-oriented) "social mental acts," as that opposition was established in the introduction to "Group Psychology"? Must we not infer that sociality is inscribed from the outset in the Narcissus complex? That the Narcissus complex is therefore not a Narcissus complex, and that the object is not an object? The relation of "subjects" to their leader is no longer one of ob-ject orientation or op-position but something else, wholly other.

Preliminary confirmation of these inferences comes in Freud's hasty modification of his definition of the love object. To say that the object of *Verliebtheit* is narcissistic is not enough. It still has to be defined more specifically as an object that "serves as a substitute for some unattained ego ideal of our own" (p. 112). The clarification is essential, and all its implications need to be spelled out here. First of all, overvaluation in love is attributed to an idealization: "It is even obvious, in many forms of love-choice, that the object serves as a substitute for some unattained ego ideal of our own" (p. 112).

An explanation for this has already been provided in the third section of "On Narcissism," as a note reminds us:

Being in love . . . exalts the sexual object into a sexual ideal. . . . The sexual ideal may enter into an interesting auxiliary relation to the ego ideal. It may be used for substitutive satisfaction where narcissistic satisfaction encounters real hindrances. . . . What possesses the excellence which the ego lacks for making it an ideal, is loved. ["On Narcissism," pp. 100–101]

But what is this ego ideal that is replaced by a substitute, that is, by the sexual object and/or the sexual ideal? It is time to recall the definition provided in "On Narcissism": the ego ideal is what one "would like to be," and so it is an identificatory *model* (the model according to which the internal ego ideal is formed, the moral agency, and so on). "On Narcissism" is not quite as explicit as this, perhaps, but our reading of the chapter on identification in "Group Psychology" leaves no further room for doubt, because that chapter describes the *vorbildliche Identifizierung* (formative identification) with the father of Oedipal prehistory in precisely the same terms: the father is the one the child wants to "be like," the child "takes his father as his ideal," and so on. Either these statements mean nothing at all, or they mean that the ego maintains a relation of "being," of identification with its ideal (whether external or internal)—and not a relation of "having," or object orientation, not even a narcissistic one.

By the same token, all these considerations clarify the importance of Freud's modification of the definition of *Verliebtheit*. Underneath its anodyne appearance, the modification implies a total reversal of perspective. To say that "the object has been put in the place of the ego ideal" ("Group Psychology," p. 113) is to state clearly that it replaces (represents, serves as substitute for) an identificatory model of the ego. And this, in turn, amounts to an acknowledgment of the character of the bond with the leader—not as object-oriented and loving, but quite simply as identificatory. For if the political love object puts itself in the place of the ideal, it must do so *as a model*: it puts itself in the place where the ego would like to be, in the identificatory place of the ego. Why continue to speak of an "object," then? Because it incarnates externally the internal ideal of the ego? Because what is involved, as Freud says about the schema that he appends to the end of Chapter 8, is an external object, an *äusseres Objekt*? Or because it is especially important not to say that what is involved is a model, because the difference between the object bond with the leader and the bonds of identification must be maintained at all costs?

These questions are not superimposed artificially on the text. They arise on their own, in an obscure and overtly awkward paragraph that immediately follows the formula cited above. Freud is engaging in a very significant speculation on the difference between *Verliebtheit* and identification. He begins by announcing that this difference is "easy to define" (p. 113). In the case of identification, the ego is enriched at the expense of the object, by introjecting its properties; in the case of *Verliebtheit*, it is impoverished to the benefit of the object, which absorbs it completely. The criterion is thus economic: appropriation/disappropriation, profit/loss, gain/sacrifice. But such an economy, as Freud is quick to note, does not facilitate the intended differentiation. Rather, it points up oppositions that do not exist, for erotic expropriation can still be described as an introjection, as a domestication of the object within a narcissistic, egoic economy. Since the opposition between ego and object turns out to be nonessential from this vantage point, it is no longer clear how *Verliebtheit* is opposed to identification.

Yet Freud insists on opposing them, and that is why he attempts to formulate a new and more basic distinction. In identification, the object is "lost," as the ego is transformed according to its model (*nach dem Vorbild des verlorenen Objektes*), whereas in *Verliebtheit* the object is maintained, preserved. *Verliebtheit*, in other words, still allows the object to subsist as object, lets it be. And where, then, might it be? It is in front of the ego, "outside" it, *other*. This alterity of the other, this ob-ject orientation of the object, is what identification does not respect, what it suppresses violently by introjecting it (*incorporating* it, since we are obviously dealing with regressive identification here and, behind that, oral devouring).

This paragraph cannot be understood if we fail to see that "object," here, no longer designates anything but exteriority or alterity vis-à-vis the ego. Whatever is not ego, whatever resists egoic assimilation, one way or another, is defined as "object." But that is also why the new distinction proves to be inadequate in turn. For if "object" signifies "external to the ego," "non-ego," we see at once that this minimal definition is just as valid for the identificatory model as for the libidinal object. Is not the *Vor-bild* what I see *before* me? Is it not the *Ideal* precisely inasmuch as *I am not it* (not yet)? If this is so, and if *Verliebtheit* respects the object's objectality, the same can also be said of identification—and their difference is once again impossible to detect. Hence Freud's interrogative objection: "Is it quite certain that identification presupposes that object-cathexis has been given up?" (p. 114).

The difference between *Verliebtheit* and identification is thus not so easy to define; it is, in fact, impossible to determine. However, the wholly negative lesson of this passage must not conceal the positive hypothesis that is introduced here in interrogative form: there are thus two types or regimes of identification, depending on whether identification absorbs (devours) the object (the *model*-object, it must be understood) or whether, on the contrary, it allows the object to subsist outside the ego. Now it must be obvious that this distinction between "idiopathic" identification and "heteropathic" identification—to borrow Scheler's useful terminology[57]—is formulated in exactly the same terms as the distinction that was to be established between *Verliebtheit* and identification. It is just as if Freud, having tried in vain to map out the distinction between object bond and non-object bond on the basis of the *Verliebtheit*/identification opposition, abruptly slipped it in between *two types of identification*. The stakes of this sort of strategic retreat are clear: it is a matter of preserving at all costs the "object-oriented" specificity of the bond with the father, at the price of making concessions at the level of its "erotic" nature. For it is absolutely *necessary* that the political bond be different from the bonds among group members—otherwise, the leader would no longer be a leader. Similarly, it is absolutely necessary that it be an ob-ject-oriented bond in the sense we have just indicated, maintaining the object as object and keeping the other as other—without which everything would boil down to the same thing, to the undecidable violence of the Same.

Shall it be said, then, that the bond with the leader is a bond of "heteropathic" identification, and thus different from, or opposed to, a bond of "idiopathic" identification? Yes and no. Yes, in that the *Verliebtheit*/identification opposition is no longer satisfactory. No, because to declare that explicitly would be to destroy "Group Psychology's" entire argument, retroactively. Thus Freud appears to be leaving the distinction between the two types of identification unexamined—as if he were no longer concerned with this overly "delicate" question—only to turn around and smuggle the distinction back in: "Can there be no identification while the object is retained? And before we embark upon a discussion of this delicate question, the perception may already be beginning to dawn on us that yet another alternative embraces the real essence of the matter, namely, *whether the object is put in the place of the ego or of the ego ideal*" (p. 114).

And that is that. We have scarcely begun to understand ("the perception may . . . be beginning to dawn") when we are expected to have understood everything. For Freud might well have offered some clarifications on that "other alternative," might have explained in what respect it is an alternative and in what respect it is other, especially since this "alternative" provides the definitive formula (*Formel*) for the "libidinal constitution of groups," and by the same token supplies the essay's conclusion: the group (the "primary group") would be, in fact, "*a number of individuals who have put one and the same object in the place of their ego ideal and have consequently identified themselves with one another in their ego*" (p. 116).

But Freud does not give us much more to go on. What, precisely, is the nature of the bond with an object-put-in-the-place-of-the-ego-ideal? In particular, how does it differ fundamentally from the ego ideal? These questions remain unanswered. Chapter 11, although it deals explicitly with the ego ideal, is in this regard a complete disappointment. It does spell out the consequences of the differentiation between the ego and the ego ideal, the relations these two agencies maintain between themselves, and so on, but it sheds no light on the nature of the bond with the (object replacing the) ideal. Is this bond ultimately based on love, *Verliebtheit?* Or on identification? We are left with question marks in these exceptionally "delicate" areas.

Since Freud leaves us to our own devices at the most critical moment, we shall have to try to reconstitute—to "construct," in the analytic sense—the argument that his analysis covertly subtends. First, *it goes without saying* that the bond with the object-put-in-place-of-the-ideal is not and can no longer be based on *Verliebtheit*. It must be something other, as Freud discreetly indicates in Appendix E of "Group Psychology," where *Verliebtheit* is said to be "a condition in which there is only room for the ego and the object" (p. 142) and is opposed to *another* relation to the object (we shall soon see which one) in which the object is put in the place of the ideal. *Verliebtheit* must therefore be based on identification, but a different identification from the one that causes the model-object to disappear in the ego. That is what had "already [begun] to dawn on us": putting the object in the place of the ego ideal means putting it in that identificatory place where the ego would like to be, *but where it cannot or must not be itself.* In other words, it means identifying oneself with a model with which one does not identify completely, according to which one governs oneself, but from a distance. Idiopathic versus heteropathic identification: instead of identifying the other with oneself, one identifies oneself with the other, who therefore, in spite of everything, remains an other, or—putting it more simply—who *remains.* The object-in-the-place-of-the-ideal is the unassimilable object in all senses, inimitable and uneatable.

A hint that Freud has in mind this type of identification with an unassimilable ideal appears in Appendix A, in the only passage where he offers any supplementary information on the "distinction between the identification of the ego with an object and replacement of the ego ideal by an object" (p. 134). This distinction is illustrated by two examples, which teach how an example is to be followed. The bad example, the one not to be followed, comes first: it is that of the soldier who identifies with the leader whom he has taken as his ideal. This soldier gets things all mixed up: he puts the object-put-in-the-place-of-the-ideal in the place of the ego and ends up making a fool of himself. What this first example shows is that one must not, or cannot, put oneself in the place of the ideal. The bond with the leader is not a bond of identification, at least not if "identification" means "taking oneself for another." But the second example, which is evidently the good one, obliges us to reconsider that schema. This is the example of Christians, to whom the Church *prescribes* the "imitation of Jesus Christ." In this case, one must identify with the ideal, follow the example of Christ, love others as He loved them.

The Christian, then, is apparently supposed to do what the soldier is not supposed to do. But appearances can be deceiving. According to Freud, the second example does not contradict the first, first of all because the identificatory prescription is never anything more than a secondary (accessory) addition to the love relation. The Church introduces a supplement, something "more" that "goes beyond the constitution of the group" (p. 135). And a supplement, as we all know, is what may be omitted with impunity. A second, supplementary reason is that the Christian prescription asks the impossible. The imitation of Christ is impracticable, it is prescribed *as impracticable*: "one can be a good Christian and yet be far from the idea of putting oneself in Christ's place" (pp. 135–36). Such an idea would be not foolish but crazy. Since the model remains infinitely transcendent (since mimetic mediation remains radically "external," as Girard would probably say)[58] there is no reason to fear that the imitator might mistake himself for the one imitated, that he might absorb the ideal in his own ego, as in the case of the foolish soldier. It follows that identification with the ideal, which is forbidden in the Army, may be prescribed by the Church—since such identification is in any event impossible. One may indeed identify oneself with the ideal, but only insofar as that ideal is—and must be—inaccessible. The Church, in sum, enjoins the imitation of an inimitable model, orders the faithful to identify *without* identifying: "Imitate me / do not imitate me."

However, this discussion still offers us only the most tenuous of clues. The (impossible) identification with an ideal is evoked here only as a particular example going "beyond the constitution of groups," and one that should not authorize us to draw any conclusions about its relation to the ideal in general. Nevertheless, the peculiar Christian injunction, as we have just expressed it, should put the informed reader of Freud on the alert, for these are the very terms used in Chapter 3 of "The Ego and the Id" to define the "categorical imperative" addressed to the ego by the ego ideal: "Be/do not be like me (the father)." There is no reason not to turn to this text (written two years after "Group Psychology") to confirm our suspicions, though this involves taking a detour and disturbing the chronology somewhat.

It is as if "The Ego and the Id" provides a retrospective explanation of a problematics of identification-with-the-ideal that "Group Psychology" had been withholding, inhibiting. In the later text we learn, first of all, that behind the ego ideal "there lies hidden an individual's first and most important identification, his identification with the father in his own personal prehistory" ("Ego and Id," p. 31).[59] The ego ideal or superego (there is no conceptual difference between these two terms, notwithstanding what has been said in France in the wake of Lagache and Lacan) derives from the primary identification, that is, from a purely mimetic identification, "direct and immediate and . . . earlier than any object-cathexis" (p. 31). More precisely, it constitutes the post-Oedipal reinforcement of that identification. Thus there is no ambiguity at all: the ego ideal is indeed that with which one identifies. But clarifications are needed. Why and how does one identify? In other words, why and how does the "reinforcement" of the primary identification come about? Two hypotheses are proposed in this connection, and the second is of particular interest.

The first hypothesis is that the primary identification is reinforced by way of a secondary (regressive) identification with the love objects abandoned at the time of the destruction of the Oedipus complex. This is the hypothesis of bisexuality or the double Oedipus complex. Since the child is considered to be originally bisexual, "masculine" *and* "feminine," two superimposed Oedipal triangles would always be involved—identification with the father and love for the mother, plus love for the father and identification with the mother—so that the renunciation of both objects when the Oedipus complex is destroyed would be balanced by two regressive identifications. Thus, for example (but everything is organized in terms of this particular example), primary identification with the paternal *model* of the positive complex of the little boy turns out to be reinforced by a secondary identification with the lost paternal *object* of the inverse, negative complex; the process as a whole leaves in its wake the "modification of the ego" known as "ego ideal or super-ego." The advantage of this hypothesis, obviously, is that it should make it possible to uncover, beneath the ideal or superegoic identification, a love bond: it is through love for the father that one would identify with him. Then, too, it has the second but by no means secondary advantage of making it possible to explain the "exit" from Oedipal rivalry, the reason for the destruction of the Oedipus complex: since the rival is simultaneously a love object, we can finally understand why the ego puts an end to the hostilities and agrees to give up the other love object to the rival. The ideal identification, the "reinforced" identification, would then be the good identification, the loving identification that makes it possible to be the other in *his* place, which is not *mine*.

And yet there is still a need for a second hypothesis. Why? Because it is not clear, finally, why the mechanism of identification with the lost object would put an end to rivalry. Saying that one identifies with the rival of the positive complex because one loves him in the negative complex perhaps accounts for the reinforcement of the identification, but it does not explain why this reinforcement would necessarily be accompanied by an attenuation of hatred. After all, to identify with the loved father is also, in the same double gesture, to identify with the father-rival, to put oneself in the father's place vis-à-vis the mother and, in the extreme case, to "devour" him, kill him, and so on. In short, the more one loves (in the negative complex), the more one hates (in the positive complex). Regressive identification, far from leading to the decline of the Oedipus complex, can do nothing but revive it and bring it to a paroxysm. Endlessly. The morality of all this (and morality itself, as we shall see) thus holds that one must not identify at all—or else must identify without identifying. This is the second hypothesis, which now attributes the formation of the ego ideal (its "reinforcement") to an anti-identificatory identification:

The super-ego is, however, not simply a residue of the earliest object-choices of the id; it also represents an energetic reaction-formation against those choices. Its relation to the ego is not exhausted by the precept: "You *ought to be* like this (like your father)." It also comprises the prohibition: "You *may not be* like this (like your father)—that is, you may not do all that he does; some things are his prerogative." This double aspect [*Doppelangesicht*] of the ego ideal derives from the fact that the ego ideal had the task of repressing the Oedipus complex; indeed, it is to that revolutionary event that it owes its existence. Clearly the repression of the Oedipus complex was no easy task. The child's parents, and especially his father, were perceived as the obstacle to a realization of his Oedipus wishes; so his infantile ego fortified itself for the carrying out of the repression by erecting this same obstacle within itself. It borrowed strength to do this, so to speak, from the father, and this loan was an extraordinarily momentous act. [p. 34]

This, according to Freud, is the beginning of morality (conscience) and law, these being obviously exhausted on their negative side in the purely formal requirement not to imitate. Before it has any content at all, the law announces, imperatively and categorically, that one must not identify. How this antimimetic interdiction forms the (formal) heart of morality in general is now easy to grasp: not to identify with the other (more precisely, not to identify the other with oneself) is the only way of respecting the other as other, without doing him violence. The Law is of the Other. It is thus, by the same token, a Law of the Subject. "Do not be like me": this is understood, positively, prescriptively, as "Be yourself," "Be original," "Be a subject." The origin of morality is simultaneously the origin of the subject, in the sense that there is no subject (identifying itself as ego through difference from the other) except a moral subject, morally instituted. The Law assigns the subject, assigns it to being. Thus would emerge from the Oedipal chaos, where all is in all and the ego in the other, a subject finally identified, identifiable, capable of entering into normal, normed, regulated relations with others.

That, at least, is what could be said if this very "subject" did not *have to identify itself in order to be a subject.* Let us schematize: the law that assigns the subject exists, *a priori*, before any subject, prior to any subjective identity and any differentiation from others. Thus it cannot take the form of an external interdiction, uttered by another and addressed to the subject, since there is not yet a subject (moral, respectful, and so on). Put in more Freudian terms, the law that forbids identification with the Oedipal rival is uttered by the rival with whom one is identifying, and thus it has no legal authority whatever. As a result, there is no choice but to identify with the law that says one must not identify; there is no choice but to imitate (or "internalize," or introject) the model that says that one must not imitate it ("internalize" it, introject it). Such is the about-face or reversal from which the ego ideal derives—the double-sided, two-faced ideal: one identifies with the father (the rival) so as not to identify with him (so as not to be his rival). Not *out of* love, consequently, but *in order* to be able to love him. Without this internal transmutation of identification, without this "reinforcement" of identification against itself, without this "borrowing" of a strength destined to repress the "loan," no subject would ever emerge from the Oedipus complex. The law, the double law that assigns the subject, is thus stated as follows: "Identify without identifying." Or, more simply still: "Identify yourself *as* a subject."

The ambivalence, the dual value of identification as Freud uses the concept, now comes fully to light. We noted this earlier in connection with the birth of "social feeling": identification is simultaneously marked with the sign of hatred, a non-bond with the other, *and* with the sign of the positive, peaceful bond with the other. It is now clear that this ambivalence resurfaces at the very heart of the Oedipal law, the law that in fact ought to institute the passage from bad (rivalrous) identification to good (ideal) identification. That law binds twice over: it bonds and unbonds the subject, and thus it has all the characteristics of a *double bind*, as Girard has so aptly noted.[60] One can only submit to it by transgressing it; one can only obey it by violating it: not to identify with the father is impossible except on the condition of identifying with him. Consequently, one is *always guilty*. This bewildering, terrifying, insane law prescribes the crime that it punishes, and the law is inescapable (it is older than the subject, which therefore will not have been able to oppose it): "Where I was, you must be—guilty, infinitely guilty of devouring me into yourself." It is a law that destroys itself, of its own accord, at the very moment it is promulgated, and simultaneously destroys the (moral) subject it assigns. The birth of morality here is also its abortion, and the subject is aborted as well. "Identify yourself *as* a subject": this injunction wrests the so-called subject's identity away at the very mo-

ment it is assigning that identity, thus condemning the so-called subject to a nameless guilt (the "unconscious feeling of guilt," as Freud
calls it here and elsewhere).

The moral of all this—and morality in general—is thus that the
only possible morality is an impossible one; necessarily impossible.
One must not identify, yet one cannot fail to identify. The "subject"—here is the unbelievable "ethics of psychoanalysis," if the
point must be pressed—has to be "itself" in and through the assimilating destruction of the other, in and through a double bind, a double bond or band (*Bindung/Entbindung*) that makes it unbond itself
while bonding itself and bind itself while unbinding itself: thus it is
at once absolved and at fault. Hence the merciless, insatiable nature
of the "law," hence the inexplicable "sadism" of the superego: the
more one identifies with the Father, the guiltier one is; the more one
respects the law, the more one is punished; the more "moral" one is,
the more intense one's "feeling of guilt," one's "moral anxiety" (this
will be the paradox, the irreducible paradox, of "Civilization and Its
Discontents"). If identification is the subject's original law *and* original sin, then it is indeed true, as Freud had suggested in "Totem and
Taboo" (*SE* 13:67–68) that consciousness (*Bewusstsein*) is born as
conscience (*Gewissen*)—but only if we add that this birth (presumably birth itself, well in advance of the Oedipus complex) gives rise
to the being-conscious-of-itself only by stealing it from itself, prior
(internally) to itself, and thus also by destroying, by definition, morality as respect for Law or for the Other's Voice. For how can I hear
and respect the "voice of conscience" as such (how can I hear *myself*
say "*you* must"), since I do not exist in advance, before I identify
myself with it, in it? Since I am its echo, but before there is any
listening? Identity with oneself, because it is enjoined, is permeated
at the outset by an otherness whose law it immediately transgresses.
"I identify, thus I am—guilty."

Let us retranslate all this into a more (?) Freudian vocabulary: "I
cannot repress Oedipal rivalry except by identifying myself with the
rival, thus by intensifying the rivalry." The Oedipal triangle is a vi-
cious circle. Like it or not, identifying in order not to identify, identifying without identifying, still and always amounts to identifying,
absorbing the other in oneself, putting the object into the ego, and

so on. This being the case, do we not return to the situation that was already one of regressive identification? Can it still be maintained that identification-with-the-ideal is *opposed* to regressive identification like an "energetic reaction-formation," given that their mechanism is the same and that the former must first of all and necessarily take the path of the latter, must borrow its strength in order to be able to repress it? Must we not say, rather, that the "reinforcement" of identification that presides over the formation of the ego ideal reinforces and revives the Oedipus complex that it was thought to repress? In short, that *one does not exit from the Oedipus complex?* The Oedipus complex, finally, feeds on its own destruction, and it is by that very token indestructible. To persuade ourselves that this is indeed the case, we need only juxtapose the passage in which Freud describes the entrance into the Oedipus complex and the one in which he describes the exit from it, the destruction of the Oedipus complex. They say the same thing: they both describe the same guilty (ambivalent) identification with the other. Here, first, is the entrance into the Oedipus complex: identification with the father and love for the mother remain independent of each other, Freud reminds us, "until the boy's sexual wishes in regard to his mother become more intense and his father is perceived as an obstacle to them; from this the Oedipus complex originates. . . . Henceforward his relation to his father is ambivalent; it seems as if the ambivalence inherent in the identification from the beginning had become manifest" ("Ego and Id," p. 32). (And the "entrance" had thus begun well in advance of the triangular Oedipus complex, from the time of the primary double bind/bond/band.) Then the exit: "The child's parents, and especially his father, were perceived as the obstacle to a realization of his Oedipus wishes; so his infantile ego fortified itself for the carrying out of the repression by erecting this same obstacle within itself" (p. 34).

There is clearly no difference between the entrance to and the exit from the Oedipus complex, between Oedipal (Oedipizing) identification and post-Oedipal (de-Oedipizing) identification: the same obstacle is involved in both cases, and the same identification with the same obstacle. And if the ambivalence of the Oedipal identification refers back, before the triangular rivalry, to the double bond/band of oral incorporation, the very same thing must be said of the "double face" of the ideal, superegoic identification. For how is the ego ideal formed? "The Ego and the Id" replies: by identification. But *Thomas Woodrow Wilson* goes further: by *devouring, cannibalizing* identification. The "end" of the Oedipus complex repeats its earliest "beginning"—its interminable prehistory:

> Equally unable to kill his father or to submit utterly to him, the little boy finds an escape which approximates removal of his father and nevertheless avoids murder. He identifies himself with his father. Thereby he satisfies both his tender and hostile desires with respect to his father. He not only expresses his love and admiration for his father but also removes his father by incorporating his father in himself as if by an act of cannibalism. Thenceforth he is himself the great admired father. . . . This almighty, omniscient, all-virtuous father of childhood, as a result of his incorporation in the child, becomes an internal psychic power which in psychoanalysis we call the Ego-Ideal or the Super-Ego. [*Thomas Woodrow Wilson*, p. 40]

It would be hard to find a better formulation: the father (the ideal, the model-object) is *put in the place of the ego*, and everything is settled by a repetition of the absolutely primal scene of the devouring of the *Urvater*, as described in "Totem and Taboo": "I, the Ego, am the father." Or else, establishing a link with what "Group Psychology" had to say about the Christian ideal and the imitation of Christ: "I am the Father, the Son and the Holy Spirit, I am God Himself." Every ideal comes sliced up, cut to pieces, chewed up and digested in advance. Every law (it is the "Law," it is "I") is already eaten, consumed, used up. And as we learn from "Totem and Taboo," obedience must therefore always have been "deferred," retrospective.[61]

What is important here for our purposes, however, is that Freud, who describes this situation, at the same time refuses to draw any conclusions from it. It is as though he were beating a last-minute retreat, in extremis before the paradox of the law, while struggling to cut through the double bind that he himself brings to light. How? By differentiating identification with the ideal from regressive identification: unlike regressive identification, identification with the ideal is not an identification *of the ego*—or at least not entirely. The father, ideal-model-object, is incorporated, to be sure, but not into the ego—only into a *part* of the ego, a part that is different from, and even opposed to, the ego proper—namely, the topological agency known as "ego ideal" or "superego." Identification and even incorporation ("Be like the father") thus occur, but the other nevertheless remains other, is maintained as other ("Do not be like the father"). The external model-object is introjected within, like an internal foreign body, in such a way that the ego finds itself *confronted with* its father *inside itself*. The categorical imperative shifts from outside to inside, taking on the form of a voice of the conscience commanding the ego from a position of intimate transcendence, in the mode of an auto-*hetero*-nomy.

The use of this topological instantiation is easy to grasp. It allows the difficulty to be split in two; it allows the double bind to be divided in half through a doubling of its realm of application. The identificatory prescription then applies to the part of the ego called "ego ideal," the identificatory interdiction to the ego itself. Thus "one" can obey the law without transgressing it, since "one" actually consists of two agencies, one of which identifies while the other does not (really) do so.

Has the paradox been disposed of, then? It is simple enough to show that it has not. On the one hand, the part of the ego that is to be identified with the father also makes itself guilty—by right, as it were—of the crime of identification. And the ego, on the other hand, will be no less guilty of failing to identify. It can never live up to the sublime and terrible imperative: "No matter what the Ego may actually achieve in life, the Super-Ego is never satisfied with the achievement. It admonishes incessantly: You must make the impossible possible! You can accomplish the impossible! You are the Beloved Son of the Father! You are the Father Himself! You are God!" (*Thomas Woodrow Wilson*, pp. 41–42). But let us set these considerations aside. Let us pretend to believe that the double bind is undone, and, granting Freud his improbable cleavage of the subject, let us tally up his logical, topological operations.

It is clear, now, that the ideal agency—hereafter termed IE—is *different* from the egoic agency, E. E does not include IE—or else includes it without including it, which amounts to saying that E identifies without identifying with IE. IE indeed remains an *ideal* for E, an inaccessible model that E can and must imitate, to the extent that imitation will always remain external and the model will remain inimitable, transcendent. The same holds true, of course, when an external object, O, puts itself within IE, in the place of IE. O will remain external to E, since IE was already external. There is, consequently, no danger that O will come into E, in the place of E. For that is the very danger against which this entire topology is constructed: at all costs, O must not disappear into E, the other has to remain an Object, an Other with a capital O. IE has precisely the function of ensuring that this differential gap between O and E is respected. It represents, within the topology, the necessity (ethical, political) of safeguarding the topological in general, the topological spacing (the forum) between ego and others. For the ego ideal may occasionally authorize the ego to absorb it, to merge with it (and we then have manic triumph or, in the social order, the feast, which always repeats the totemic meal, cannibalistic ingestion, in one form or another).[62] But these are exceptions to the rule, and they themselves are regulated. The rule holds that the ego ideal forbids *truly* devouring identification and punishes it cruelly when it occurs (then we have melancholy or, in the social order, the mourning that follows a feast or sacrifice). The ego ideal, in other words, regulates relations with others by regulating the proper distance from others—that is, to borrow Brecht's term, the *distanciation* of identification.

Let us bring to a close this (overly) rapid recapitulation of the theory of the ego ideal. Has it really led us far afield from "Group Psychology"? Quite the contrary, it should allow us to better understand the enigmatic "formula" of groups and to spell out, finally, the precise nature of the distinction between the political bond and social bonds. If the political bond is defined as being a relation to an object put in the place of the ego ideal, then we have confirmed that we are dealing here with a bond of "heteropathic" identification: the Father-Leader represents the ideal of crowd members, an ideal with which they can and must identify (to whom they must submit, whom they must obey, and so on, since his will is theirs), but without being required or able really to identify (that would be to destroy his authority, the authority of the Other).

As for the social bond, it is initially possible to suppose that such bonds derive from devouring, "idiopathic" identification, since Freud defines them as identifications with objects put into the ego, and since on that basis they are incapable of generating nonviolent relations to others. But by specifying that group members "[identify] with one another in their ego" *because* they have put the same object "in the place of their ego ideal," Freud implies that they identify with one another *inasmuch as they do not (really) identify with the object*. Thus morality and politics are safe: the members of the group identify with one another, although not by virtue of a shared object love, as Freud has repeated throughout the essay (for that love is the root of rivalry and violence), but on the basis of a shared non-identification with the Father (which is the basis of morality, of ethico-political respect for the other). Identifying without (really) identifying, identifying with one another as being identically subjected to the law that forbids (really) identifying with one another, group members then identify themselves as moral subjects, political subjects: respectful sons of the Father, brothers respectful toward one another as they all are toward the Father.

Now, what is presupposed by this whole construction (which we have "constructed," reconstructed, ourselves)? Clearly, the emergence of the distinction between the ego and the ego ideal, that is, the conjoined emergence of subjects and law. The entire edifice of "Group Psychology" rests, in the last analysis, on this distinction. Without the institution of this elementary distance between the ego and the Father, there would be neither ego nor Father (neither God nor Master), nor would there be distanced relations with "brothers." But it is also clear that Freud can establish (institute, found) this distinction only if he cuts arbitrarily, arbitrally, into the double bind that conjointly (dis)institutes or (un)founds the subject and the law in their impossible distinction. For the law (the ego ideal, the Other, the Father, the Name of the Father, or whatever one wishes to call it) will always be "I," the Ego, in my impossible identity. And the basis, the founding bond of society, is thus itself without foundation. The edifice of society has no basis.

Have we not come back to the old conundrum with which Freud earlier confronted Bernheim: "Christopher bore Christ; Christ bore the whole world; Say, where did Christopher then put his foot?" ("Group Psychology," p. 89)? If we must now readdress this abyssal question to Freud, it is not only because the theory of the ego ideal has caused us to lose our footing; it is also because the theory has led us back to the abyss of *hypnosis*. For we now discover that this abyss is what brings about the bond with the ideal, the binding or supporting bond of society.

It surfaces (resurfaces, rather) toward the end of Chapter 7, right after Freud has introduced his distinction between the bond with the object-put-in-the-place-of-the-ego-ideal and the (bondless) bond with the object-put-in-the-place-of-the-ego. And it surfaces or resurfaces in the place of *Verliebtheit*, in other words, in the place of what had, until then, supplied the paradigm for the relation to the ideal. To be sure, Freud seems at first to be assimilating the hypnotic state to the state of being in love. From *Verliebtheit* to hypnosis, he says at the outset, is only a short step. We find in each case the same submission with respect to the other, the same docility, the same credulity, the same absence of criticism: in each case, the words of the other have the value of law, even at the expense of reality. In each case, as a result, the object has taken the place of the ego ideal. Hypnosis and *Verliebtheit* would both fit into the "formula" of authority: "No one can doubt that the hypnotist has stepped into the place of the ego ideal" (p. 114)—like the object of being in love, then. But there is a "but": "It is only that everything is even clearer and more intense in hypnosis, so that it would be more to the point to explain being in love by means of hypnosis than the other way round" (p. 114).

This reversal signifies that hypnosis does not come into play as a second example of the relation to the ideal object, an example *parallel* to that of *Verliebtheit*. This new example, in fact, is more exemplary than the first. Hypnosis would exhibit the relation to the ideal object in all its purity; it would manifest, in other words, its essence or quintessence. Why? Because it would be pure, purified of all sexual goal-orientation, *even inhibited as to its aim*:

The complete absence of impulsions which are uninhibited in their sexual aims contributes further towards the extreme purity of the phenomena. The hypnotic relation is the unlimited devotion of someone in love, but with sexual satisfaction excluded; whereas in the actual case of being in love this kind of satisfaction is only temporarily kept back, and remains in the background as a possible aim at some later time. [p. 115]

Hypnosis, a pure relation to the ideal object, would thus be a love purified of all love. But this definition, as we see, transcends the limits of love and exceeds itself, overflows its own bounds. If hypnosis exemplifies the relation to the ideal object more purely than *Verliebtheit*, it is not because it is, so to speak, more "loving" than love, but because it is no longer loving at all. From *Verliebtheit* to hypnosis, what we find is not continuity but rupture, and rupture means now that the pure relation to the ideal object is nonlibidinal, nonerotic.

The object-put-in-the-place-of-the-ego-ideal, then, is not loved —it hypnotizes. Medusa-like, it paralyzes, freezes, the ego. And this object is the Leader, the *Führer*. For the political bond that binds the members of the group to their shared ideal object can at last be named: it is the hypnotic, hypnotico-suggestive bond. The *Führer* hypnotizes his "subjects," and that is how he maintains the cohesion of the social body. This proposition is not to be taken metaphorically, according to Freud. Indeed, he insists that hypnosis is not just an illustration of the bond with the Leader-who-replaces-the-ideal, it *is* that bond itself. Hypnosis already *is* a group of two, and the group *is* a multiple hypnosis: "The hypnotic relation is (if the expression is permissible) a group formation with two members. Hypnosis is not a good object for comparison with a group formation, because it is truer to say that it is identical with it. Out of the complicated fabric of the group it isolates one element for us—the behaviour of the individual to the leader" (p. 115).

Now this conclusion (for it is Freud's last word on the question of authority, power, politics, thus on the social, and so on) in turn gets away from itself. It oversteps the boundaries of psychoanalysis, which extends beyond itself, as it were, so as to find itself outside itself right in the middle of itself. This is so for several reasons.

Hypnosis as Enigma

First, this conclusion exceeds the limits of psychoanalysis because it concludes with a riddle, a *Rätselwort*. Hypnosis, which is supposed to explain the enigma of groups, is itself an enigma:

Hypnosis would solve the riddle of the libidinal constitution of groups for us straight away, if it were not that it itself exhibits some features which are not met by the rational explanation we have hitherto given of it as a state of being in love with the directly sexual trends excluded. There is still a great deal in it which we must recognize as unexplained and mysterious. [p. 115]

This passage implies that the *libidinal* constitution of the group necessarily remains a riddle for psychoanalysis, because its constitutive element, hypnosis, eludes the libidinal model. Coming after an essay entirely devoted to demonstrating the libidinal character of hypnosis *and* the group, the avowal, it must be admitted, is actually a *reversal*. Where Chapter 4 of "Group Psychology" ("Suggestion and Libido") promised to overturn the prevailing explanation of groups by way of hypnosis, by making hypnosis an effect or appearance of the libidinal, Chapter 8 ("Being in Love and Hypnosis") overturns this overturning—which amounts, quite simply, to returning to the starting point. It is a turn for nothing, in short, but at the end of it psychoanalysis itself has been quite overturned, canceled out. For virtually all the resources of psychoanalysis, here called "ego analysis," have been mobilized in the struggle against so-called group psychology. And with what outcome, finally? The enigma of the hypnosis *of* the ego, the enigma of group psychology at the heart of ego analysis. It turns out that psychoanalysis is a mystery to itself—foreign to itself, *unheimlich*.

A Model-less Identification

But that is not all. The objection may quickly be raised that although hypnosis may escape the libidinal model, it nevertheless fits the formula "bond with an object-put-in-the-place-of-the-ego-ideal," by means of which psychoanalysis would retain its full encompassing capacity, all its theoretical power. And in fact, Freud understands it in just this way; for him, the analysis (division, topical cleavage) of the ego (ego vs. ego ideal) is manifestly valid as an explanation of the hypnotic phenomenon, and not vice versa. Hypnosis then has to be understood as a bond of "heteropathic" identification, as we saw earlier; it has to be understood as a repetition of the relation to the very first ideal-model-object, that is, to the paternal figure. The recapitulating conclusion of Appendix E says just this:

Hypnosis resembles being in love in being limited to these two persons [the ego and the object], but it is based entirely on sexual impulsions that are inhibited in their aims and puts the object in the place of the ego ideal. *The group* multiplies this process; it agrees with hypnosis in the nature of the instincts which hold it together, and in the replacement of the ego ideal by the object; but to this it adds identification with other individuals, *which was perhaps originally made possible by their having the same relation to the object.* [p. 143; emphasis added]

But here is where we must break with Freud, for if there is identification in hypnosis, it is certainly not of the heteropathic type, certainly not identification with an *ideal*. Such is the strangeness of the hypnotic relation (and Freud should have known this, considering how much interest he had shown, earlier, in hypnosis and suggestion) that it entails no relation with the other—as object, model, or figure. What in fact is the "relation"[63] between the hypnotized person and the hypnotist? A relation of letting go of the self, or of being seized by the other, a relation of submission—that is the immediate answer. But the submission in question is *blind*, exactly as the eye is blind to itself. It is a submission that does not "see" (nor does it hear, or perceive in any way) the one to whom it is submitting, any more than it "sees" itself as submission to the other. To say, as Freud does further on, that the hypnotized individual is fascinated, mesmerized by the look, the sight (*Blick, Anblick*) of the hypnotist (p. 125) is to be mesmerized oneself, blinded by the hypnotic *spectacle*. Freud's description is a description "in the third person"; it is valid only for the spectator who is present at the scene of suggestion, who sees the hypnotized individual see the gaze of the hypnotist, and so on. The hypnotized individual himself (but who is "he"?) does not see any of that, involved as he is *in* the scene, in that entirely other scene where he executes (acts, plays, mimes) the order of the hypnotist *without seeing or knowing that an order is involved and that the order is addressed to him by another person.*

Freud had already said this, in his own way, in the "Note on the Unconscious in Psycho-Analysis" of 1912. In the case of posthypnotic suggestion (and, we may add, in the case of hypnotic suggestion in general), he explained that the hypnotist's order remains *unconscious*. It remains unconscious, more precisely, as an order, that is, as an injunction or suggestion made by another. The order, to be sure, is executed, acted out, "translated into action," and this is done consciously. The subject knows that he must, without fail, do this or that. But he does not know why, nor where this imperious duty, this incomprehensible *Zwang*, originates: "But not the whole of [the order] emerged into consciousness: only the conception of the act to be executed. All the other ideas associated with this conception—the order, the influence of the physician, the recollection of the hypnotic state, remained unconscious even then" ("Note on the Unconscious in Psycho-Analysis," *SE* 12: 261).[64]

As a result, everything related to the hypnotist's intervention remains unavailable to consciousness. The hypnotist is not represented to consciousness, and his power is all the more absolute and complete in that he does not appear, does not present himself as such. He is obeyed blindly, to the very extent that the hypnotized individual forgets that he is obeying *him*. In hypnosis, in other words, we find a *forgetting of the other*.[65] It is true that at the time, in keeping with his more consistent doctrine of the unconscious, Freud construed that forgetting as the forgetting of a *representation* (the *idea* of order, the *memory* of the hypnotic state) acting on the basis of an unconscious memory. But that is a point on which we must once again break with him (and here it means breaking with the psychoanalytic concept of the unconscious). To say that the scene of the injunction subsists in the form of an unconscious representation would be to presuppose that the hypnotized individual had earlier lived it, perceived it as a present event, and thus as a re-presentable, rememberable event. In short, it would presuppose a subject to whom that event had happened, to whom the event had presented itself as an experience: the hypnotized person would have been present at the injunction, would have replied ("Here I am!") to the other's call, submitting *himself* to *him* with full awareness, awareness of himself and of the other.

Now the hypnotic injunction—like every injunction, perhaps, like every imperative[66]—sets aside this schema, which is that of simple communication between two subjects, usually called "sender" and "receiver." For if the hypnotized person could represent the order to himself as an order, if he were content to respond to a "*you must*" addressed to *him*, there would quite simply be no hypnosis, which is, properly speaking, a subjection, in the very strong sense of this word: the subject is rendered subject, assigned as subject. The hypnotic commandment does not present itself to a consciousness that is already there to hear it; rather, it takes hold of it (and posits it) prior to itself—in such a way that it never presents itself to consciousness. It falls into a radical "forgetting" that is not the forgetting of any memory, of any (re)presentation. It gives no order *to* a subject; it orders the subject. Or again, to borrow a term from Heidegger (however astonished he would have been to see himself convoked in such an argument), he *destines* his receiver or *destinataire*: he determines him in his most proper being, gives him his own selfhood even as he withholds himself in that donation.

Thus, when the hypnotized person says "I"—for example, "I am thirsty"—he says it in the name and in the place of the hypnotist who has intimated to him the order to be thirsty; "you must" is immediately transformed into "I want." Far from replying, then, to the discourse of the other, the hypnotized person quotes it in the first person, acts it out or repeats it without knowing that he is repeating.[67] He does not submit himself *to* the other, he *becomes the other*, comes to be like the other—who is thus no longer an other, but "himself." No property, no identity, and in particular no subjective liberty precede the commandment, here. The commandment enjoins the subject, intimates the "I," and orders him, as it were, to be free (once again a double bind: "Be [a] subject," "Be yourself," "Be free," and so on). That is why, at the same time, it obliges beyond any obedience, beyond any *desire* for submission and any *voluntary* servitude. Enjoining the free spontaneity of the subject, it withdraws from what it enjoins: the subject, thus assigned, does not know that he is obeying.

This commandment, having seized the hypnotized person before (he was) "himself," has never appeared to him as such, has never stood up before him,[68] so that he plies himself freely—at least so he believes (it is obvious that this freedom is not an auto-nomy, unless "freedom" and "autonomy" are understood apart from the metaphysics of the subject). Commanding freedom, the hypnotic order commands without commanding in the usual sense, from the standpoint of a radical forgetting (or a "past") that delivers the subject to "himself," liberates his ineffable and somnambulic "spontaneity."

Thus this commandment converges quite precisely with the definition (a psychologizing one, to be sure, but that hardly matters here) that Freud had earlier given of suggestion, in his preface to Bernheim's *Suggestion*:

It is worth while considering what it is which we can legitimately call a "suggestion." No doubt some kind of psychical influence is implied by the term; and I should like to put forward the view that what distinguishes a suggestion from other kinds of psychical influence, such as a command or the giving of a piece of information or instruction, is that in the case of suggestion an idea is aroused in another person's brain which is not examined in regard to its origin but is accepted as though it had arisen spontaneously in that brain. ["Preface to Bernheim," *SE* 1: 82]

The suggestive injunction is not information, quite simply because it *forms* the subject (here called "brain") prior to any communication. In short, hypnosis involves the birth of the subject—perhaps not a repetition of the birth event,[69] but birth as repetition, or as primal identification: in it the subject comes into being (always anew: this birth is constantly repeated) as an echo or duplicate of the other, in a sort of lag with respect to its own origin and its own identity. An insurmountable lag, then, since it is a constitutive one, and one that without any doubt constitutes the entire "unconscious" of the subject, prior to any memory and any repression. The (constraint to) repetition, as Freud has indeed said, is the unconscious itself. It is a "resistance of the id," as we learn from "Inhibitions, Symptoms and Anxiety" (*SE* 20: 160)—to be more precise, it is an insistence of the id, which has never appeared but does not cease not to appear, causing me thus to appear, *myself*.

These few remarks hardly cover the formidable set of problems raised by the hypnotic relation. However, they should suffice to show that this singular "relation" is a relation of non-relation, is not a relation to an *other*. In particular, it is not at all a relation of identification with a paternal figure or with an ideal model, as Freud attempts to imagine it ("[hypnosis puts] the object in the place of the ego ideal," and so on). If it is absolutely necessary to speak of identification in connection with hypnosis (and why not, in fact? the hypnotized individual *is* the hypnotist—himself), then it is necessary to point out, at the very least, that this identification is of the idiopathic type. The so-called object is not put in the place of the ego ideal, here, but rather in the place of the ego: this latter comes to (be in) the place of the other, which thus will never be present to him as an object or ideal model—it will have been immediately "absorbed" in and as (the) ego.

In this sense, hypnosis leads us back to the very type of identification—devouring identification—whose relation to the ideal Freud was trying to define. The Law of the Other is quite literally *assimilated* in it, and this brings us back once again to the paradox of the conjoined (un)constitution of "subject" and "law," of "self" and "other." (We need to be more skeptical than ever of the image of absorption or devouring assimilation. Here we have to imagine— but it is no doubt *unimaginable*, in the strict sense—that no mouth, no bodily envelope precedes incorporation. All things considered, incorporation must instead be viewed as an *incarnation*: one subject emerges incarnating the other, body and soul. The same skepticism is called for, of course, with regard to the term we have used for the sake of convenience, that is, "*idio*pathy": no "own" precedes identification. There is indeed appropriation, but to the profit of no preexisting subject: an improper propriation.)

By making hypnosis the example par excellence of the relation to the (object-put-in-the-place-of-the) ego ideal, and consequently of the relation to authority in general, Freud thus says too much and not enough about it. He says too much because this example manifestly eludes the metapsychological "formula" that it is supposed to illustrate, that is, the *theoretical* distinction between the ego and the ego ideal (Ego vs. Father, Ego vs. Leader, and so on): he manages to imply, in spite of himself, as it were, that the possibility of authority and power demand to be thought through, rigorously, *prior to the theory (and) the subject*. Yet Freud also does not say enough because, by persisting in enclosing hypnosis within the framework of his theoretical "formula," he closes off or inhibits all the questions that might have arisen in this regard. Everything ends up being modeled on the image of the Hypnotist-Leader-Father rising up in front of the subject(s) and overwhelming him (or them) with a glance—a sort of ultimate dead-bolt lock to keep out the formless, unfigurable threat of the group-of-two (or several), that is, of the id which is without subject(s), without identity (or identities), without Father and without Power, neither one nor two but the Same. Thus psychoanalysis marks its limit twice: once by pointing toward what exceeds that limit, a second time by refusing to cross it.

The Confrontation with Social Psychology

One final way to characterize this sort of internal overflowing of psychoanalysis is to underline the fact that this is precisely where psychoanalysis encounters the positions of its "other," so-called social or group psychology. The constructions of Le Bon and Tarde are similarly bound up with the hypnotic power of the leader, so that it is difficult to see, in the end, in what way Freud's contribution is profoundly original. Far from finding some sort of resolution, the confrontation with social psychology opens, finally, onto a very spectacular identification with the adversary, and this inability to define its difference from its other marks an unmistakable *failure* for psychoanalysis.

That is, a failure of individual psychology. We must remember that the entire "difference" of psychoanalysis with respect to social psychology lay in its claim to ground the collective in the individual (in the love of individuals), whereas Le Bon, Tarde, or McDougall established it at the outset in a collective-being (hypnotic suggestibility) that came before any individuality. And this difference came to be supported, within Freud's own argument, by the difference postulated between the individual bond with the Ideal-Father-Chief and the social bonds of identification that were supposed to derive from it. It is this latter difference that Freud abolishes, at the end of the road, by identifying the bond with the leader and the hypnotic bond. For how can the bond with the leader be distinguished from bonds of identification—"suggestive" bonds of identification?[70] Is this not tantamount to acknowledging that what is involved, in both cases, is the same type of "bond" (mimetic, sympathetic, or empathetic, whatever one wishes to call it for the sake of convenience)? And thus that the "Father" is a brother? Or that there is no Leader-Father *different* from the "brothers," any more than there are "brothers" different from the ego—from myself? Hence the difference between individual and social psychology becomes undiscoverable. From this point on, no individual, no individual psychology is available to support, uphold, or subtend group psychology. Group psychology, in the form of hypnosis, invades everything, up to and including the relation of the ego to its ideal. There is no more ego, now, except when it is permeated by another, primordially intimated and broached in its very intimacy—in short, suggested.

Moreover, Chapter 10 of "Group Psychology" takes on the task of developing the thesis—a disconcerting one, to say the least, if we recall the essay's original plan—of the *anteriority* of group psychology with respect to any individual psychology. This was also Gustave Le Bon's thesis, as we recall. And it was implied in Freud's remarks in advance, when he borrowed the theme of the regressive character of crowd psychology from Le Bon, thus implying that crowd psychology was older, more "primary" than individual psychology. But it is clear at the same time that this chronological anteriority can no longer be that of an individual unconscious, as Freud still presumed in Chapter 2. If the unconscious primary processes and group psychology are one and the same thing (absence of negation, delay, reflection, will, and so on), this must now be understood in the sense of an unconscious that is older than any individual subject. It follows that the quest for origins broached by Freud does not stop with the history of the individual but opens up, just as it does for Le Bon, onto the collective prehistory of humanity.

That is the motif, first of all, of the inherited, hereditary unconscious (the id). Since the history of the individual (ontogenesis) turns out to be incapable of supplying the origin and the explanation of the hypnotic relation, we shall go looking for them a notch further up, in phylogenesis. Hypnosis is supposed to be the trace of a more ancestral psychology, that of primitive man. Individual history then repeats this collective prehistory; the beginning of mankind begins all over again with every individual:

Hypnosis . . . [is] an inherited deposit from the phylogenesis of the human libido. ["Group Psychology," p. 143]

The hypnotist awakens in the subject a portion of his archaic heritage which had also made him compliant towards his parents and which had experienced an individual re-animation [*eine individuelle Wiederbelebung*] in his relation to his father. [p. 127]

But this prehistory, in turn, fails to open up access to an earlier individual. There was no beginning at the beginning-again. Regression or *regressus* is here *in infinitum*, and now we know why: because the primitive unconscious (the unconscious of primitive individuals) was (always) already "inherited"—transmitted, bequeathed, suggested by another. If we wish to make hypnosis a legacy, we have to presume that this legacy is primordial and that it has never belonged to anyone. The other was always already at the (originless) origin of the individual, and everything—that is to say, history—had thus begun in *pre*-individual *pre*history. And this, then, is the motif of what must be called the collective unconscious or, more precisely (so as not to fall back into the rut of Jungianism), the unconscious-as-collective. Here it is, waiting to be read. The first psychology of humanity (ours, even now) was collective: "We must conclude that the psychology of groups is the oldest human psychology; what we have isolated as individual psychology, by neglecting all traces of the group, has only since come into prominence out of the old group psychology, by a gradual process which may still, perhaps, be described as incomplete" (p. 123).

And this "psychology," this thought, belonged to no subject. Being common to all (communing them), it belonged to no one. There was no one to think anything at all, and yet *That* provided something to think about, to feel, to desire. In the beginning was not a subject, nor even a sum of subjects, but *That*: the group, the horde, or the primitive *band*.

The psychology of such a group, as we know it from the descriptions to which we have so often referred—the dwindling of the conscious individual personality, the focusing of thoughts and feelings into a common direction, the predominance of the affective side of the mind and of unconscious psychical life, the tendency to the immediate carrying out of intentions as they emerge—all this corresponds to a state of regression to a primitive mental activity, of just such a sort as we should be inclined to ascribe to the primal horde.*

*What we have just described in our general characterization of mankind must apply especially to the primal horde. The will of the individual was too weak; he did not venture upon action. No impulses whatever came into existence except collective ones; there was only a common will, there were no single ones. An idea did not dare to turn itself into an act of will unless it felt itself reinforced by a perception of its general diffusion. This weakness of the idea is to be explained by the strength of the emotional tie which is shared by all the members of the horde. [pp. 122–23]

In the beginning, then, was the band—that is, if we have understood correctly, the bond (rather than the group). From the beginnings (they are lost in the depths of time, and they will thus always have been numerous, plural), *That* bound men, enjoined them and adjoined them beyond themselves—unbinding and delivering them (*Entbindung*, in German, also means childbirth). *That*—who is It? No one at all. The bond, being older than the subjects that it enjoins and adjoins, is not one of them—it is detached from them, unbound from them. (It is only for convenience that we might want to call it the Mother: Mother Nature who likes to encode herself, a hypnotizing Mother acting out of the depths of her night. Or a group in difference from itself.)

The failure of individual psychology follows. But we might also speak of the "triumph" of individual psychology. For no doubt Freud, by conceding everything to "group psychology," irremediably spills psychoanalysis beyond its own limits. But in doing so, he confronts what already constituted the limit of so-called group psychology, namely, the inability to think the group through to the very end: beyond the individual, beyond the subject—that is, beyond power. Let us recall that, for Le Bon and Tarde, everything came to freeze or fixate around the figure of the Hypnotist-Leader, an all the more "prestigious" and fascinating figure in that it came out of nowhere, explained everything without explaining itself. Where *That*—the id—was, an ego arrived, omnipotent and self-sufficient—in short, a Narcissus. Now it is this same theoretical—and political—gesture that Freud repeats here, with a fidelity and a brutality that can only be labeled somnambulistic. Here it is, waiting to be read. Right after describing the primitive band, that is, archaic (a)subjectivity and an-archy, Freud proceeds—with a myth, the "scientific myth" of the primitive Narcissus-Father:

Further reflection will show us in what respect this statement requires correction. Individual psychology must, on the contrary, be just as old as group psychology, for from the first there were two kinds of psychologies, that of the individual members of the group and that of the father, chief, or leader. The members of the group were subject to ties [*gebunden*] just as we see them to-day, but the father of the primal horde was free [*frei*]. His intellectual acts were strong and independent even in isolation, and his will needed no reinforcement from others. Consistency leads us to assume that his ego had few libidinal ties; he loved no one but himself, or other people only in so far as they served his needs. To objects his ego gave away no more than was barely necessary.

. . . The leader himself need love no one else, he may be of a masterful nature, absolutely narcissistic [*absolut narzisstisch*], self-confident and independent. [pp. 123–24]

"Dreams Are Completely Egoistic" (II)

We are left, then, with a myth.

For it would be pointless to try to comment on this at once intimidating and derisory myth. In a way, there is nothing to seek beyond what it says. It says what it says, no more and no less. It states, dictates, decrees, institutes the Political (and the) Subject.

It says that at the origin was an Ego, a Father, a leader, a solitary, absolute Subject, not bound in any attachment. And it tells how the "sons" ("sons," because not-Fathers, not-Subjects) gathered together one day to kill the Father, to take his place. But this band of criminals, the story goes on to say, could not take the place of the Subject. Beyond the fact that these sons became subjects only by proxy, *in the place of* the father (hence the inexpiable remorse that held them in its grip: they were not subjects on their own), beyond the fact that these brothers had had to band together, bind themselves together *for* the murder and *through* the murder (they were too weak, so they chopped up the body and devoured it together), no one of them could take *the* place of the Father. That place—the place of the Subject—was unique. There was room for only One, and succession was therefore impossible. Let us listen to what we are told:

None of the group of victors could take his place, or, if one of them did, the battles began afresh, until they understood that they must all renounce their father's heritage. They then formed the totemic community of brothers, all with equal rights and united by the totem prohibitions which were to preserve and to expiate the memory of the murder. ["Group Psychology," p. 135]

The father's heritage, in short, was untransmittable. Transmitted, bequeathed, *given*, it was annulled by the same token: it was no longer, then, an absolute power, an autonomous and sovereign subjectivity. For power to change hands without being usurped, the murder would have had to be carried out by another Narcissus. Everything would have had to begin with a death struggle between two solitary and independent self-consciousnesses. But that was not what happened. On the son's side, what was primary was servitude, and it was consequently impossible to escape from it. Thus the sons immediately lapsed back into group psychology (which, indeed, they had never abandoned).

It was only much later that the first individual detached himself from the group, unbound himself and delivered himself—*was born*. He was a poet, the "first epic poet." He *imagined* the Subject, imagined the struggle unto death between two Narcissuses. Let us listen (all this is recounted, recited, in the epic manner):

He who did this was the first epic poet; and the advance was achieved in his imagination [*in seiner Phantasie*]. This poet disguised the truth with lies in accordance with his longing. He invented the heroic myth. The hero was a man who by himself [*allein*] had slain the father—the father who still appeared in the myth as a totemic monster. Just as the father had been the boy's first ideal, so in the hero who aspires to the father's place the poet now created the first ego ideal. [p. 136][71]

But this *epos*, in fact, was a drama. This *diegesis* was a *mimesis*. The poet pretended to be recounting the exploits of another, but that other was "he." In his *Phantasie*, he identified with the Father, *played* the Father. He put himself in the role of the Father (*in die Rolle des Vaters*), or (and it amounts to the same thing) he put himself in the place of the one who was putting himself in the place of the Father. He put himself, *ego*, in the place of his ideal. This fantasy or dream was completely egoistic:

The myth, then, is the step by which the individual emerges from group psychology. The first myth was certainly the psychological, the hero myth. . . . [The poet] goes and relates to the group his hero's deeds which he has invented. At bottom this hero is no one but himself. Thus he lowers himself to the level of reality, and raises his hearers to the level of imagination. But his hearers understand the poet, and, in virtue of their having the same relation of longing towards the primal father, they can identify themselves with the hero. [pp. 136–37]

The subject is thus born in myth, in fantasy, in art. The first subject of humanity (or the second, if we count the Father) was a *genius*, in the proper sense of the word: creating, procreating, generating his own narcissistic ideal, he auto-generated himself; by giving himself to himself as his own model, he gave himself to himself, gave himself birth. A perfect circularity, which is that of God the Father, absolute Narcissus: he imagined *himself*. But a dreamed circularity, as well: he himself *was the other*, with whom he identified. This genius, in reality, was an aborted genius.

Here, as a result, is a myth, the myth of the mythic birth of the subject, recounted by Freud. Once again, there is nothing to say about it, for when he recounts how the very first subject had auto-generated himself by recounting himself in a myth, Freud is of course recounting *himself* in his entirety. That poet, that brilliant *Dichter*, is "he." And that hero with whom the poet identifies in his fantasy, that absolute Orphan bringing down the absolute Father, is also "he." And that Orphan-Father, arising out of nowhere at the origin of history, innate and immortal (unkillable, unconquerable), is again "he."

"Me," "Myself," and "I": all this (psychoanalysis, in short) was nothing but a great egoistic dream—that of "Sigmund Freud," but also "ours," that of the throng of parricidal listeners and readers. A subject will be born here, identifying itself with all positions, assassinating everyone and playing all the roles. Without being born, then. This birth will have been merely mythical, fantasmatic, fictive, and doubtless nothing (no Father, no Narcissus, no Master) has preceded the situation of *Dichter*—that is, of actor, mime. Everything will have begun through the angle—the primordial angle—of an identification without model, an identification that is blind. And nothing, as a result, will have ever really begun. We shall always have been (in) this waking, somnambulic (posthypnotic) dream, prior to any lucidity. This dream (this throng) is ourselves, it is you and it is I, *ego*.

Notes

Notes

A key to abbreviations of works frequently cited in the text and the Notes can be found in the Note on Abbreviations, pp. xi–xii.

Dramatis Personae

1. See "The Neuro-Psychoses of Defense," *SE* 3: 45–46, and *Studies on Hysteria*, *SE* 2: 122.

2. See also Freud's letter to Fliess of December 22, 1897: "Have you ever seen a foreign newspaper after it has passed the censorship at the Russian frontier? Words, sentences and whole paragraphs are blacked out, with the result that the remainder is unintelligible. A 'Russian censorship' occurs in the psychoses, and results in the apparently meaningless deliria" (*Origins*, Letter 79, p. 240).

3. See, for example, Freud's article on "The Unconscious": "To require that whatever goes on in the mind must also be known to consciousness is to make an untenable claim. . . . The conventional equation of the psychical with the conscious is totally inexpedient," etc. (*SE* 14: 167–68).

4. Jacques Lacan, *The Four Fundamental Concepts of Psycho-Analysis*, ed. Jacques-Alain Miller, trans. Alan Sheridan (New York, 1978), p. 24.

5. Ibid., p. 36.

6. Ibid., pp. 47, 225–26.

7. We know that, for Freud, access to an instinct comes only through its "psychical representatives"—or, better still, that instinct *is* this representing (*Repräsentanz*) itself. The following passage of "The Unconscious" makes this clear: "An instinct can never become an object of consciousness—only the idea that represents the instinct [*die Vorstellung, die ihr repräsentiert*] can. Even in the unconscious, moreover, an instinct cannot be

represented otherwise than by an idea. If the instinct did not attach itself to an idea or manifest itself as an affective state, we could know nothing about it" (*SE* 14: 177). That is why, as we read in the sentence immediately preceding, "the antithesis of conscious and unconscious is not applicable to instincts" when instincts are understood as pure somatic processes: "we" have in fact no knowledge (no con-science) of the instinct before it comes to (re)present itself to us—whether in consciousness *or in the unconscious*. It is clear that the unconscious psyche maintains the same relation to the instincts that the conscious psyche does, namely, that of a subject to *its* representations (here, to its *Vorstellungen*, since according to Freud the *Affekt* represents the instinct before consciousness alone).

8. See, among other texts, Martin Heidegger, *Nietzsche*, vol. 4, *Nihilism*, trans. Frank A. Capuzzi (San Francisco, 1979), pp. 102–18, and "The Age of the World Picture," in Martin Heidegger, *The Question Concerning Technology and Other Essays*, trans. William Lovitt (San Francisco, 1977), pp. 115–54.

9. This is even how the certitude of the *Cogito* is introduced, as Jacques Derrida has shown: "Whether I am mad or not, *Cogito, sum*. Madness is therefore, in every sense of the word, only one *case* of thought (*within* thought)" (*Writing and Difference*, trans. Alan Bass [Chicago, 1978], p. 56).

10. Freud makes this assertion repeatedly, from the "Project for a Scientific Psychology" (*SE* 1) to "The Ego and the Id" (*SE* 19): the unconscious is in partnership with representations of things, which are capable of becoming conscious only through their association with representations of words. In this sense, unconscious thought is always conceived as visual thought, on the model of preconscious fantasies and dream-like hallucinations: "The state of psychical rest was originally disturbed by the peremptory demands of internal needs. When this happened, whatever was thought of (wished for) was simply presented in a hallucinatory manner, just as still happens to-day with our dream-thoughts every night. . . . It is probable that thinking was originally unconscious, in so far as it went beyond mere ideational presentations and was directed to the relations between impressions of objects, and that it did not acquire further qualities, perceptible to consciousness, until it became connected with verbal residues. . . . With the introduction of the reality-principle one species of thought-activity was split off; it was kept free from reality-testing and remained subordinated to the pleasure principle alone. The activity is *phantasying*" ("Formulations on the Two Principles of Mental Functioning," *SE* 12: 219–22).

11. This illustration of the division of the subject through the self/other duality recurs often in Freud, for example, in the article on "The Unconscious," Part I (*SE* 14), and in "The Question of Lay Analysis" (*SE* 20: 188): "Everyone is aware that there are some things in himself that he would be very unwilling to tell other people or that he considers it altogether out of

the question to tell. These are his 'intimacies.' He has a notion, too—and this represents a great advance in psychological self-knowledge—that there are other things that one would not care to admit *to oneself*: things that one likes to conceal from oneself and which for that reason one breaks off short and drives out of one's thoughts if, in spite of everything, they turn up. Perhaps he may himself notice that a very remarkable psychological problem begins to appear in this situation—of a thought of his own being kept secret from his own self."

12. Jean-Paul Sartre, *Being and Nothingness: An Essay on Phenomenological Ontology*, trans. Hazel E. Barnes (New York, 1956), pp. 50–57.

13. Ibid., pp. 51–52.

14. *Meditation II*: "What then is it that I am? A thinking thing. What is a thinking thing? It is a thing that doubts, understands, affirms, denies, wills, abstains from willing, that also can be aware of images and sensations" (*Descartes' Philosophical Writings*, trans. Norman Kemp Smith [London, 1952], p. 206).

"Dreams Are Completely Egoistic"

Parts of this chapter appeared in an earlier version in *Analytiques*, 3 (Paris, May 1979). The epigraphs on pp. 10 and 16 are from *The Interpretation of Dreams*, pp. 67 and 50, respectively.

1. The dream has been generally known in French as "le rêve de la belle bouchère" (the dream of the butcher's beautiful wife), at least since Jacques Lacan discussed it in his 1956–57 seminar, "Les Formations de l'inconscient"; he returned to the topic in "The Direction of the Treatment and the Principles of Its Power," in *Ecrits: A Selection*, trans. Alan Sheridan (New York, 1977), pp. 226–80.

2. *Aneignung*, as Lacan pointed out in a session of the seminar cited in note 1, signifies appropriation as taking properly speaking—a taking possession. The *eigen*, the subjective property, is here inseparable from a theft, a *usurpation* of identity, or else a violent *assimilation*. One may, if one chooses, consider all of what follows as a commentary on this violence of property/propriety, on that strange "event"—*Ereignis*—that summons up the proper in and through deappropriation: *a-propriation* (Derrida).

3. Lacan, "Direction," pp. 262–63.

4. This is the mechanism of "recuperation" that Freud had described in "Draft N" (letter to Fliess, May 31, 1897): "Hostile impulses against parents (a wish that they should die) are also an integral part of neuroses. . . . At periods in which pity for one's parents is active—at times of their illness or death . . . one of the manifestations of grief is . . . to reproach oneself for their death (*cf.* what are described as 'melancholias') or to punish oneself in a hysterical way (by putting oneself into their position with an idea of retribution) with the same states [of illness] that they have had. The

identification which takes place here is, as we can see, merely a mode of thinking and does not relieve us of the necessity for looking for the motive" (*Origins*, p. 207). More than twenty-four years later, Freud comes back to the same idea in Chap. 7 of "Group Psychology": a girl, for example, may identify with a morbid symptom of her mother's (with a single one of her traits), and identification then signifies "a hostile desire to take her mother's place: 'You wanted to be your mother, and now you *are*—anyhow so far as your sufferings are concerned.' This is the complete mechanism of the structure of a hysterical symptom" (p. 106).

5. It is in fantasies (waking, dreaming, unconscious) that the wish is fulfilled, and nowhere else: "The motive forces of phantasies are unsatisfied wishes, and every single phantasy is the fulfilment of a wish, a correction of an unsatisfying reality" ("Creative Writers," p. 146).

6. On this point, the irreducibility of the fantasy of desire to the satisfaction of a need, one must of course refer to the work of Jacques Lacan and his school; see, for example, Jean Laplanche and J.-B. Pontalis, "Fantasme originaire, fantasme des origines, origines du fantasme," in *Les Temps Modernes*, no. 215 (April 1964): 1861–68; and Serge Leclaire, "Langage et Inconscient" (in collaboration with Jean Laplanche), in *L'Inconscient, VIᵉ colloque de Bonneval* (Paris, 1966), pp. 108ff.

7. Let us recall that, for Freud, the fantasy is doubly present in the dream. At the dream's source, first of all, it is an unconscious fantasy, which is an "element in the dream-thoughts" (*Dreams*, p. 491). Then, on its surface, it is a waking fantasy or daydream, which is used by the secondary elaboration for the construction of the dream's "façade." Freud adds that the latter plunges its roots into the former, and so it turns out that the dream's "façade" is "available for use in the material of the dream-thoughts." See *Dreams*, pp. 491ff., and also the commentaries by Laplanche and Pontalis ("Fantasme," pp. 1858–59) and Jean-François Lyotard (*Discours, figure* [Paris, 1971], pp. 261ff.).

8. Laplanche and Pontalis, "Fantasme," p. 1860.

9. Thus it is no accident that the letters to Fliess in which the theory of fantasy is progressively sketched in as wish fulfillment (and no longer as a simple "mnesic symbol" of trauma) are also the ones in which the motif of identification intervenes almost obsessively. The letters in question are those of 1897 (*Origins*, pp. 181–82, 197–200, 207–9) that tacitly pave the way for the abandonment of the *neurotica*, that is, of the theory of the "seduction scene" (Letter 69). We know, moreover, that it is also at this point that the fantasmatic *Szene* takes on a properly *theatrical* meaning, as can be seen from the famous Letter 71, in which Freud compares the content of the incestuous fantasies dredged up in his self-analysis to that of the tragedy of *Oedipus Rex*, making clear at the same time that the relation of the subject to the fantasy is identical to that of the spectator to the drama represented: "The gripping power of *Oedipus Rex* . . . becomes intelligible.

. . . The Greek myth seizes on a compulsion which everyone recognizes because he has felt traces of it in himself. Every member of the audience was once a budding Oedipus in phantasy" (*Origins*, pp. 223–24). The relation of "recognition" (*anagnorisis*) reproduces the one that occurs in the fantasy, and we are dealing here with a relation of identification: the spectator identifies with the transgressor-hero who fulfills the wish in his place, just as the agoraphobe, for example, identifies in his fantasy with a prostitute working the streets (pp. 181–82). Jean Starobinski deserves much credit for having first drawn attention to the pertinence of the theatrical model in Freud, in his "Hamlet et Freud" (preface to Ernest Jones, *Hamlet et Oedipe* [Paris, 1967]); Gilles Deleuze and Félix Guattari (*Anti-Oedipus: Capitalism and Schizophrenia*, trans. Robert Harley, Mark Seem, and Helen R. Lane [New York, 1977]) and more recently Jean-François Lyotard ("Pardelà la représentation," preface to Anton Ehrenzweig, *L'Ordre caché de l'art* [Paris, 1974]) have drawn on this work for a critique of "representative theatricality" in Freud.

10. "I must have been prepared at all times in my *Ucs.* [unconscious] to identify myself with Professor R., since by means of that identification one of the immortal wishes of childhood—the megalomaniac wish—was fulfilled" (p. 556).

11. *Dreams*, p. 250: "Children are completely egoistic [*absolut egoistisch*]; they feel their needs intensely and strive ruthlessly to satisfy them—especially as against the rivals, other children, and first and foremost as against their brothers and sisters." See also pp. 124, 155, 268–71, 441, etc.

12. Such diffraction of the ego into several "part-egos" occurs in the "psychological novel" that is mentioned in "Creative Writers," p. 150.

13. *Dreams*, p. 277: "The dream-thoughts and the dream-content are presented to us like two versions of the same subject-matter in two different languages. Or, more properly, the dream-content seems like a transcript of the dream-thoughts into another mode of expression, whose characters and syntactic laws it is our business to discover by comparing the original and the translation."

14. *Republic*, 392c–98b. "When [the poet] delivers a speech as if he were someone else, shall we not say that he then assimilates thereby his own diction as far as possible to that of the person whom he announces as about to speak? . . . And is not likening one's self to another in speech or bodily bearing an imitation [*mimeisthai*] of him to whom one likens one's self?" (393c; trans. Paul Shorey; Loeb Classical Library ed. [London, 1969], pp. 227–29). This passage has been discussed by Gérard Genette ("Frontiers of Narrative," in his *Figures of Literary Discourse*, trans. Alan Sheridan [New York, 1982]), and Philippe Lacoue-Labarthe ("Typographie," in his *Mimesis des articulations* [Paris, 1975]). My discussion owes a great deal to this latter article, a remarkable text on which I shall draw in all that follows.

15. "The first wishing seems to have been a hallucinatory cathecting of

the memory of satisfaction" (*Dreams*, p. 598). "An impulse of this kind is what we call a wish; the reappearance of the perception is the fulfilment of the wish; . . . the aim of this first psychical activity was to produce a 'perceptual identity' " (p. 566); and so on.

16. Laplanche and Pontalis, "Fantasme," p. 1868.

17. Ibid.

18. These analyses are carried out in René Girard's *Deceit, Desire, and the Novel: Self and Other in Literary Structure*, trans. Yvonne Freccero (Baltimore, Md., 1965); *Violence and the Sacred*, trans. Patrick Gregory (Baltimore, Md., 1977); *Critique dans un souterrain* (Lausanne, 1976); and *Things Hidden Since the Foundation of the World*, trans. Michael Metteer and Stephen Bann (Stanford, Calif., 1987).

19. The term is Roland Barthes's, in *A Lover's Discourse: Fragments*, trans. Richard Howard (New York, 1978), pp. 136–37.

20. The mimetic relation Girard described corresponds fairly closely to the domain of the "imaginary" or "dual" relation that Lacan had already explored, starting with his earliest work on "paranoic knowledge," (*De la psychose paranoïaque dans ses rapports avec la personnalité* [Paris, 1932]), through the writings that focus on the "mirror stage" (*Ecrits* [Paris, 1966], pp. 93–193 [partial trans. in *Ecrits: A Selection*, pp. 1–29], and "La Famille," in *L'Encyclopédie française*, vol. 8, art. 40). Cf. also the following passage from "Aggressivity in Psychoanalysis" (*Ecrits: A Selection*, p. 19) in connection with the "transitivity" of the "mirror stage": "During the whole of this period, one will record the emotional reactions and the articulated evidences of a normal transitivism. The child who strikes another says that he has been struck; the child who sees another fall, cries. Similarly, it is by means of an identification with the other that he sees the whole gamut of reactions of bearing and display, whose structural ambivalence is clearly revealed in his behaviour, the slave being identified with the despot, the actor with the spectator, the seduced with the seducer. . . . It is in this erotic relation, in which the human individual fixes upon himself an image that alienates him from himself, that are to be found the energy and the form on which this organization of the passions that he will call his ego is based. This form will crystallize in the subject's internal conflictual tension, which determines the awakening of his desire for the object of the other's desire: here the primordial coming together (*concours*) is precipitated into aggressive competitiveness (*concurrence*), from which develops the triad of others, the ego and the object." Beyond the many important terminological differences (the "imaginary" refers principally to the visible, to a "visual *Gestalt*," which in theory should not be the case with mimesis), there is no doubt that Lacan's approach converges with (and anticipates) Girard's. However, the convergence breaks down where Lacan introduces—alongside the imaginary relation to the *petit autre* and transcending it from the vantage point

of the "Other's place"—a symbolic "intersubjective" relation with respect to which "imaginary factors," in spite of their inertia, "figure only as shadows and reflections" ("Seminar on 'The Purloined Letter,'" trans. Jeffrey Mehlman, in *Yale French Studies* 48: 40); see also Lacan's *Le Moi dans la théorie de Freud et dans la technique de la psychanalyse*, the section entitled "Au delà de l'imaginaire, le symbolique" (Paris, 1978). We may well wonder, though, whether Girard is not doing much the same thing when he manages to exempt Christianity from mimetic violence, considering how good he is at spotting it—far from the structural anthropology on which Lacan depends—at the foundation (the unstable, strictly speaking *unstabilizing* foundation) of the other symbolic institutions. But this last question—the question, in short, of original sociality, *preceding* any symbolic institution (and any "scapegoat")—would lead us too far afield. We shall take it up later on, with reference to "the primal band."

21. Melanie Klein, *Envy and Gratitude* (London, 1957), pp. 36–37: "The envious relation to the mother expresses itself in an excessive Oedipus rivalry. *This rivalry is much less due to love of the father* than to *envy of the mother's possession* of the father and his penis. . . . The father (or his penis) has become an *appendage* to the mother and *it is on these grounds* that the girl wants to rob her mother of him" (emphasis added). (Klein's French translator notes the multiple resonances of the term "appendage": appurtenance, adjunct, accessory, appendix, and so on.) It is clear that Klein's way of generating the Oedipal triangle is quite different from Freud's: it is not love for a parent that leads to rivalry with a third party (the other parent or the other child), but rather rivalry that orients love toward a third-party object. It would suffice, in short, to replace "envy" with "mimesis" in order to produce the triangle of desire as Girard outlines it.

22. Jean Laplanche, *Life and Death in Psychoanalysis*, trans. Jeffrey Mehlman (Baltimore, Md., 1976), pp. 15, 22. The theory of the attachment of the sexual instincts to the self-preservative instincts is developed by Freud in "Infantile Sexuality," the second of his "Three Essays."

23. On the Lacanian theory of the "attachment" (if we may use the term) of desire to demand, see Lacan, *Ecrits: A Selection*, pp. 263ff. and 285ff., along with the still unpublished seminars of 1955–56 and 1956–57, "La Relation d'objet" and "Les Formations de l'inconscient."

24. "I have avoided sex," Freud wrote to Fliess with reference to *Dreams*, "but 'dirt' is unavoidable" (*Origins*, Letter 117, September 6, 1899). The "dirt" here is the entire complex of ambitious, social-climbing desires that make up, as Marthe Robert accurately notes, "the most powerful driving force behind the personal dreams analyzed in *The Interpretation of Dreams*." (On all this, see Marthe Robert, *From Oedipus to Moses*, trans. Ralph Manheim [Garden City, N.Y., 1976], Chap. 3, "Ambition Thwarted.")

25. See also *Dreams* (p. 268, n. 1): "The appearance in dreams of things of great size and in great quantities and amounts, and of exaggeration generally, may be another childish characteristic. Children have no more ardent wish than to be big and grown-up and to get as much of things as grown-up people do." Hence the notion of "great man," as "Moses and Monotheism" (*SE* 23: 110) adds.

26. On the ludic origin of fantasy, see also "Formulations on the Two Principles of Mental Functioning," (*SE* 12: 218–19, para. 2) and "Family Romance" (*SE* 9: 238).

27. See Philippe Lacoue-Labarthe's commentary, "Note sur Freud et la représentation," in *Digraphe*, no. 3 (Paris, 1974). The identification in question here is that of the spectator, but the same mechanism applies to the poet as well. Just as the daydream is "egoistic," as "Creative Writers" states, so novels are "egocentric": the hero masks the author's ego—in other words, the author identifies with him.

28. The theatrical metaphors are Freud's: "This, then, was the complete game [*Spiel*, also "play"]—disappearance and return. As a rule one only witnessed its first act, which was repeated untiringly as a game in itself, though there is no doubt that the greater pleasure was attached to the second act. . . . He compensated for this, as it were, by himself staging the disappearance and return of the objects within his reach. . . . It may perhaps be said in reply that [the mother's] departure had to be enacted as a necessary preliminary to her joyful return. . . . But . . . the first act, that of departure, was staged as a game in itself and far more frequently than the episode in its entirety, with its pleasurable ending" ("Beyond Pleasure," pp. 15–16).

29. In a well-known passage, Bataille argued against Hegel that death cannot be looked "in the face" except by way of the spectacle, that is, by way of sacrificial or tragic representation: "In sacrifice, the sacrificer identifies with the animal killed. Thus he dies in seeing himself die, and even, in a way, through his own will, a willing weapon of sacrifice. But this is a comedy! . . . It is a matter, at least in tragedy, of identifying ourselves with some character who dies, and to believe we are dying whereas we are still alive. What is more, imagination pure and simple is enough, but it has the same meaning as the classical subterfuges, the spectacles or the books to which many people resort" (Georges Bataille, "Hegel, la mort et le sacrifice," in *Deucalion*, no. 5 [Neuchâtel, 1955], pp. 33–34). Now it is to that same "comic" logic of spectacular representation (of death, of pain) that Freud appeals in order to *confirm* the domination of the pleasure principle. The paradigm of "economic" play (representation, repetition) is indeed tragedy, and Freud reiterates—echoing all of Western poetics since Aristotle—that tragedy is an imitation in which one takes pleasure: "Finally, a reminder may be added that the artistic play and artistic imitation carried

out by adults, which, unlike children's, are aimed at an audience, do not spare the spectators (for instance, in tragedy) the most painful experiences and can yet be felt by them as highly enjoyable" ("Beyond Pleasure," p. 17). We may and must conclude, as Lacoue-Labarthe does ("Note sur Freud"), that, if there is a repetition "beyond" the pleasure principle (an an-economic representation), it has to be sought far from the theatrico-spectacular model and from the prevailing concept of imitation: that is what we are attempting to do here.

30. Also art, since poetic creation presumed to be modeled on the *Schauspiel*, functions in turn in "Creative Writers" as a paradigm for art in general. Hence it is clear that comprehension of both fantasy and art depends, in the last analysis, on what is meant here by *Spiel*, that is, mimesis. In other words, are we dealing with a scenic representation (like the theatrical *spectacle*)? Or rather, as I am inclined to believe, with a "properly" mimetic activity (like the actor's "play"-acting)?

31. Cf. the interpretation of Dostoevski's "death attacks" in "Dostoevsky and Parricide," *SE* 21.

32. It is essential to take into account the correction Freud made six years later, in "Some Psychical Consequences of the Anatomical Distinction between the Sexes" (*SE* 19: 255): "Even after penis-envy has abandoned its true object, it continues to exist: by an easy displacement it persists in the character-trait of *jealousy*. . . . While I was still unaware of this source of jealousy and was considering the phantasy 'a child is being beaten,' which occurs so commonly in girls, I constructed a first phase for it in which its meaning was that another child, a rival of whom the subject was jealous, was to be beaten. This phantasy seems to be a relic of the phallic period in girls. The peculiar rigidity which struck me so much in the monotonous formula 'a child is being beaten' can probably be interpreted in a special way. The child which is being beaten (or caressed) may ultimately be nothing more nor less than the clitoris itself, so that at its very lowest level the statement will contain a confession of masturbation, which has remained attached to the content of the formula from its beginning in the phallic phase till later life." On this topic, see Jacques Nassif, "Le Fantasme dans 'On bat un enfant,'" *Cahiers pour l'Analyse*, no. 7 (March–April 1967), and Jean-François Lyotard, "Discours, figure, l'utopie du fantasme," in his *Discours, figure*, pp. 327–54 (I am particularly indebted to the fifth paragraph of this chapter).

33. Klein, *Envy and Gratitude*, especially pp. 6ff. (on the difference between envy, jealousy, and greed); Hanna Segal, *Introduction to the Work of Melanie Klein* (New York, 1973), pp. 27ff.

34. See Elsa Köhler, *Die Persönlichkeit des dreijahrigen Kinder* (Leipzig, 1926), and Henri Wallon, *Les Origines du caractère chez l'enfant* (Paris, 1934). Maurice Merleau-Ponty saw this research as a way to get around solipsism

(psychologistic or transcendental) through the exploration of a "syncretic sociability" that would antedate the self/other differentiation ("Les Relations avec autrui chez l'enfant," Sorbonne course, 1950–51). I can subscribe to this position if I add, with Lacan, that transitivism immediately opens onto aggressiveness (and "understanding of others" onto hatred): this primary "sociality" is also a primary a-sociality. I shall come back to this point.

35. On this topic, see Laplanche, *Life and Death*, pp. 98ff.

36. On "construction," see "Constructions in Analysis," *SE* 23. On "recollection," see "Remembering, Repeating and Working-Through (Further Recommendations on the Technique of Psycho-Analysis, II)," *SE* 12.

37. Jean-François Lyotard, "Par-delà la représentation," preface to Anton Ehrenzweig, *L'Ordre caché de l'art* (Paris, 1974).

38. On the specularization of mimesis in Plato, see Lacoue-Labarthe, "Typographie."

39. Freud adds: "I should not be surprised if it were one day possible to prove that the same phantasy is the basis of the delusional litigiousness of paranoia" ("Child," p. 195).

40. Aristotle, *De anima*, trans. R. D. Hicks (Amsterdam, 1965), Book 3, Chap. 3, p. 129: "And, since sight is the principal sense, imagination [*phantasia*] has derived even its name from light [*phaos*], because without light one cannot see."

41. For what follows, see *Dreams*, pp. 135–40 and 192–93.

42. Is it a coincidence, moreover, that the analysis of this dream calls forth, concerning the ambivalence of friendship and hatred, the following quotation from a speech by Brutus in *Julius Caesar*: "As Caesar loved me, I weep for him; as he was fortunate, I rejoice at it; as he was valiant, I honour him; but, as he was ambitious, I slew him"? Is it a coincidence that Freud concludes that he himself "had been playing the part of Brutus in the dream," and goes on to add: "Strange to say, I really did once play the part of Brutus. I once acted in the scene between Brutus and Caesar from Schiller before an audience of children. I was fourteen years old at the time and was acting with a nephew who was a year my senior" (*Dreams*, p. 424)? To confirm the identificatory character of the rivalry that opposed Freud to R. in the dream of "the uncle with the yellow beard" (where R. is identified with Freud's uncle), let us quote the following note as well: "It will be noticed that the name Josef plays a great part in my dreams (cf. the dream about my uncle). My own ego finds it very easy to hide itself behind people of that name, since Joseph was the name of a man famous in the Bible as an interpreter of dreams" (p. 484, n. 1). By competing with R. (= Joseph), Freud is thus competing with "himself."

43. It is clear that Freud fills all the slots and plays all the parts: he names and is named, abuses and is abused, beats and is beaten; he is anti-Semite and Jew. Here is renewed confirmation of our earlier position on

the "egoism" of dreams and fantasy: the "self" is everywhere, but everywhere identifying with an "other" (nonreflexive identification with the Minister, specular identification with R. and N.). It is on this basis that we shall subscribe to what Laplanche and Pontalis say about the impossibility of assigning the subject to *one* of the places of the original fantasy ("Fantasme," p. 1861); to what Cornelius Castoriadis says about "the indistinction of the subject and non-subject," in the "constituting fantasy" (*L'Institution imaginaire de la société* [Paris, 1975], pp. 387ff.); and to C. Stein's thesis on wish fulfillment as infantile and megalomanic nondifferentiation of subject and object ("Rome imaginaire," in *L'Inconscient*, no. 1 [Paris, January–March 1967]).

44. See also the analysis of the "revolutionary dream" (*Dreams*, pp. 215ff.).

45. See the note added in 1923 to "Fragment of an Analysis of a Case of Hysteria" (the Dora case): "The longer the interval of time that separates me from the end of this analysis, the more probable it seems to me that the fault in my technique lay in this omission: I failed to discover in time and to inform the patient that her homosexual (gynaecophilic) love for Frau K. was the strongest unconscious current in her mental life. . . . Before I had learnt the importance of the homosexual current of feeling in psychoneurotics, I was often brought to a standstill in the treatment of my cases or found myself in complete perplexity" (*SE* 7: 120, n. 1).

46. It is of course obvious—even if Freud does not say so clearly, during this period (1900)—that the hysterical triangle described here is nothing but the classic Oedipal triangle (the subject, the love object, the rival model).

47. Cf. "Psycho-Analytic Notes," p. 64, and "Some Neurotic Mechanisms in Jealousy, Paranoia and Homosexuality," *SE* 18: 225ff.

48. Lacan, "Direction," p. 261.

49. Here is one example of this literature, among many others: "These [hysterical] patients are veritable actresses: they do not know of a greater pleasure than to deceive . . . all those with whom they come in touch. The hysterics who exaggerate their convulsive movement . . . make an equal travesty and exaggeration of the movements of their soul, their ideas and their acts. . . . In one word, the life of the hysterics is nothing but one perpetual falsehood" (Jules Falret, "Folie raisonnable ou Folie morale," in *Etudes cliniques sur les maladies mentales* [Paris, 1890], p. 502, quoted by Ilza Veith in *Hysteria, the History of a Disease* [Chicago and London, 1965], p. 211).

50. Since Freud praised Jean Martin Charcot for it, see "Bericht über meine Studienreise nach Paris und Berlin," 1886 (in J. and R. Gicklhorn, *Sigmund Freuds akademische Laufbahn im Lichte der Dokumente* [Vienna, 1960]) and also Charcot's obituary, 1893 (Sigmund Freud, *Gesammelte Werke* [Frankfurt and London, 1952–68], vol. 1).

Ecce Ego

The epigraph on p. 53 is from *The Complete Works of Friedrich Nietzsche*, trans. Anthony M. Ludovici (New York, 1911), 17: 1. On p. 94 the epigraph from Bernart de Ventadour is from *Chansons d'amour*, trans. Moshé Lazar (Paris, 1966), p. 181; the epigraph from Wagner is from act 2, scene 2, of *Tristan und Isolde*, trans H. and F. Corder (Leipzig, 1904), pp. 648–52.

1. See, for example, "A Metapsychological Supplement to the Theory of Dreams" (*SE* 14: 223): "We know that dreams are completely egoistic and that the person who plays the chief part in their scenes is always to be recognized as the dreamer. This is now easily to be accounted for by the narcissism of the state of sleep. Narcissism and egoism, indeed, coincide; the word 'narcissism' is only intended to emphasize the fact that egoism is a libidinal phenomenon as well; or, to put it another way, narcissism may be described as the libidinal complement of egoism."

2. C. G. Jung, *Psychology of the Unconscious: A Study of the Transformations and Symbolisms of the Libido*, trans. Beatrice M. Hinkle (New York, 1916).

3. Freud wonders about this himself, with "perceptible uneasiness" ("On Narcissism," p. 77). But his intent is to discredit in advance all "speculation" in this area, and to propose to retain a dualism solidly based on "observation" and "empirical interpretation." Does this really do away with the uneasiness, though? We are entitled to doubt it, since none of Freud's stated reasons for maintaining dualism justifies (quite the opposite is true) the introduction of an ego libido whose inherently composite character Freud had just specifically announced: "As regards the differentiation of psychical energies, we are led to the conclusion that to begin with, during the state of narcissism, they exist together and that our analysis is too coarse to distinguish between them; not until there is object-cathexis is it possible to discriminate a sexual energy—the libido—from an energy of the ego-instincts" (p. 76).

4. Cf. Jean Laplanche and J.-B. Pontalis, "Ego-Libido/Object-Libido," in *The Language of Psychoanalysis*, trans. Donald Nicholson-Smith (New York, 1974), pp. 150–151, n. 6. See also Jean Laplanche, *Life and Death in Psychoanalysis*, trans. Jeffrey Mehlman (Baltimore, Md., 1976), p. 67.

5. Freud used the term "narcissism" for the first time in connection with homosexuality. He noted in 1910 that the homosexual identifies with his mother in order to repress the love he feels for her, "and takes his own person as a model in whose likeness he chooses the new objects of his love. . . . He finds the objects of his love along the path of *narcissism*, as we say; for Narcissus, according to the Greek legend, was a youth who preferred his own reflection to everything else and who was changed into the lovely flower of that name" ("Leonardo da Vinci and a Memory of His Child-

hood," *SE* 11: 100); see also "The Sexual Aberrations," *SE* 7: 144, n. 1 (note added in 1910), in "Three Essays," and an article written in 1911 by Otto Rank, "Une Contribution au narcissisme," in *Topique*, no. 14 (Paris, 1974).

6. See François Roustang, *Dire Mastery: Discipleship from Freud to Lacan*, trans. Ned Lukacher (Baltimore, Md., 1982), Chap. 3, esp. pp. 45–46; I shall lean heavily upon Roustang's analyses from here on. In connection with the "Fliess affair," I shall take for granted a certain familiarity with the abundant and indispensable material collected by Max Schur in *La Mort dans la vie de Freud* (Paris, 1975), in particular Chap. 9 ("Disciples et amis. Le réveil des anciens conflits"), in which Schur forcefully suggests that the "Jung affair" repeated the scenario of the "Fliess affair." (See, for example, p. 328: "Freud's relation with Fliess was characterized by a profound ambivalence, accentuated both by the intensity of Freud's positive feelings and, on Fliess's side, by the hostile assault which brought the relationship to an abrupt end. This intense ambivalence creates a link between the conflict with Fliess and, to a lesser extent, the relationship with Jung on the one hand, and the deeper level of the earliest ambivalence-laden conflicts on the other.")

7. Cf. Roustang, *Dire Mastery*, p. 54.

8. Freud's writing offers numerous hints of this proximity, always in the margins of the "Fliess affair." To Jung, he writes that his work on the Schreber case has revived his own "Fliess complex" (*Letters*, pp. 378–80). His letter of October 6, 1910, to Ferenczi is even more explicit: "You have observed that I no longer have any need to expose my personality completely. . . . Since the Fliess affair, this need has been completely suppressed. A portion of homosexual cathexis has been withdrawn and used for the enlarging of my ego. I have succeeded at the very point where the paranoic fails" (that is, at the point where Fliess had failed). See also, in this regard, the conclusion of "Psycho-Analytic Notes," where Freud evokes the "striking conformity" between Schreber's delusions and psychoanalytic theory (*SE* 12: 78).

9. On projection and rejection, see "The Neuro-Psychoses of Defense" (1894) and "Further Remarks on the Neuro-Psychoses of Defense" (1896), *SE* 3: 58–59 and 174–85. On autoerotism, see Letter 125 to Fliess (September 9, 1899): "The lowest of the sexual strata is auto-erotism, which renounces any psychosexual aim and seeks only local gratification. . . . Hysteria (and its variant, obsessional neurosis) is allo-erotic; the main highway it follows is identification with the loved person. Paranoia dissolves the identification again, re-establishes all the loved persons of childhood . . . and dissolves the ego itself into extraneous persons. So I have come to regard paranoia as a surge forward of the auto-erotic tendency, a regression to a former state" (*Origins*, pp. 303–4).

10. Freud returns several times to this difference between neurotic

repression, which merely displaces the libidinal cathexis onto a fantasmatic object-substitute, and psychotic "repression," which decathexes even "thing-presentations" themselves; cf. "On Narcissism," p. 74; "The Unconscious," *SE* 14: 196–97, 203–4; and "Neurosis and Psychosis," *SE* 19: 150–51.

11. Jacques Lacan proposed the term "foreclosure" for this psychotic rejection, to differentiate it even more clearly from repression, which always presupposes (which *is*) the "symbolization" of the repressed. This symbolization is what would be lacking in psychosis; what has been foreclosed then returns, in a nonsymbolized form, "in the real." Thus Lacan goes quite far in the direction opened up by Freud, since the rejection no longer even belongs to the (or a) subject, but to a "lack" in the constitution of subjectivity as such (it would remain to be seen how what has been foreclosed can simply appear, and to whom it would thus appear). On all these questions, see Jacques Lacan, "Réponse au commentaire de Jean Hyppolite sur la 'Verneinung' de Freud," in *Ecrits* (Paris, 1966), pp. 384–93, and "On a Question Preliminary to Any Possible Treatment of Psychosis," in *Ecrits: A Selection*, trans. Alan Sheridan (New York, 1977), pp. 199–201, 217–21; see also his unpublished seminar "Les Psychoses," especially the session on December 7, 1955.

12. Freud wrote to Jung: "May I suggest that you should not use the term autoerotism as inclusively as H. Ellis, that it should not include hysterical utilizations of libido, but only truly autoerotic states, in which all relations with objects have been abandoned" (*Letters*, p. 191).

13. Daniel Paul Schreber's *Memoirs of My Nervous Illness* (trans. Ida Macalpine and Richard A. Hunter [London, 1955]) is recommended reading in this connection; the text makes clear to what extent the "overvaluation of the ego itself" exceeds the sexual sphere to which Freud tries to confine it. Schreber does assert that the power of destruction-attraction he exercises on the "divine rays" is a function of the intensity of the "sensation of voluptuousness" he experiences in his own body (p. 94 and elsewhere). But this voluptuousness is precisely a megalomanic voluptuousness, directly linked with the "enlargement of the ego": to enjoy, to enjoy *all the time*, is to come through with flying colors against "God Flechsig," in a sort of sexual gigantomacy on which "the Order of the World" depends and which puts Schreber in the position of Savior of humanity. He will either be the "female harlot" that the persecuting voices represent him to be—a prostitute handed over to God Flechsig in order to be *possessed* by him, then "forsaken" (pp. 75, 77, etc.)—or he will be able to turn this humiliating situation to his own advantage by making "the Order of the World" depend on his *own* pleasure, in a sacred prostitution that will elevate him to the status of God's wife. Schreber's erotheocosmology is never anything but a way of answering the question "Who?" (*Who* am I? He or I? Nothing or

everything?). As for equating the voluptuous body of Schreber with a sexual object, this would mean failing to understand that he is literally *sacrificed* to pleasure (this is one of the meanings of the Schreberian *Versöhnung*, as Lacan pointed out [*Ecrits: A Selection*, p. 207]) and, as such, *transfigured*: body enlarged to the dimensions of the universe (since he has "swallowed" it whole), radiant body haloed with a "crown of rays" (p. 88), redeeming body from which will come forth a race of "new human beings out of Schreber's spirit" (p. 111), and so on.

14. Jung does not miss a chance to underline the convergence somewhat perfidiously, since he presents his genetic concept of the libido as a solution to the difficulties that had ensnared Freud in the Schreber case (*Letters*, p. 471). Indeed, Jung might well have had in mind a passage such as the following: "Are we to suppose that a general detachment of the libido from the external world would be an effective enough agent to account for the 'end of the world'? Or would not the ego-cathexes which still remained in existence have been sufficient to maintain rapport with the external world? To meet this difficulty we should either have to *assume that what we call libidinal cathexis (that is, interest emanating from erotic sources) coincides with interest in general*, or we should have to consider the possibility that a very widespread disturbance in the distribution of libido may bring about a corresponding disturbance in the ego-cathexes. But these are problems which we are still quite helpless and incompetent to solve" ("Psycho-Analytic Notes," pp. 73–74; emphasis added).

15. This is not always the case. The persecutor is sometimes of the opposite sex, and Freud goes to a good deal of trouble to explain this, in "A Case of Paranoia Running Counter to the Psycho-Analytic Theory of the Disease" (*SE* 14: 263–72).

16. On this topic, see A. de Waehlens, *La Psychose. Essai d'interprétation analytique et existentiale* (Louvain-Paris, 1972), pp. 146–47.

17. Cf. Jacques Lacan, *De la Psychose paranoïaque dans ses rapports avec la personnalité* (Paris, 1975 [reprint ed.]), pp. 263–74; also "Propos sur la causalité psychique," in *Ecrits*, p. 169. Furthermore, we may wonder whether erotomania is not a sort of delirium of triumphant jealousy, the overwhelming certainty of being loved by *him* coming back to affirm the triumph over *her*, the feminine rival who is somehow associated with the erotomanic individual. This hypothesis (which is not Freud's, although it does not challenge the idea of sexual identity between the victim of delusion and his or her "object") would provide a better explanation of the frequent development of the delusion of jealousy into erotomania. See, on this topic, Daniel Lagache's excellent remarks in "Erotomanie et jalousie" (in his *Oeuvres*, vol. 1 [1932–46], Paris, 1977): the "satisfied pride" of the erotomanic would correspond to the "wounded pride" of his jealous counterpart, just as megalomania corresponds to the idea of persecution.

18. Here we are following the "chronology" of delusion established by Freud in the theoretical section of "Psycho-Analytic Notes," where the delusion of grandeur of the narcissistic ego is placed in primary position, since it is presumed to come before the delusions of persecution, jealousy, and so on (pp. 72–73). In the first two sections, devoted to the interpretation of the Schreber case, he considers the theme of the delusional megalomanic (Schreber's divine marriage) rather as a *secondary* compromise destined to get the ego-agency to accept the "feminine wishful phantasy" (pp. 32, 47–48).

19. Schreber, *Memoirs*, p. 57. Octave Mannoni has quite correctly noted that the delusion had opened up onto a "conflict of prestige, authority, and knowledge" (in his *Clefs pour l'imaginaire ou l'autre scène* [Paris, 1969], pp. 90–92).

20. René Girard has made this quite clear, especially with regard to the "literary" and "philosophical" follies of Hölderlin and Nietzsche. I am greatly indebted to Girard's analyses and will draw on them heavily in all that follows: *Violence and the Sacred*, trans. Patrick Gregory (Baltimore, Md., 1977), pp. 155–58; "Système du délire," in *Critique dans un souterrain* (Lausanne, 1976); and "Superman in the Underground: Strategies of Madness—Nietzsche, Wagner and Dostoevsky," in *MLN*, 91, no. 6 (1976), pp. 1161–85.

21. Let us not be too unfair: Freud also says that there is rivalry between the victim of delusion and his double, since he (Freud) combines the interpretation of delusion through the libidinal "phases" and "vicissitudes" with an Oedipal deciphering of Schreber's delusional state, which leads him to equate Flechsig with Schreber's older brother, and God with his father ("Psycho-Analytic Notes," pp. 50ff.). The fact remains that these two versions are curiously dissociated (the Oedipal problematics virtually never comes into question in Part III, which is of particular interest to us here), and this is probably not a coincidence. In fact, to blend the two decodings would presuppose being able to say why the Oedipal *rival* (paternal, fraternal) arouses a homosexual *love*. But Freud never responds to that question, except perhaps in the briefest of notes: "In the same way, Schreber's 'feminine wishful phantasy' is simply one of the typical forms taken by the infantile nuclear complex" (p. 55, n. 3). This "typical" form will be studied only later, under the heading of an inverted Oedipus complex, and by way of all sorts of difficulties to which we shall return at the appropriate moment. It should suffice for now to know that with regard to delusion, combining an interpretation based on the Oedipal reality and an interpretation based on homosexuality is a not self-evident undertaking, without a thoroughgoing revision of the Oedipal schema (see in this connection the notes on the Schreber case presented in "A Seventeenth-Century Demonological Neurosis" [1923], *SE* 19: 91–92).

22. See also Freud's letter of March 9, 1911, about Fliess to Abraham (in *A Psycho-Analytic Dialogue: The Letters of Sigmund Freud and Karl Abraham*, trans. Bernard Marsh and Hilda Abraham [New York, 1965], p. 103): "Do not forget that it was through him that both of us came to understand the secret of paranoia . . . ; I once loved him very much." (I should like to thank Patrick Ach for pointing out this passage.)

23. Jung, as Roustang points out (*Dire Mastery*, pp. 45–46), was not mistaken, all the more because the allusion to Fliess was included in a letter in which Freud, for the first time, called him "dear friend" (and no longer "dear colleague"): "The reference to Fliess—surely not accidental—and your relationship with him impels me to ask you to let me enjoy your friendship not as one between equals but as that of father and son. This distance appears to me fitting and natural" (*Letters*, p. 71). Only such a distance could have stemmed the mimetic escalation (symmetrical, to use Gregory Bateson's terminology) implied in the "communist" relation of equal to equal.

24. "If we review the ingenious constructions which were raised by Schreber's delusion in the domain of religion . . . , we can gauge in retrospect the wealth of sublimations which were brought down in ruin by the catastrophe of the general detachment of his libido" ("Psycho-Analytic Notes," p. 73). Freud repeats this at the end of "On Narcissism," just at the moment—and it is hardly a coincidence!—when he is building bridges in the direction of "collective psychology": "The frequent causation of paranoia by an injury to the ego, by a frustration of satisfaction within the sphere of the ego ideal, is thus made more intelligible, as is the convergence of ideal-formation and sublimation in the ego ideal, as well as the involution of sublimations and the possible transformation of ideals in paraphrenic disorders" ("On Narcissism," p. 102).

25. Georg Wilhelm Friedrich Hegel, *Phenomenology of Spirit*, trans. A. V. Miller (Oxford, 1977), p. 105.

26. René Girard, *Things Hidden Since the Foundation of the World*, trans. Michael Metteer and Stephen Bann (Stanford, Calif., 1987), Chap. 1, A, "Acquisitive Mimesis and Mimetic Rivalry," and Book 3, Chap. 1, F, "From Object Rivalry to Metaphysical Desire." For example: "To untie the knot of desire, we have only to concede that everything begins in rivalry for the object. The object acquires the status of a disputed object and thus the envy that it arouses in all quarters becomes more and more heated" (p. 294).

27. We need only think, for example, of the phases of "spite" and "hatred" that follow, according to Gaëtan de Clérambault, the phase of erotomanic "hope." (In any event, clinical reality constantly blends together erotomania/jealousy/persecution types, so that it would be quite presumptuous to seek to distinguish them at all costs.) "Aimée," the patient analyzed in Lacan's thesis, maintained a relationship of erotomanic idyll with the

Prince of Wales, one of persecution with the actress Z. and the writer P. B., and one of jealousy with her husband.

28. Schreber, *Memoirs*, pp. 86–91. As we know, it was after a suicide attempt in his mother's apartment that Schreber was admitted to Professor Flechsig's clinic (pp. 64–65). Freud takes very little interest in the suicidal dimension of the end-of-the-world delusion. However, it is clear that that delusion kept Schreber oscillating between (manic) megalomanic exaltation and (melancholic) suicidal depression, so that in the end it is impossible to differentiate between the two phases (between victory over the double and the double's victory, between hetero-aggression and auto-aggression, and so on). Freud would surely have been more attentive to all this a few years later, after his analysis of manic-depressive states ("Mourning and Melancholia," *SE* 14) and his identification of the "death instinct."

29. Schreber, *Memoirs*, pp. 97–98. See Lacan's remarks on this topic, in *Ecrits: A Selection*, pp. 208–9.

30. Here the question of philosophic madness ought to arise—the madness of philosophers and philosophy as madness. For example, is there not a profound congruence between the modern era of metaphysics (determination of the being as being-itself, presence to self in certitude, subject[iv]ity, and so on) and the movement of madness itself? Between the modern concept(s) of madness (alienation, for example) and madness itself? These questions have been addressed by Jacques Derrida, in "La Parole soufflée" (*L'Ecriture et la différence* [Paris, 1967]); by Philippe Lacoue-Labarthe, in "Typographie" (*Mimesis des articulations* [Paris, 1975]), in "L'Oblitération" (*Le Sujet de la philosophie* [Paris, 1979]), and in "La Césure du spéculatif" (*Hölderlin, L'Antigone de Sophocle* [Paris, 1978]); and of course by Freud: "The complaints made by paranoics also show that at bottom the self-criticism of conscience coincides with the self-observation on which it is based. Thus the activity of the mind which has taken over the function of conscience has also placed itself at the service of internal research, which furnishes philosophy with the material for its intellectual operations. This may have some bearing on the characteristic tendency of paranoics to construct speculative systems" ("On Narcissism," p. 96). "It must be confessed that the expression and content of our philosophizing then begins to acquire an unwelcome resemblance to the mode of operation of schizophrenics" ("The Unconscious," *SE* 14: 204).

31. "His Majesty the Baby," Freud writes in "On Narcissism" (p. 91), echoing "His Majesty the Ego" discussed in "Creative Writers" (p. 150); the ego "comes up against limits to its own power in its own house," it is not an "absolute ruler" ("A Difficulty in the Path of Psycho-Analysis," *SE* 17: 141, 143); the megalomanic "creates autocratically a new external and internal world" ("Neurosis and Psychosis," *SE* 19: 151); "the unbounded self-love (the narcissism) of children regards any interference as an act of *lèse majesté*" (*Dreams*, p. 255, n. 2, added in 1919); and so on. Conversely,

if Narcissus is always a tyrant, the tyrant is always a Narcissus: in "Group Psychology" Freud says that the narcissism of the primitive tyrant (the *Urvater*) was absolute (p. 124). The narcissistic libido is thus the tyrannical impulse.

32. *Desire* for power, and not *will* to power. As Girard strongly suggests, Nietzsche's "madness" is perhaps entirely located in that relentless inflection of the desire for power (resentment) toward a will to power (will to will). Cf. Girard's "Superman in the Underground," pp. 1169ff.

33. Laplanche and Pontalis, *Vocabulary of Psychoanalysis*, "Ego-Libido/Object-Libido," pp. 150–51.

34. Ibid., p. 150: "'Object' and 'ego' in these compound terms refer to the point to which the libido is directed, not its point of departure." But why attempt to dispel the ambiguity at all costs? The German *Ichlibido* is no clearer (moreover, Laplanche and Pontalis recognize that their approach raises difficulties "with more than terminological implications").

35. Among other passages, see "The Libido Theory," a chapter added to "Three Essays" in 1915 (Part III, Chap. 3): "Psychoanalysis . . . affords us assured information only on the transformations that take place in the object-libido, but is unable to make any immediate distinction between the ego-libido and the other forms of energy operating in the ego" (p. 218).

36. "On Narcissism," p. 76: "This part of the allocation of libido necessarily remained hidden from us at the outset." "Three Essays," p. 218: "The narcissistic libidinal cathexis of the ego is the original state of things, realized in earliest childhood, and is merely covered by the later extrusions of libido, but in essentials persists behind them."

37. On Freudian *Spekulation* in general, see Gilles Deleuze, *Présentation de Sacher Masoch* (Paris, 1967), pp. 28–29, 111ff.; Rodolphe Gasché, "La Sorcière métapsychologique," in *Digraphe*, no. 3 (Paris, 1974); Jean-François Lyotard, "De l'apathie théorique," in *Critique*, no. 333 (Paris, 1975); and Jacques Derrida, "Legs de Freud," in *Etudes freudiennes*, nos. 13–14 (Paris, 1978; reprinted in his *La Carte postale*, Paris, 1980).

38. Not that the study of illness and hypochondria does not bring up some very interesting questions. For example, "the question of what makes it necessary at all for our mental life to pass beyond the limits of narcissism and to attach the libido to objects" ("On Narcissism," p. 85). The answer is found, in keeping with the (un)pleasure principle, in the necessity to *defer* the painful, indeed death-giving "stasis" implied by the accumulation of excess libido in the ego. Narcissism is thus not simply inaccessible to observation, it is quite simply impossible, *unlivable*—exactly like the "inertia principle" of Freud's "Project for a Scientific Psychology" of 1895 (*SE* 1) or the "Nirvana principle" (that is, the pleasure principle as death instinct) of the 1920's. Narcissus defers to Love, as Thanatos to Eros, and this is speculation itself: the speculation of death.

39. Some of these changes are closely linked with the introduction of

narcissism, even if this is not immediately obvious. It is clear, for example, that Freud's move to account for primitive orality by incorporation and identification takes him back to a point prior to the self-preservation/sexuality distinction and to any *object relation*: the "object" is then "what he himself is": "The first [pregenital organization] is the oral or, as it might be called, cannibalistic pregenital sexual organization. Here sexual activity has not yet been separated from the ingestion of food; nor are opposite currents within the activity differentiated. The *object* of both activities is the same; the sexual *aim* consists in the incorporation of the object—the prototype of a process which, in the form of identification, is later to play such an important psychological part" (added in 1915 to "Three Essays," Part II, Chap. 6, p. 198).

40. Cf. Girard, *Things Hidden*, Book 2, Chap. 4, F ("Narcissism: Freud's Desire"): Freud "fails to see that, far from *incongruous* for the being whose desire (as he puts it) is object-directed, the choice of intact narcissism is absolutely imperative since it is 'narcissism' and nothing else that desire always needs" (p. 374). The issue of translation is not insignificant, for it is only by inflecting the *Inkongruenz* of the German text into "incongruity" that Girard and his collaborators can accuse Freud of failing to recognize the narcissistic character of object-oriented love and can integrate his theory of love into a more powerful theory that would see its blindness: "The more I think of the *Inkongruenz* that Freud sees as residing in the choice of the woman with intact narcissism as the preferred object for object-oriented desire, the more I appreciate why Freud had to present this choice as he did, and dismiss as inconsequential its incongruous aspects. . . . There is certainly something incongruous—according to the dictionary, something that does not quite fit the situation Freud envisages, something that does not conform, in other words, to psychoanalytic theory. . . . A critique is not effective until it succeeds in integrating the *Inkongruenz* of the earlier theory into some new theory and makes it disappear within the context of the new theory" (p. 380). All these formulas could be reversed: by dint of wishing too much to see what Freud does not see, one fails to see that Freud *also* sees the narcissistic character of overvaluation in love, that is, the narcissistic character of the choice of the "incongruent" object. ("He does not see that what he calls overvaluation of the object in object-oriented desire is the same thing as what he describes under the label 'intact narcissism'" [p. 397, Jean-Michel Ourghourlian].) The *Inkongruenz* of the "previous theory" only becomes incongruous for the "new theory" because the latter insists at all costs on making the former a univocal, congruent theory, identifiable with its most manifest intended meaning. This takes absolutely nothing away from the relevance of Girard's analyses, but rather puts this relevance in context: the incongruence of the Freudian positions on narcissism finally escapes theoretical identification and is thereby more "pow-

erful" than the critiques that have been addressed to it. A "Freudian desire" exists, there is no doubt about it; but this desire grows shadowy and inhibited; it passes into its other—and it is no longer "Freud's."

41. "On Narcissism," p. 100: "The development of the ego consists in a departure from primary narcissism and gives rise to a vigorous attempt to recover that state."

42. Denis de Rougement, *Love in the Western World*, trans. Montgomery Belgion (New York, 1956), p. 55 (and, more generally, all of Book 1).

43. See also Freud's "Introductory Lectures on Psychoanalysis," *SE* 16: 417–18.

44. "The object-choice [the 'type' Freud is analyzing consists in choosing the 'whore'] which is so strangely conditioned, and this very singular way of behaving in love, have the same psychical origin as we find in the loves of normal people. They are derived from the infantile fixation of tender feelings on the mother, and represent one of the consequences of that fixation. In normal love only a few characteristics survive which reveal unmistakably the maternal prototype of the object-choice" ("A Special Type of Choice of Object," *SE* 11: 168–69).

45. Philippe Lacoue-Labarthe has pointed out (in personal conversation) that the expression Freud used, *sich etwas gefallen lassen*, translated as "plaire" by Laplanche, can also mean "to tolerate" or "put up with something" (or someone)—which would of course lead in the direction of the self-sufficiency of the narcissistic woman. The fact remains that Laplanche's translation is just as valid, and that the context of the sentence (the need to be loved) seems to weigh in its favor.

46. *Meditation III*: "Finally, as regards my parents, even though all that I have ever held concerning them were true, it would not follow that it is they who conserve me, nor that they have brought me into being in so far as I am a thinking thing" (*Descartes' Philosophical Writings*, trans. Norman Kemp Smith [London, 1952], p. 229).

47. On this *regressus in infinitum*, see Laplanche, *Life and Death in Psychoanalysis*, p. 109.

48. Here we are touching on what Philippe Lacoue-Labarthe has proposed to call "typography" (impression of type, modeling, fashioning, fictioning, etc.): see his article "Typographie," pp. 257ff.

49. See, among many other passages, Jacques Lacan, *Le Séminaire I, Les Ecrits techniques de Freud* (Paris, 1975), pp. 140–41.

50. No doubt this difficulty accounts for the fact that Lacan progressively abandoned the analysis of the imaginary in favor of the nonspecularizable, under the aspects of language, the Symbolic, the Other, and so on. Nevertheless, it must be noted, in the absence of a more detailed analysis, that the distinction between a *refente* or a *clivage* by (and in) the symbolic *grand Autre* and an alienation of the ego in the imaginary *petit autre*

(always denounced as a "lure" or "misrecognition") makes it possible to identify the subject as Other and thus to *verify* it, where consideration of the imaginary relation alone did not preclude the introduction of a very fertile uneasiness as to the status of the subject. On this issue, see Jacques Derrida, "Le Facteur de la vérité," in *Poétique*, no. 21 (Paris, 1975), pp. 123–24 and 137ff. (reprinted in his *La Carte postale*).

51. It is noteworthy that the expressions *Idealich* and *Ichideal* are absolutely interchangeable (as will be, later on, the terms *Ichideal* and *Über-ich*). Thus we must not be too eager to find indications of a conceptual difference here, as Lacan is when he proposes to distinguish the ego ideal, understood as an agency of symbolic law, from the ideal ego, understood as an agency of imaginary captation (*Le Séminaire I, Les Ecrits techniques de Freud*, Chap. 11; see also "Remarque sur le rapport de Daniel Lagache," in *Ecrits*, pp. 671ff.). Freud confuses precisely these two levels, and there is the heart of the problem: the problem, let us say, of the *narcissistic law*, of autoheteronomy.

52. It will have become evident that the difficulty we are concerned with is none other than that of the operation of the Holy Spirit. I am grateful to Eric Michaud, whose attentive reading reminded me of this obvious connection.

The Primal Band

This chapter owes a great deal to Jean-Luc Nancy and Philippe Lacoue-Labarthe, on whose teaching much of my argument is based (traces of this teaching are found in their article "La Panique politique," in *Cahiers Confrontation*, no. 2, on which I rely more heavily than my scattered references may suggest); and to Eric Michaud, who generously shared with me his knowledge of late-nineteenth-century "hypnotic" theories (Hippolyte Bernheim, Gustave Le Bon, and so on). This chapter is gratefully dedicated to them. It may be considered an expanded version of a talk given in May 1980 ("Journées Confrontation": *Le Lien social*) and reprinted under the same title in *Le Lien social*, a collective publication (Paris, 1981). The epigraph on p. 128 is from *Humanisme de l'autre homme* (Montpellier, 1972), p. 68. The first epigraph on p. 153 is from *The Politics of Obedience: The Discourse of Voluntary Servitude*, trans. Harry Kurz (Montreal, 1975), p. 52.

1. It would be far preferable to use the term "*Mass* Psychology" and not "Group Psychology," as Strachey's translation maintains, or even "Crowd Psychology," as others have proposed. If it is true, as recent French translators (P. Cotet, A. Bourguignon et al., 1981) point out, that "the title *Massenpsychologie und Ich-Analyse* was inspired by Le Bon's *Psychologie des foules*," the fact remains that the term "*Masse*" introduces distant political connections that it seems important to retain (see n. 37, below, and also

S. Moscovici's excellent treatment of the question, "Quand traduira-t-on Freud en français?" in *Le Monde du Dimanche*, 11 Jan. 1981). Thus although I have relied on the Strachey translation here in citing Freud, I have often preferred to use the term "mass psychology" in my own text.

2. "The transformation of 'bad' instincts is brought about by two factors working in the same direction, an internal and an external one. The internal factor consists in the influence exercised on the bad (let us say, the egoistic) instincts taken in its widest sense. By the admixture of *erotic* components the egoistic instincts are transformed into *social* ones. . . . We have learned that the *external compulsion* exercised on a human being by his upbringing and environment produces a further transformation towards good in his instinctual life—a further turning from egoism towards altruism" ("Thoughts for the Times on War and Death," *SE* 14: 282–83).

3. In this connection, the precautionary notes Martin Heidegger sounded in paragraphs 25 and 26 of *Being and Time* are as pertinent as ever: as long as we continue to speak in terms of "subject," of "ego"—in other words, of *subjectum*—we shall remain at the level of the simple subsistence of a plurality of subjects and, by the same token, at the level of the definitively mysterious question of how "an ontological bridge from one's own subject, which is given proximally as alone, to the other subject, which is proximally quite closed off," might be established (*Being and Time*, trans. John Macquarrie and Edward Robinson [New York, 1962], p. 162).

4. See André Akoun's preface to Gustave Le Bon, *Psychologie des foules* (Paris, 1975); Jean Stoetzel, *La Psychologie sociale* (Paris, 1978), pp. 261ff.

5. "To-day the claims of the masses are becoming more and more sharply defined, and amount to nothing less than a determination to destroy utterly society as it now exists, with a view to making it hark back to that primitive communism which was the normal condition of all human groups before the dawn of civilisation" (Gustave Le Bon, *The Crowd: A Study of the Popular Mind* [London, 1952], p. 16). It is apparent that the "psychopathology" of the social bond is accompanied, for Le Bon, by a pessimistic (and prophetic) diagnosis: the time to come will be that of the masses elevated to the status of subject, "the age we are about to enter will be in truth the *era of crowds*" (p. 14). Le Bon develops his theses further in *Psychologie du socialisme* (1898), *La Révolution française et la Psychologie des révolutions* (1912), and other texts.

6. Le Bon, *The Crowd*, pp. 28–29.

7. Ibid., p. 206. A few lines earlier, with respect to the ideal, Le Bon writes: "The crowd has become a people, and this people is able to emerge from its barbarous state. However, it will only entirely emerge therefrom when, after long efforts, struggles necessarily repeated, and innumerable recommencements, it shall have acquired an ideal. The nature of this ideal is of slight importance; whether it be the cult of Rome, the might of Ath-

ens, or the triumph of Allah, it will suffice to endow all the individuals of the race that is forming with perfect unity of sentiment and thought" (p. 205).

8. Ibid., p. 205.   9. Ibid., p. 156.

10. Ibid., pp. 29–30.   11. Ibid., pp. 36ff.

12. Telepathy, also called "mental suggestion" (by analogy with the merely verbal suggestion of the hypnotist), was fascinating at the time to many scholars: Janet, Bergson, William James, Richet, and Lombroso, to mention only a few (later, we shall find Jung, Ferenczi—and Freud). Le Bon does not mention telepathy directly, but it comes up in Gabriel Tarde's *Les Lois de l'imitation* (Paris, 1895, 2d ed.), a work whose arguments Le Bon borrowed and amplified in *The Crowd*. In Tarde's text we find the following: "Perhaps, in order to fully understand sociality in its relative form [imitation, 'imitativity'], the only one in which in varying degrees it actually occurs, it may be well to conceive of it, hypothetically, as perfect and absolute. In its hypothetical form it would consist of such an intense concentration of urban life that as soon as a good idea arose in one mind it would be instantaneously transmitted to all minds throughout the city" (Gabriel Tarde, *The Laws of Imitation*, trans. Elsie Clews Parsons [New York, 1903], p. 70). This dream of direct communication—or sociality— without intermediaries comes up again in Freud's text; Freud then quite oddly concedes to the telepathy thesis all that he denied the thesis of suggestion: "If only one accustoms oneself to the idea of telepathy, one can accomplish a great deal with it—for the time being, it is true, only in imagination. It is a familiar fact that we do not know how the common purpose comes about in the great insect communities: possibly it is done by means of a direct psychical transference of this kind. One is led to a suspicion that this is the original, archaic method of communication between individuals and that in the course of phylogenetic evolution it has been replaced by the better method of giving information with the help of signals which are picked up by the sense organs. But the older method might have persisted in the background and still be able to put itself into effect under certain conditions—for instance, in passionately excited mobs" ("New Introductory Lectures," *SE* 22: 55). Thus the mass bond may have to be thought of as a telepathic umbilical cord.

13. The articles Freud devoted to hypnosis and to suggestion in the 1890's are available in *Pre-Psycho-Analytic Publications and Unpublished Drafts*, *SE* 1. In these texts Freud can be seen to oscillate between Charcot's "somatic" theory of hypnosis and Bernheim's more "psychological" theory; Freud finally comes down in favor of the latter.

14. All the necessary information on this "discovery" can be found in the works of H. F. Ellenberger, *The Discovery of the Unconscious* (London, 1970); L. Chertok and R. de Saussure, *Naissance du psychanalyste* (Paris,

1973); and D. Barrucand, *Histoire de l'hypnose en France* (Paris, 1967). It is noteworthy that Freud always appeals to hypnosis as well as to dreams when he is attempting to "prove" the phenomenon of the unconscious (cf. "The Unconscious," *SE* 14: 168–69, and "A Note on the Unconscious in Psycho-Analysis," *SE* 12: 261ff.; "Introductory Lectures on Psycho-Analysis," *SE* 15: 103–4; "Ego and Id," p. 13). It was while observing Bernheim, Freud writes elsewhere, that he "received the profoundest impression of the possibility that there could be powerful mental processes which nevertheless remained hidden from the consciousness of men" ("An Autobiographical Study," *SE* 20: 17).

15. See, for example, Hippolyte Bernheim, *L'Hypnotisme et la suggestion dans leurs rapports avec la médecine légale* (Paris, 1897), Chap. 1: "I have defined suggestion: any idea accepted by the mind. . . . We have established that all suggestions tend to be carried out, that all ideas tend toward action. Translated into the language of physiology, that means that every brain cell stimulated by an idea stimulates the nervous fibers that have to carry out that idea. . . . Hearing a suggestive waltz causes our body to vibrate in unison with the waltz; and even though we are not waltzing, even though we are making an effort not to waltz, if someone were to register the movements of our body with an instrument, a pattern would be obtained sketching out the unconscious choreographic movements of our machine. . . . What is called hypnotism is nothing other than the stimulation to activity of a normal property of our brain, suggestibility." Defined in this way, Bernheim's "suggestibility" corresponds fairly closely to what others preferred to call "sympathy" (Ribot, Bergson) or "empathy [*Einfühlung*]" (Lipps)—that is, a *mimic* relation to the feelings of others: "In man, infectious laughter or yawning, walking in step, imitating the movements of a rope-walker while watching him . . . are cases of physiological sympathy" (Théodule Armand Ribot, *The Psychology of the Emotions* [London, 1897], p. 232; see also Henri Louis Bergson, who makes the connection between sympathy and suggestibility in *Time and Free Will: An Essay on the Immediate Data of Consciousness*, trans. F. L. Pogson [London, 1910], pp. 13–19). It is that corporal mimesis that would then be called unconscious, because nonreflective, *reflex* (E. Michaud, "Le Réflexe," unpublished manuscript).

16. Le Bon, *The Crowd*, pp. 31–32.

17. Ibid., p. 119.

18. Ibid., pp. 117–18.

19. Ibid., pp. 124–30. All these quotations come from Chap. 3 of Book 2 of Le Bon's *The Crowd* ("The Leaders of Crowds and Their Means of Persuasion"). We may compare Le Bon with the following passage by Tarde: "Therefore, in the beginning of every old society, there must have been, *a fortiori*, a great display of authority exercised by certain supremely

imperious and positive individuals. Did they rule through terror and imposture, as alleged? This explanation is obviously inadequate. They ruled through their *prestige*. The example of the magnetiser alone can make us realise the profound meaning of this word. The magnetiser does not need to lie or terrorise to secure the blind belief and the passive obedience of his magnetised subject. He has prestige—that tells the story" (Tarde, *Laws of Imitation*, p. 78).

20. "Group Psychology," pp. 76–77: "We cannot avoid being struck with a sense of deficiency when we notice that . . . the person who is to replace the hypnotist in the case of the group is not mentioned in Le Bon's exposition." Freud continues to reproach the psychosociologists for having neglected the importance of the leader in group psychology.

21. Or almost in the dark, that is. When Le Bon spells it out, he is led straight to the almost untenable edge of his own discourse: "The leader has most often started as one of the led. He has himself been hypnotised by the idea, whose apostle he has since become. . . . The men of ardent convictions who have stirred the soul of crowds . . . have only exercised their fascination after having been themselves fascinated first of all by a creed" (*The Crowd*, pp. 118–19). This is an important statement, for, taken to the extreme—and here that is the political extreme—it implies that the leader is no more a subject (is no less hypnotized) than those he leads. But Le Bon does not take the idea much further.

22. The unmasterable unleashing of the crowd was also Freud's fear, as revealed in certain passages of his correspondence. Marthe Robert points these out and comments: "It would be no exaggeration to call Freud's fear of crowds a phobia, for it was not based on any real danger, and he seems to have expressed it from the start by an analogy which would provide him much later with the central idea of his observations on sociology, namely an analogy between "the people" and the deeper strata of the human psyche. Between the masses and the unconscious he saw a connivance verging on complicity, which endangers the highest values of consciousness and the achievement of the individual" (*From Oedipus to Moses*, trans. Ralph Mannheim [Garden City, N.Y., 1976], pp. 45–46). This is a phobia of the unconscious, then, and one that must refer to some fear of the unmasterable, if it is true that phobias have the function of warding off the uncontrollable surfacing—panic—of anxiety.

23. This is quite explicit in Tarde, who turned to "psychologists"—that is, to Bernheim, Delboeuf, and Féré—in search of the ultimate explanation of sociality. The social bond is imitation, and imitation is suggestion, "person-to-person suggestion, which constitutes social life": "I think . . . that I am conforming to the most rigorous scientific method in endeavoring . . . to throw light upon the mixed and complicated social tie, as we know it, by means of a social tie which is very pure, which is reduced to

its simplest expression, and which is so happily realised for the edification of the sociologist in a state of somnambulism" (Tarde, *Laws of Imitation*, p. 76). William McDougall, in *An Introduction to Social Psychology* (London, 1960), put suggestion on the same plane as imitation and sympathy, defining all three as an "interaction" between two individuals leading to "the assimilation of the actions and mental state of the patient to those of the agent": assimilation bearing on "presentations" (ideas) in the case of suggestion, on affects in the case of sympathy, and on bodily movements in the case of imitation (pp. 77–79). We can see, then, that Freud is not reading too much into McDougall's text when he proposes to see in sympathy (or "sympathetic induction of emotion") a phenomenon of affective *suggestion*.

24. Cf. "On Psychotherapy," *SE* 7: 260–61.

25. "The Ego and the Id" warns the analyst against the temptation "to play the part of prophet, saviour and redeemer to the patient. Since the rules of analysis are diametrically opposed to the physician's making use of his personality in any such manner, it must be honestly confessed that here we have another limitation to the effectiveness of analysis; after all, analysis does not set out to make pathological reactions impossible, but to give the patient's ego *freedom* to decide one way or the other" (p. 50, n. 1). See also Jacques Lacan's highly instructive remarks in *Le Séminaire I, Les Ecrits techniques de Freud* (Paris, 1975), pp. 34ff.

26. On the relationships Freud establishes between transference (*Übertragung*) and thought transmission (*Gedankenübertragung*), see François Roustang's excellent article, "Suggestion over the Long Term," in *Psychoanalysis Never Lets Go*, trans. Ned Lukacher (Baltimore and London, 1980), pp. 43–65.

27. The lecture that follows, "Analytic Therapy," only complicates the problem. Indeed, Freud makes an effort to differentiate the use of suggestion in psychoanalytic treatment from the use Bernheim made of it, but he never calls into question the *identity* of the phenomenon at stake in both contexts; he goes so far as to speak of "psychoanalytic suggestion" in connection with transference (*Introductory Lectures*, *SE* 16: 448). We shall come back to this point.

28. "It may be remarked, by the way, that, outside hypnosis and in real life, credulity such as the subject has in relation to his hypnotist is shown only by a child towards his beloved parents, and that an attitude of similar subjection on the part of one person towards another has only one parallel, though a complete one—namely in certain love-relationships where there is extreme devotion. A combination of exclusive attachment and credulous obedience is in general among the characteristics of love" ("Psychical [or Mental] Treatment," *SE* 7: 296).

29. "Fragment of an Analysis of a Case of Hysteria," *SE* 7: 117: "It is

true that . . . there is usually a sort of blind dependence and a permanent bond between a patient and the physician who has removed his symptoms by hypnotic suggestion; but the scientific explanation of all these facts is to be found in the existence of 'transferences' such as are regularly directed by patients on to their physicians."

30. "Three Essays," p. 150, and also p. 150, n. 1: "In this connection I cannot help recalling the credulous submissiveness shown by a hypnotized subject towards his hypnotist. This leads me to suspect that the essence of hypnosis lies in an unconscious fixation of the subject's libido to the figure of the hypnotist, through the medium of the masochistic components of the sexual instinct."

31. In Sandor Ferenczi, *Oeuvres complètes*, vol. 1 (Paris, 1982), p. 107ff. See also, in the same volume, "Suggestion and Psychoanalysis" (1912).

32. Later, in "An Outline of Psycho-Analysis," Freud writes: "The aim of [Eros] is to establish ever greater unities and to preserve them thus—in short, to bind together; the aim of [the other basic instinct] is, on the contrary, to undo connections and so to destroy things" (*SE* 23: 148).

33. See also Chap. 4 of "The Ego and the Id," which deals with the vital *Verbindung* of the cells and, more generally, the *Verbindung* or *Vermischung* of the two basic varieties of instincts.

34. Le Bon, *The Crowd*, p. 73.

35. I have borrowed this "translation" of the German *Bindung* from Jacques Derrida and his analysis of the "bindinal economy" in Freud's "Beyond the Pleasure Principle" ("Spéculer—sur 'Freud,'" in Derrida's *La Carte postale*, Paris, 1980).

36. So it is, for example, that Freud's "Thoughts for the Times on War and Death" calls peoples and states "the collective individuals of mankind" (*SE* 14: 278).

37. See Hannah Arendt, *The Origins of Totalitarianism* (New York and London, 1973), Chap. 10, "A Classless Society." Arendt quotes Le Bon as one of the ideological references of fascism (p. 316, n. 21), and rightly so: the Fascist ideologues, beginning with Hitler and Mussolini, were very well acquainted with the theses popularized by Le Bon, and applied them explicitly, so that it is not an exaggeration to say that *The Crowd* finds its political enactment in the Fascist mass. This point sheds some light on the strange congruence between the Freudian *Massenpsychologie* and the Fascist reality, which Bataille had already pointed out in "La Structure psychologique du fascisme" (in his *Oeuvres complètes*, vol. 1 [Paris, 1970], p. 356; see also Jacques Lacan's remarks in *Ecrits*, p. 475; Eric Michaud makes the Hitler–Le Bon–Freud connection in "L'Art face à la crise, 1929–1939," in documents in the possession of the University of Saint-Etienne).

38. Nancy and Lacoue-Labarthe, "La Panique politique," *Cahiers Confrontation*, no. 2, pp. 42–43 (see also, in the same volume, Claude Lefort,

"L'Image du corps et le Totalitarisme"). On the (more than metaphoric) metaphor of the "body politic," see the classic work of E. Kantorowitz, *The King's Two Bodies* (New York, 1957), and also Judith E. Schlanger, *Les Métaphores de l'organisme* (Paris, 1971).

39. See, for example, McDougall's *An Introduction to Social Psychology*, p. 79: "Sympathetic induction of emotions is displayed in the simplest and most unmistakable fashion by many, probably by all, of the gregarious animals. . . . One of the clearest and commonest examples is the spread of fear and its flight-impulse among the members of a flock or herd."

40. "Inhibitions, Symptoms and Anxiety," *SE* 20: 122: "Eros desires contact because it strives to make the ego and the loved object one, to abolish all spatial barriers between them. But destructiveness, too, which (before the invention of long-range weapons) could only take effect at close quarters, must presuppose physical contact, a coming to grips."

41. See above, pp. 113–26.

42. The text of "Group Psychology" continues as follows (p. 105): "The cannibal, as we know, has remained at this standpoint; he has a devouring affection for his enemies and only devours people of whom he is fond." The same gesture is made in "The Ego and the Id" (p. 29, n. 2): "An interesting parallel to the replacement of object-choice by identification is to be found in the belief of primitive peoples, and in the prohibitions based upon it, that the attributes of animals which are incorporated as nourishment persist as part of the character of those who eat them. As is well known, this belief is one of the roots of cannibalism and its effects have continued through the series of usages of the totem meal down to Holy Communion. The consequences ascribed by this belief to oral mastery of the object do in fact follow in the case of the later sexual object-choice." If we add that Chap. 7 of "Group Psychology" ends with a long note that refers to "Totem and Taboo" and to the "early history of the human family," it will be clear that the problematics of primary identification must be read as a *prehistoric* problematics, in every sense: we are dealing with what precedes the history of the ego, but also the history of humanity. These passages are discussed in their own right by Nancy and Lacoue-Labarthe in "La Panique politique," and by Jean-Louis Tristani, *Le Stade du respir* (Paris, 1978), pp. 123ff.

43. On this whole "matrical" problematics, it is indispensable to refer to Nicolas Abraham's studies of the mother-child "dual union," understood as "nonseparated-separated" or "separation included in the nonseparated" (*L'Ecorce et le noyau* [Paris, 1978], especially pp. 396ff.), as well as Imre Hermann's *L'Instinct filial* (Paris, 1972).

44. The proposition that the womb-mother is not an object can be supported by a large number of Freudian texts. Examples include *Thomas Woodrow Wilson: A Psychological Study*, by Sigmund Freud and William C. Bullitt (Boston, 1967), p. 37: "The libido first stores itself in love of self:

Narcissism. . . . To be sure, even an unweaned child has a love-object; the breast of his mother. He can, however, do nothing but to introject this object into himself and treat it as a part of himself"; "An Outline of Psycho-Analysis," *SE* 23: 188: "To begin with, the child does not distinguish between the breast and its own body; when the breast has to be separated from the body and shifted to the *outside* because the child so often finds it absent, it carries with it as an *object* a part of the original narcissistic libidinal cathexis"; and "Inhibitions, Symptoms and Anxiety," *SE* 20: 130: "Birth is not experienced subjectively as a separation from the mother, since the foetus, being a completely narcissistic creature, is totally unaware of her existence as an object." I owe this last reference (and the idea of searching for others) to a discussion with Jean-Luc Nancy.

45. Here we are dealing with what Jacques Lacan isolated and "translated" under the name of "identification with the unary feature" (= with a signifying, iterable mark); Lacan seeks to see it as the structuring identification of the subject (= of desire), as opposed to primary identification, called "mystical." His unpublished 1962 seminar "Identification," in which the term is introduced, thus explains that it is only on the level of the second identification that the dimension of the Other appears; now "the appearance of this dimension of the Other is the emergence of the subject"; "desire . . . must, and can only, constitute itself within the tension created by this relation to the Other." Defined as incorporation, primary identification would, on the contrary, bring us back to before the Other, thus before the subject, toward a union or a mystical body: "There is no way to bring it into play, except to rejoin it through a thematics that has already been elaborated, going back to the most ancient mythical, even religious traditions, under the name of 'mystical body.' . . . A Church is constituted from a body, and it is not for nothing that Freud, defining for us the identity of the ego in its relations with what he is calling, at that point, *Massenpsychologie*, refers to the bodily nature of the Church. But how can I get you to start from there without giving way to all sorts of confusions and believing that, as the term 'mystical' indicates clearly enough, it is along very different paths from those where our experience seeks to lead us?" (seminar of March 28, 1962). The logic that presides here over the methodical exclusion of primary identification is implacable, and it is the logic of the subject itself: for there to be any subject, there *must* be some Other; hence it follows that the constitutive identification must *not* inextricably blend the self and the other, must not be based on incorporation or devouring. Otherwise, it would be *de*constitutive of the subject. The discourse of the Other, it is clear, is organized like a powerful defense of the subject.

46. "Introjection" and "incorporation" are nearly synonymous terms for Freud, who often uses them interchangeably, even though the latter is really the "prototype" of the former, strictly speaking. Thus we need not be more

rigorous than he on this point, at least at the level of commentary (on the reasons—legitimate ones, moreover—for introducing a sharper distinction between the two processes, see Maria Torok, "Maladie du deuil et Fantasme du cadavre exquis," in Abraham, *L'Ecorce et le noyau*).

47. Let us recall the following passage: "Identification expresses a resemblance and is derived from a common element [*Gemeinsames*] which remains in the unconscious. Identification is most frequently used in hysteria to express [*Ausdrück*] a common *sexual* element [*einer sexuellen Gemeinsamkeit*]" (*Dreams*, p. 150).

48. "Mourning and Melancholia," *SE* 14: 250. Hysterical identification "is the expression of there being something in common, which may signify love [*einer Gemeinschaft, welche Liebe bedeuten kann*]" (p. 250).

49. This "single trait" is not the same thing as a "common element" or "something in common." In fact, the *einziger Zug* represents the *Gemeinsamkeit*, which itself represents-accomplishes the desire for an object. It is indispensable to eliminate this ambiguity, for otherwise there is no way to grasp the difference between hysterical identification with a third person and secondary identification of the "Dora" type: the latter also focuses on "a single trait," but this feature is borrowed from the object by virtue of a direct, *immediate* identification. In this respect, the excessive lengths to which Lacan took the *einziger Zug* increased the ambiguity, to the extent that identification may be partial in the case of secondary identification as well as in that of hysterical identification. Hence the Chinese puzzle proposed to the commentators who, going back to Freud via Lacan, seek the famous identification with the "unary feature" sometimes in the direction of the second identification (cf., for example, the anonymous article on "Le Clivage du sujet" in *Scilicet*, vols. 2/3 [1970]: 109), sometimes in the direction of the third (cf. Tristani, *Le Stade du respir*, p. 136), and with just as much reason.

50. See above, pp. 11–16.

51. To avoid falling into the general confusion over this passage, let us spell things out. Freud gives *three* examples of hysterical identification through symptoms, after which he categorizes identifications in general into *three* types (primary, secondary, and triangular). But these two enumerations do not coincide, if only because the primary identification, which appears in the second list, cannot be found in the first. There is thus no reason to ask, as Jean Laplanche does (in *L'Angoisse, Problématiques I* [Paris, 1980], pp. 343–44), why Freud speaks of three types of identification, whereas "there were four of them at the start" (one primary identification plus three hysterical identifications through symptoms). The first and the third examples of the first list both fall into the third category of the second list—which thus produces, if my arithmetic is correct, *three* types.

52. The fact that what is involved here is an identification with the oth-

er's *unrequited* love—that is, as Lacan insisted, with the other's *desire*—of course changes nothing. The desire for a fundamentally lost object (*objet petit a*, to use the official terminology) remains a desire for an object.

53. The individual sentiment is understood to be anterior even to *Einfühlung*, for Freud points out twice that *Einfühlung* is not explained by identification: "Another suspicion may tell us that we are far from having exhausted the problem of identification, and that we are faced by the process which psychology calls 'empathy' [*Einfühlung*] and which plays the largest part in our understanding of what is inherently foreign to our ego in other people" ("Group Psychology," p. 108); "We are very well aware that we have not exhausted the nature of identification with these examples taken from pathology, and that we have consequently left part of the riddle of group formations untouched. A far more fundamental and comprehensive psychological analysis would have to intervene at this point. A path leads from identification by way of imitation to empathy, that is, to the comprehension of the mechanism by means of which we are enabled to take up any attitude at all towards another mental life" (p. 110, n. 2). But these remarks, if they seem to make *Einfühlung* the "last instance of identification," as Nancy and Lacoue-Labarthe point out quite correctly ("La Panique politique," pp. 45ff.), remain quite elliptical in the last analysis, and this is no accident. In fact, the *Einfühlung* that is "well-known to philosophers" was never anything but another name for what McDougall called "sympathy," that is, the apprehension of the affects of another person by way of a mimic, automatic and involuntary reproduction of that person's gestures (see Le Bon's *The Crowd*, pp. 31–32, and endnote 24 above). To the extent that the whole point of Freud's argument is tacitly directed against McDougall's "sympathy" ("sympathy is born of identification"), it would have been completely self-contradictory to set *Einfühlung*-sympathy at the basis of identification. And Freud does this only by allusion, without going any further. It should also be noted in passing that the *Einfühlung* and the "sympathy" in question here have nothing to do with Husserl's *Einfühlung* or Scheler's "sympathy." Scheler, for example, cannot speak harshly enough about Lipps's *Einfühlung*: this latter, unlike true sympathy, would not give us access to the experiences of another person *as that other person*. And when Scheler objects, in his commentary on Chap. 7 of "Group Psychology," that sympathy is not born of identification, because it "supposes precisely a certain phenomenological distance between the *selves*," it is at the price of assimilating Freud's hysterico-triangular identification to Lipps's *Einfühlung*, where that distance is "abolished" (Max Scheler, *Nature et formes de la sympathie* [Paris, 1971], pp. 37–38). But this assimilation, as we now understand, rests upon a misunderstanding. Dealing with the question of *Einfühlung*, the psychoanalyst and the phenomenologist find themselves for once on the same side.

54. Cf. Jean-Pierre Vernant, "Ambiguïté et renversement. Sur la structure énigmatique d'Oedipe Roi,'" in J.-P. Vernant and P. Vidal-Naquet, *Mythe et tragédie en Grèce antique* (Paris, 1972), pp. 114ff. See also Jacques Derrida's admirable "Pharmacie de Platon," in his *La Dissémination* (Paris, 1972), especially pp. 146ff.

55. "Civilization and Its Discontents," *SE* 21: 95: "Human life in common is only made possible when a majority comes together which is stronger than any separate individual and which remains united against all separate individuals. The power of this community is then set up as 'right' in opposition to the power of the individual, which is condemned as 'brute force.'" It is noteworthy that the "social contract" of girls is of exactly the same type as the one among brothers in the primal horde after they have killed their father (cf. "Totem and Taboo," *SE* 13: 144).

56. "On the Universal Tendency to Debasement in the Sphere of Love," *SE* 11: 183: "The overvaluation that normally attaches to the sexual object [is] reserved for the incestuous object and its representatives."

57. Scheler, *Nature et formes de la sympathie*, p. 59: "In the idiopathic type, it is the foreign *ego* that is absorbed and assimilated by my own *ego* . . . ; in the heteropathic type, on the contrary, it is my *ego* (in the formal sense of the word) that is attracted, captivated, hypnotized by another formal *ego*." Scheler may have drawn this distinction from his reading of "Group Psychology," whose theses he discusses at length in the second edition of his book.

58. On the Girardian distinction between the (good) external mediation, which excludes mimetic rivalry, and (bad, modern) internal mediation, which provokes it, see René Girard, *Deceit, Desire, and the Novel: Self and Other in Literary Structure*, trans. Yvonne Freccero (Baltimore, Md., 1965), pp. 9–14 (on page 2, external mediation is related quite straightforwardly to the imitation of Christ).

59. A note refers here to a more complex prehistory: "Perhaps it would be safer to say 'with the parents'" ("Ego and Id," p. 31, n. 1). Thus, as Freud later states in *Thomas Woodrow Wilson*, there would be "two primary identifications with the father and the mother" (p. 45). But this indication, which is obviously such as to upset the Oedipal schema, is quickly bypassed. *First phase:* Identification would focus on the bearer of the penis, thus also on the mother, since the child does not know the anatomical difference between the sexes—or rather, knows only one sex, *that of the father.* (The primary identification, as "Group Psychology" said, "has nothing to do with a passive or feminine attitude . . . ; it is on the contrary typically masculine" [p. 105].) *Second phase:* "In order to simplify my presentation, I shall discuss only identification with the father" ("Ego and Id," p. 31, n. 1). This "simplification," besides conveniently putting off all questioning of the Oedipal triangle (positive or negative, it hardly matters), also makes it possible

to get around the intimidating possibility of a maternal ego ideal or Superego—a mother-law (law of the mother).

60. René Girard, *Violence and the Sacred*, pp. 147–49. On the double bind (double constraint, paradoxical injunction, pragmatic paradox), cf. Gregory Bateson, *Steps to an Ecology of Mind* (New York, 1972), and P. Watzlawick, J. Helmick-Beavin, and D. Jackson, *Pragmatics of Human Communication* (New York, 1967).

61. "Totem and Taboo," *SE* 13: 143: "What had up to then been prevented by [the father's] actual existence was thenceforward prohibited by the sons themselves, in accordance with the psychological procedure so familiar to us in psycho-analyses under the name of 'deferred obedience.'"

62. "Group Psychology," p. 131: "The separation of the ego ideal from the ego cannot be borne for long . . . , and has to be temporarily undone. In all renunciations and limitations imposed upon the ego a periodical infringement of the prohibition is the rule; this indeed is shown by the institution of festivals, which in origin are nothing less nor more than excesses provided by law and which owe their cheerful character to the release which they bring." Here a note refers to "Totem and Taboo," *SE* 13: 142: "Cannibal savages as they [the members of the patriarchal horde] were, it goes without saying that they devoured their victim as well as killing him. The violent primal father had doubtless been the feared and envied model of each one of the company of brothers; and in the act of devouring him they accomplished their identification with him, and each one of them acquired a portion of his strength. The totem meal, which is perhaps mankind's earliest festival, would thus be a repetition and a commemoration of this memorable and criminal deed, which was the beginning of so many things—of social organization, of moral restrictions and of religion."

63. "Rapport" (here translated as "relation") was Mesmer's word for the "harmonious" circulation of the "magnetic fluid" between the hypnotist and his subject. The term was still in use in Charcot's and Bernheim's day (though it had shed its "fluid" connotations), and Freud had used it in his "Psychical [or Mental] Treatment" in 1890 to designate the reduction of "the subject's universe" to the hypnotist himself (*SE* 7: 295). We find it again here, coupled with "transference": "The hypnotist avoids directing the subject's conscious thoughts towards his own intentions, and makes the person upon whom he is experimenting sink into an activity in which the world is bound to seem uninteresting to him; but at the same time the subject is in reality unconsciously concentrating his whole attention upon the hypnotist, and is getting into an attitude of *rapport*, of transference on to him" ("Group Psychology," p. 126). All that is said here about the hypnotic "rapport" thus applies also to "transference."

64. The following paragraph of "Note on the Unconscious in Psycho-Analysis" continues: "The idea of the action ordered in hypnosis not only became an object of consciousness at a certain moment, but the more strik-

ing aspect of the fact is that this idea grew *active*: it was translated into action as soon as consciousness became aware of its presence. The real stimulus to the action being the order of the physician, it is hard not to concede that the idea of the physician's order became active too. Yet this last idea did not reveal itself to consciousness, as did its outcome, the idea of the action; it remained unconscious, and so it was *active and unconscious* at the same time" (*SE* 12: 261).

65. Or else, to echo François Roustang, *there is no other* (in his *Psychoanalysis Never Lets Go*, p. 108). This book appeared too late for me to take into account, as I would have liked, Roustang's important studies, "Transference: The Dream" and "The Game of the Other," neither of which had been published previously. I can thus only allude to them, since my analyses intersect with Roustang's, which in my view cannot be ignored.

66. Emile Benveniste, as read by Jean-Luc Nancy ("Notre Probité!" [on truth in the moral sense in Nietzsche], in *Revue de théologie et de philosophie*, 112 [1980], and "La Voix libre de l'homme," in *Les Fins de l'homme* [Paris, 1981], pp. 179ff.). It is still difficult—no doubt because we are too close to the question—to assess the extent to which our hypotheses on hypnotic injunction converge with the research Nancy has undertaken, with quite different(?) objectives, on the Kantian imperative.

67. This is precisely the definition Freud always gives of the transferential *Wiederholung* and *Agieren* (we shall return to this).

68. The hypnotist's commandment has never stood up before the hypnotized person even under the unbearable (blinding, thus invisible) aspect of Jehovah delivering the Law to his people: "How does the hypnotist manifest [his power, 'animal magnetism,' *mana*]? By telling the subject to look him in the eyes; his most typical method of hypnotizing is by his look. But it is precisely the *sight* of the chieftain that is dangerous and unbearable for primitive people, just as later that of the Godhead is for mortals. Even Moses had to act as an intermediary between his people and Jehovah, since the people could not support the sight of God" ("Group Psychology," p. 125).

69. A repetition of the birth event is what Rank suggested in *The Trauma of Birth* (London, 1929). However, in this connection we have to reiterate Freud's objection to Rank's overall thesis: birth is not an event at all, since it is the advent of the subject, *before* any event. (Cf. "Inhibitions, Symptoms and Anxiety," *SE* 20: 135: "It is easy to say that the baby will repeat its affect of anxiety in every situation which recalls the event of birth. The important thing to know is what recalls the event and what it is that is recalled.") If what is at stake in hypnosis is a "second birth," then we shall have to say that this repetition does not repeat a primal event, but rather an advent that is in itself already "repetitive"—haunted by a past older than any present and any representation.

70. That "identification" is never anything but another name for "sug-

gestion" is confirmed once again in Chap. 11: the members of the group are "carried away . . . by 'suggestion,' that is to say, by means of identification" ("Group Psychology," p. 130).

71. Philippe Lacoue-Labarthe discusses this passage in *Portrait de l'artiste, en général* (Paris, 1979), pp. 89–91, and in "L'Echo du sujet," in his *Le Sujet de la philosophie* (Paris, 1979), p. 296.

Library of Congress Cataloging-in-Publication Data

Borch-Jacobsen, Mikkel.
   [Sujet freudien. English]
   The Freudian subject / Mikkel Borch-Jacobsen; translated by
Catherine Porter; foreword by François Roustang.
   p.   cm.
   Translation of: Le sujet freudien.
   Bibliography: p.
   ISBN 0-8047-1440-1 (alk. paper)   ISBN 0-8047-1839-3 (pbk.)
   1. Psychoanalysis.   2. Freud, Sigmund, 1856–1939.   I. Title.
BF173.F85B6713   1988
150.19'52—dc 19   87-30548
                                            CIP